Book
Center
2.50

Also by Drew Middleton

THESE ARE THE BRITISH (1957)

This is a Borzoi Book,

Published in New York by ALFRED A. KNOPF

THE
Supreme Choice

DIEU ET MON DROIT

THE

Supreme Choice

BRITAIN *and* EUROPE

BY

DREW MIDDLETON

New York: Alfred·A·Knopf: Mcmlxiii

L. C. catalog card number: 63–9131

THIS IS A BORZOI BOOK

PUBLISHED BY ALFRED A. KNOPF, INC.

FIRST AMERICAN EDITION

Published in somewhat different form in England by Martin Secker & Warburg Limited.

FOR JUDY

In the hope that she will
know a better world
than ours.

INTRODUCTION

THE FIRST ROUND of negotiations between Britain and the European Economic Community ended on January 29 when France wrecked the talks at Brussels just as they neared decisive success and British entry. The timing of the start of a second round of negotiations is obscure. But that there will be such negotiations between Britain and Europe is certain.

The Conservative government of the United Kingdom has declared that it intends to continue its efforts to enter the E.E.C. as long as it is in office. The Labor Party, on the other hand, is opposed to British entry, although its position is far from unanimous on this point. Consequently, a change in the British government might delay British admission to E.E.C. still further.

The world will know soon enough. A general election in Britain must be held before the autumn of 1964, and it may be held as early as May 1963. A Labor victory would increase the obstacles to British entry. Yet even now, in the aftermath of France's action, the logic of British union with Europe remains so strong that the evolution of a larger Europe, including the United Kingdom, appears almost inevitable.

Oddly enough, a conviction that the Labor Party would win the next general election played a part in the French action. Charles de Gaulle believed, his intimates say, that Prime Minister Harold Macmillan lacked the necessary political authority to take Britain into Europe. He also believed that the Labor Party, even after it had been deprived of Hugh Gaitskell's leadership, the most grievous loss the Labor movement has sustained since the death of Ernest Bevin, would win the next election.

Such certainty in the uncertain and, to him, largely unknown waters of British politics was characteristic of de Gaulle's thought and action in the days when he was barring the door to Britain. He and his ideas have since emerged as the most formidable barrier not only to Britain's entry but to the gradual development of a larger trans-Atlantic community as well. Some regard him as the rock upon which the European ship will founder; others, as the protector of Europe against American political and economic domination. One thing is indisputable: he is mortal. There is yet another factor, to be discerned from the reports of his officials, who often act more like courtiers than members of a democratic government: after five years of power, the General has become increasingly, even arrogantly confident that he and his policies are right and not open to question.

The joke, heard at Brussels, London, and Paris, "De Gaulle has an inferiority complex; he thinks he's God," has some application. Sadly enough, it is the same joke, with appropriate changes, that one heard in Berlin and Rome under the dictators.

It is easy enough to see what de Gaulle did. He postponed Britain's entry into Europe and he dealt a merciless blow to the spirit of European unity among the six members of the E.E.C. It is more important for the future of this great movement to understand why he did this, to probe the workings of his mind. By doing so, we can come to a fairer assessment of the prospects in the future.

Charles de Gaulle lives both in the past and in the future. The history of France and his own personal experience guide him. So does his view of what France and Europe will be in the future. So, we can say with reasonable certainty, does his expectation of what history will say of him one hundred, two hundred years hence.

De Gaulle, as his writings testify, has always believed in a union of continental, European states—the states which, perhaps with the addition of Spain and Portugal, now make up the economic community. He does not believe that this union could retain its cohesion if it were linked closely with Britain, a nation with global interests in its Commonwealth and its remaining colonies.

The French president's attitude toward Britain is compounded of admiration and fear. Some British characteristics he admires. But Britain's ways are not the ways for his France or his Europe. Early in the negotiations he made it clear that Britain's admission to E.E.C. depended upon her willingness to divest herself of Commonwealth and colonial connections, to become in fact a continental rather than a maritime power.

This primary objection to Britain's entry is powerfully influenced by the General's view of the Anglo-American relationship, which he quite evidently sees in terms of Roosevelt and Churchill rather than of Kennedy and Macmillan. He believes that Britain, in Europe, would be the United States's Trojan horse. Through its close ally in London, the American administration could bring political, military, and economic influence to bear upon the continental members. This would perpetuate that American domination which de Gaulle regards as injurious to the creation of a truly European union—injurious because it conflicts both with Europe as it is today and, I believe, with Europe as the General envisages that it is to develop.

Although appearances are against it, Charles de Gaulle believes today in the indispensability to France and continental Europe of the North Atlantic Treaty Organization. *Today* is the operative word. Europe is defended today by the United States. The General doubts this will be so tomorrow, meaning, in his mind, five or ten or fifteen years hence.

Then, when the transports steam westward, Europe will be on its own. It cannot be prepared to defend itself then if it lives now, and until that day, under American political leadership and military protection. Consequently, the participation of the United States in European affairs must be restricted even at the cost of speeding the military withdrawal the General expects. Meanwhile, Europe must create its own system of defense along national lines—the French nuclear striking force is an example—and evoke a "spirit of European unity" that will enable it to stand on its own and repel the political and economic pressure of the Communist bloc.

To round out this picture of what might be called a "European Europe," we have an idea of how the French president sees its relations with the Soviet Union developing. He has spoken of a Europe that stretches from the Atlantic to the Ural Mountains in Russia. This will be established, he believes, by two conditions.

The first is the development of an expansionist, aggressive Communist China whose policies will drive the Soviet Union to look to Europe for allies. The second is a change in

the Russian system, a liberalization of political and social outlook that will make the Soviets more amenable to negotiation
with Europe of the outstanding difficulties. To the General it
must appear quite reasonable that, as the Chinese pressure
mounts and Soviet society changes, the day may come, in 1975
or 1980, when a strong European community can negotiate
with the Soviet Union the reunification of Germany and the
establishment of an alliance.

Whether or not one agrees that the General's is the path
to the future, the grandeur of his thinking, the spaciousness of
his approach must be conceded. But his proposals are opposed
by no less far-sighted, no less noble ones which have become
part of the policy of the United States and which have been
adopted by hundreds of thousands of Europeans in the last
fifteen years.

These seek the creation of a larger European community
including Britain, the Scandinavian nations, Switzerland, Austria, Portugal, and perhaps someday Spain and Greece. To
such a community the United States and Canada could be
united first by economic ties and later by political co-operation.
This is the true Atlantic community that transcends the relative narrowness of a European national community and provides an effective balance against the Communist bloc.

The conflict between de Gaulle's Europe and Kennedy's
Atlantic community now has entered a crisis. With British
membership as the immediate goal, the West is about to be
convulsed with a new struggle for Europe. On the outcome will
depend what kind of Europe we are to have in the future and
perhaps what will be the future political course of great areas
such as North and Central Africa and the Middle East which
are dependent on the industrial power of Europe.

Are we to have one West, stretching from the Pacific coast to East Germany, or are we to have two, de Gaulle's Europe and the Anglo-American community? Everything de Gaulle did in January 1963 was pointed toward the former—the creation of a third force in the world. As this is written, he is winning. And he is a formidable antagonist.

Yet, although he talks and preaches of the realities of the situation in his exercise of French leadership in Europe, he appears to have forgotten that he is dealing in power politics and that these, as the term implies, depend on power. He must understand that, even in that future he glimpses a decade hence, power in its rawest military and economic forms will rest with the United States and those of its allies he has excluded from Europe.

In the end, I believe, the plans of this great, brave, lonely man will be overborne by the simple realities of power. As the cost of the nuclear age increases, it will become more and more evident that Europe cannot live without the United States, whereas the United States can do reasonably well without Europe.

All this will strike romantics who admire the French leader as unfortunate. But it is the way things happen to be. And in the forthcoming struggle for the future of Europe it is well to remember that when de Gaulle talks of European unity he is also advocating the division of the West.

This has been a difficult and satisfying book to write. Difficult because it deals with a fluid situation—the movement toward European unity. Satisfying because this is one of the most exciting developments of the century; the achievement of European unity will change the world as nothing has changed it since the emergence of the United States as a world power in the closing years of the last century. Within this decade we shall see the power relationships in the world drastically altered.

Because a Europe that includes the United Kingdom would inevitably affect the relations of the Western world with the Communist empire and with the emerging nations of Africa, I have discussed the Russian and satellite position vis-à-vis a new Europe and dealt with those aspects of the African problem that I know about from personal experience.

A book about a rapidly developing situation cannot rely for source material on authoritative texts. Most of what I have written is the result of literally hundreds of conversations with industrialists and farmers, economists and bankers, diplomats and officials. To all those from Athens to Oslo who have answered my questions and offered their views, my heartfelt thanks.

Paris
February 1963

CONTENTS

CHAPTER XIII

THE

Supreme Choice

· 1 ·

*Britain Takes the Plunge... The National Ego
and the Challenge of Europe... The Commonwealth or the European Economic Community*

O N WEDNESDAY, August 2, 1961, Harold Macmillan arose
in the House of Commons to make the most important
statement a British Prime Minister has made since, a little
more than twenty-one years before, Winston Churchill told
Parliament that although Britain's allies were in defeat and
her armies broken she intended to fight on alone. That had
been the supreme expression of British insularity in its
finest sense. What Macmillan had to say was at once a farewell
to that proud independence and an approach to a situation
new to British history. Above all, his speech was, intrinsically,
an admission of Britain's inability to maintain independent
economic, military, and political strength even faintly com-

mensurate with that of the Soviet Union and the United States
and its willingness to seek in a time of comparative peace the
kind of alliance Britain has frequently resorted to in war and
just as frequently abandoned once the war was won.

The members of the House, not usually the most im-
pressionable of men, were able to subdue their impatience to
be off on their summer vacations and to attend seriously to
what even the least sensitive recognized as a turning point in
British history. But such is the interconnection of nations
great and small today that the movement Macmillan initiated
that day will be a turning point not only in the history of his
own country but in the histories of such disparate nations as
the United States, Norway, West Germany, and the Soviet
Union. What brought Britain and the world to this turning
point, and the effect of her decision of all our affairs, is the
principal theme of this book.

The Prime Minister's first words were: "I beg to move."
He then read the Conservative motion:

> That this House supports the decision of Her Majesty's Gov-
> ernment to make formal application under Article 237 of the
> Treaty of Rome in order to initiate negotiations to see if satis-
> factory arrangements can be made to meet the special interests
> of the United Kingdom, of the Commonwealth and of the
> European Free Trade Association; and further accepts the
> undertaking of Her Majesty's Government that no agreement
> affecting these special interests or involving British sover-
> eignty will be entered into until it has been approved by this
> House after full consultation with other Commonwealth coun-
> tries, by whatever procedure they may generally agree.

So the plunge was taken. In exactly one hundred words a
thousand years of British history were undone. The people of
Britain, through their government, were embarking on a

course that ran contrary to some of their deepest convictions and most abiding traditions. Because of Britain's historic involvement in the world beyond her shores, and because the United Kingdom has played an influential role in the two great world organizations of our century, the League of Nations and the United Nations, there is a tendency to underestimate the strength of British nationalism. Yet it is impossible to understand either the exercise of world leadership by the British in the past or the decline of Britain in the present without some knowledge of how these baffling people are affected by nationalism.

The very existence of British nationalism, and its lunatic cousin chauvinism, is decried by that very powerful group which makes and molds British public opinion. With a few exceptions, such as Lord Beaverbrook, and he might be called selectively internationalist, this group is international in outlook and, on balance, to the left of center. This group played an important role in preparing the British public for an approach to the Common Market. Critics would say that the group has long influenced affairs in Britain to the point where entry into the European Economic Community was the only hope of national salvation. But powerful though the internationalists may be, they have never wholly succeeded in eliminating the stubborn, innate nationalism of the British.

Much will be said and written about this nationalism in describing the political repercussions of Britain's first and abortive try to enter Europe. Nationalism developed there in a more moderate manner than in contemporary France or prewar Germany, largely because the British have been protected by geography, the valor of their defense, and the ineptness and occasional bad luck of their enemies from those military reverses which, rather than victories, are the primary psychological impulse for nationalist excesses. The defeats of the Napoleonic wars were the seed beds for Prussian and ultimately German nationalism, and Louis Napoleon rode into the Tuilleries on a wave of nationalist fervor that had not been able to forget Waterloo. The islanders have known many defeats, but not since 1066 have they been defeated in the home islands. They have been spared invasion, occupation, and, consequently, the more rabid forms of nationalism.

In the last century, nationalism occasionally affected the public for brief periods. Indeed, the word "jingoism" is derived from a popular Victorian music-hall song:

> We don't want to fight, but, by jingo, if we do,
> We've got the men, we've got the ships, we've got the
> money, too.

But although nationalism was never elevated to a national creed, the slightest sign that this sentiment was latent in British hearts produced howls of rage at home and abroad. There was, of course, no moral outcry abroad over imperialism since, without exception, all the other major powers of the world unremittingly pursued it until the outbreak of World War I. In the building of the greatest of modern empires, however, the British were not above occasional self-righteous lectures on the superiority of their civilizing mission. The pious explanations of why they were in Bechuanaland or Burma were far more galling to rival powers than British progress in far-off continents, which they themselves, after all, were imitating.

The popular attitude toward the rest of the world, which is a basic aspect of nationalism, owes a great deal to the geographical situation of the British Isles. For one hundred years, the British generally have been both the most widely traveled of European peoples and, in regard to Europe, the most insular. British factories, clubs, cantonments, and shops dotted the Deccan and the Borneo jungles; their stamp remains on Rangoon and Accra, Wellington and Bahrein. Yet until very recently the masses maintained a cheerful ignorance of continental peoples. The British were not hostile. The upper class and the upper middle class, a very small percentage of the whole population, visited and know France and Italy. And the islanders do not share the average Frenchman's pity for anyone not born in France. Except when their furious energies were provoked by war, a process which takes a long time, the British remained indifferent to Europe. They had their Empire. They had their Commonwealth. And, "niggers begin at Calais."

This insularity was bolstered by another characteristic. "In no other society," wrote Hilaire Belloc, "is the worship of the corporate body of the nation exalted to such a height, and this worship of the native country as an idol . . . is the main cause of English homogeneity." In the past this homogeneity has been the source of great and unexpected shows of strength. It has been accounted the main reason that the United Kingdom was able to weather the staggering casualties of World War I. Some social historians attribute the comparative facility with which Edward VIII was removed from the throne to its pervasive influence.

Certainly, this homogeneity played a significant role in the sudden and effective restoration of national unity in 1940. When Winston Churchill, many years later, remarked that his defiant speeches at that time were merely the expression of the national will, he was being accurate rather than modest.

A slowly unifying Europe has challenged Britain's economy and international influence. Thus far, President de Gaulle
has prevented Britain from joining Europe. But entry into
E.E.C. still offers Britons the best chance of fulfilling national
aspirations in a changing world. They will persist in their
efforts.

The original six members of E.E.C., or, as it is popularly
known, the Common Market, embraced the concept primarily for economic reasons. But in each of these six—France,
West Germany, Italy, the Netherlands, Belgium, and Luxembourg—a few national leaders saw some form of political
co-operation as the natural outcome of a closer economic relationship. This was also true of Britain. Ultimately, the
attraction of possible leadership in Europe will outweigh the
economic arguments which originally drew the United Kingdom toward the E.E.C.

When the perceptive politician or civil servant along the
Thames looks at the Common Market as it is now constituted, he cannot see a single large state whose political stability compares with that of the United Kingdom. The British
alone have avoided revolution, invasion, and defeat. Parliamentary democracy has outlasted the French and German republics and outfought the Italian and German tyrannies. In
the late forties it was strong enough to enable the oldest of
industrial, capitalist states to develop into a welfare state.
Internal stability, based primarily on a corporate sense of
nationhood, has protected the country from the bitter political
strife, often erupting into riot, which elsewhere has accompanied, as it has in France, the dissolution of an overseas
empire.

This is a basis for optimism with regard to Britain's

opportunities in Europe. The politician and the civil servant see in the E.E.C. a structure which, although imposing enough from the outside, is endangered by certain weaknesses of its parts. Leadership, political leadership, is what is needed, and the British will be only too happy to provide it. They do not see post-Gaullist France as stable enough even to attempt it. The political succession in Bonn may be clearer; but there is a fundamental weakness in the German position, as seen from Whitehall: although many Europeans may have forgiven 1933-1945 in Germany, they have not forgotten it to the point where they are prepared to leave the political leadership of Europe in German hands.

The measure of leadership which any one country is able to exercise in a united Europe depends upon the form that unity takes. At the moment E.E.C. does not constitute an outright union. Its present tendency is toward a confederation that is a common organization affecting a limited but important area of national life, national economies, but it is also federal in the sense that the Community acts directly in some respects upon the citizens of member states. The coming crisis in Europe with regard to the political direction to be taken by E.E.C. is most likely to arise from the disputes between those who desire a federal Europe and those who favor a confederation. In the first case there would be a central federal government which would be the sovereign power. In the second there would be a permanent union whose common organization of sovereign states would not be sovereign, although it might have authority in clearly defined fields.

However, in Britain in the preparatory period the economic opportunities have been stressed most. Simply put, the argument is that competition within this huge new area will provide successful British industries with new openings for mass-produced goods and thus stimulate production and competition to a point where the United Kingdom will be able to compete on even terms with her great rivals, West Germany, the United States, the Commonwealth, and other overseas markets.

The approach to Europe aroused doubts and misgivings on both sides of the English Channel. Arguments in Britain, many of them irrelevant, have provided a contradictory picture. On one hand, say the advocates of E.E.C., this is the country's last chance for survival as a great political influence. Britain can lead Europe, once she is in it. If she remains outside, however, Europe will dominate her and will speak in more authoritative tones than London to Moscow and Washington. On the contrary, say the opponents. If Britain goes in, she loses her special position vis-à-vis the United States and her role as leader of the Commonwealth, and in matters of urgent national interest she may find herself outvoted by Italians, Germans, and French.

Setting these arguments aside for the moment, the drastic alteration of Britain's position in the last few years in relation to the E.E.C. powers, the United States, and the Soviet Union can hardly be exaggerated.

In 1963 the dynamic economic force in Europe is E.E.C. —that is, three of its members in particular, France, West Germany, and Italy. This dynamism can be seen in the expansion of industry and is also evident in export figures. But it is perhaps more important to understand it in its effect on the societies under discussion. Not only are production figures rising. There is also a forceful renaissance of popular energy directed to industrial and commercial pursuits. It may be that in the nuclear age Italians, Frenchmen, and West Germans have realized that although their countries can no longer be made great by force of arms, that even though they are overshadowed by the nuclear colossi, they can still win economic security and national well-being through economic offensives. How else can the movement of young upper-class Italians, Frenchmen, and Germans into commercial life, rather than the army or the civil service or the professions, be explained?

This phenomenon naturally raises problems. In the last year a number of senior German and French civil servants have deplored the lack of bright young recruits to their departments. Industry, they say, has been getting them all; this may be an exaggeration, but it is clear that a career in business, with its richer rewards, attracts young men who three decades ago would have gone into the military or civil services.

Britain has not been standing still. Solid advances in production, in exports, in industrial and commercial techniques have been made. But the harsh fact is that to foreigners, including citizens of these three booming continental countries, Britain seems to be standing still. We shall examine the reasons more closely later in this book. But even to the uninitiated there is a vast difference between the vibrant, hustling economic society of, say, northern Italy, and that of some sections of the British realm. There is also a sharp contrast between the outlook of Britons with regard to their commercial opportunities today and the aggressive, hopeful approach they took in 1951 when the country was emerging from the long twilight of austerity.

In its relation to Europe in recent years the United Kingdom can be compared to an old and lovely country house in the midst of its own grounds on the outskirts of a bustling modern city. The house is filled with mementoes of a glorious past; its inhabitants are civil to the pushing people in the city, but there is no need to be anything more. Now the city stretches out. Its people, with scant respect for past grandeur, are competing economically and even socially and politically with the family in the country house. The house itself is in a state of disrepair. The relatives do not visit the old home as much as they once did; they are intrigued with the fresh new outlook of the town. Does the country-house family join the sharp competition of the city, casting aside old rights to win new opportunities, or does it relapse into a long, warm twilight amid memories of other days?

In the contemporary world such a decline was inevitable for a Britain aloof from Europe. Events may arrest the process, however. A civil war in France, for instance, would disrupt the still fragile structure of continental Europe. But although this would postpone reduction of Britain's status in relation to Europe, it would not ultimately prevent it. The past is no answer; the Battle of Britain does not sell steel in Argentina against German competition.

If Britain's position, either individually or as the center of the Commonwealth, has declined in relation to Europe, it has declined much more drastically in comparison with the position of the two titans, the United States and the Soviet Union. Indeed, it has been the realization, dimly but firmly grasped by a politically adult people, that the United Kingdom can no longer compete as a world power with the American and Russian titans which has provided the basic political impetus for entry into the European Economic Community.

Secure in his own belief in the superiority of the United States, the American reader may be pardoned for asking how any Briton in the seventh decade of the century can have believed since 1945 that Britain could compete. After all, if he has traveled in the United Kingdom, he has been told often enough that the United States is the major Western power now, that the leadership of the West lies with the Americans; and, occasionally, he has been told just how that leadership should be exercised. The politically experienced know that Prime Minister Macmillan considers the British as the Greeks in America's Roman Empire. The economist knows that the City of London and the Treasury run the world-wide sterling area on reserves which are less than the capital of the Ford Motor Company.

The popular belief in Britain's position as a world power, specifically the third world power after the United States and the U.S.S.R., has died hard in the United Kingdom for a number of reasons. To consider one in the field of national psychology: it is difficult for a people who have been on top for hundreds of years to understand that the power is no longer there. This is especially true in a country where the trappings of the imperial past are not only alive but venerated. The Army may be smaller than that of Italy, but the Guards at Buckingham Palace are as smart as ever. To take another reason from the field of international relations: more Britons visit the Continent every year than ever before, but they go to the Riviera or the Costa Brava rather than to Essen or Clermont-Ferrand or Turin. They have been and still are largely ignorant of the changes brought by the European economic revolution of the last ten years.

The Commonwealth has done Britain a great deal of good. But in the attainment of a realistic approach to their own status in the world, it has done the British, and specifically the English, a great deal of harm. Britain's position as the center of the Commonwealth undeniably gave her, in the past, greater stature in the eyes of Moscow and Washington. But the tendency in Britain, which has grown paradoxically as the ties with the Commonwealth have weakened, has been to exaggerate this position.

Until quite recently Britain and the Commonwealth were compared on even terms with the United States and the Soviet Union by people who should have understood the fragility of the political ties between Commonwealth nations, the economic pressures on the old commercial arrangements, and the fact that those ties of blood, shared experience, and culture about which so many words are spilled at formal banquets now apply to only four members of the Commonwealth: Canada, Australia, New Zealand, and Britain. The cause of this gross overestimate of the power of the Commonwealth in world affairs, which was eagerly equated in the home islands with global influence, was that the Commonwealth evolved from the old Empire. Possession of the Empire did give Britain a military, diplomatic, and economic voice far louder than that to which she was entitled on the basis of the area and population of the British Isles.

Twice in this century the Commonwealth raised vast forces and sent them to fight at Britain's side on land and in the air in Europe, Africa, and Asia, and on all the oceans of the world. Indeed, the Indian Army in World War II was the largest volunteer army ever raised. Until 1939 the knowledge of this army's strength and availability kept the peace from

Suez to Singapore, very much as the United States Seventh Fleet keeps the peace today in the western Pacific.

But the Commonwealth is changing. Whatever its ultimate shape, it will not, it cannot in the modern world, be the basis for Britain's claims to world power. The Commonwealth, or at least some members of it, will still respond to Britain's call—more readily if the call from Whitehall is echoed by a more powerful voice from Washington. But other members, particularly the new states of Africa and Asia, will often stop their ears.

The essential political consequence of Britain's entry into Europe, from the standpoint of the Commonwealth, will be the abandonment by the United Kingdom of a unique position as the heart of the world-wide organism. This position was the result of many factors, some of them as concrete as the absence of duty on raw materials imported from the Commonwealth, some as intangible as the lively ghosts of red-faced and choleric English judges who sat in Accra or Colombo administering the law with a blazing incorruptibility. Continuation depended on Britain's being of the Commonwealth, not of Europe or even of an Atlantic community. Whatever happens once Britain has joined, this relationship cannot be retained.

The British quite clearly are abandoning one set of claims to be a great power in exchange for entry into a group in which, they believe, their experience and abilities will entitle them to a leading role. In this sense entry will be a political gamble. If Britain cannot be a great power in comparison with the Soviet Union and the United States, then she will play an important part in a great power, a united Europe. Nothing in international affairs is as simple as that.

But, on the whole, this change seems to represent the adjustment, conscious or unconscious, which a very large number
of Britons have made with themselves with respect to the
Common Market and the future role of their country in the
world.

Many plausible arguments have been advanced for doing nothing; they always are. Yet it required a good deal of
faith to see the survival of the United Kingdom as a great
power of the second rank, that is, in the same class as contemporary France or West Germany, if she remained wedded
to her present concept of her place in the world. On one hand
there is the slow decay of the economic and political relationships with the Commonwealth. This has been going on for
years. Ghana's drift toward totalitarianism, India's opposition
to British international policies, and, recently, sharp British
criticism of India, the leftist trend in Ceylon, the welcome by
Australian and Canadian buyers to non-British goods—the
sum total of all this ultimately is a far more serious drain on
the basic unity of the Commonwealth than more spectacular
developments such as the withdrawal of the Union of South
Africa.

On the other hand there is the steady increase in political, military, and economic strength—and consequently in
diplomatic influence—of four great political entities, the Soviet Union, Communist China, the United States, and the European Economic Community. Without Britain the latter may
not be as complete, politically and economically, as it
would wish to be. But only the most patriotic Briton can believe that E.E.C., if it continues in its present course, would
not overshadow an increasingly isolated United Kingdom in
the immediate future.

Perhaps this graceful and comfortable decline into international impotence is what the British desire. Many of them appear willing to trade any lingering pretensions to world prestige and influence for a world status not unlike that of Sweden, a country, it should be remembered, which once shook Europe from the Volga to the Rhine. Some, in fact, prefer living in the old country house, snubbing the neighbors and re-reading old tales of glory around the hearth every evening. Fortunately for the Western world, to which the British Isles have given so much, they are not in a majority.

In this book we shall be concerned with the new generations in Europe. A new generation is moving toward the top in Britain. We shall examine its leaders and its ideas in detail later. Now it suffices to note that this generation has come to terms with the altered position of Britain in the world. It is not content to live in the past. Nor is it so beguiled by the image of the Commonwealth, superimposed in the minds of an older generation upon a fading picture of world-wide Empire, that it believes that in Britain's present straits the Commonwealth offers insurance for the continuation of the home islands as a world power. I am not writing about the Angry Young Men of the left or the brassy, closely shaven young men of the right who believe that Britain's destiny lies in copying the methods and techniques of Madison Avenue. The people who are attempting to change Britain by bringing her into Europe and then arousing and exerting her resources of intelligence, experience, and energy are in fact the most visionary, the most imaginative of the generation now in its forties.

They know that something is wrong. And they are not content to accept it. They see no virtue in a continued decline in proud isolation. They are the activists of modern Britain. They understand, instinctively, that the old Britain is dead.

We must turn now to that death and what brought it about. History offers few more terrible, poignant, and remorseless accounts than that of the decline of British power. And, if we look at the world around us, few that have led to so much bloodshed, suffering, and misery in what is laughingly called the civilized world.

· 2 ·

What Happened to the British?... The Mature Strength of 1939 ... Changes in Power Relationships ... Empire into Commonwealth ... Competition with Europe ... The Outlook for the Sixties

To look back to Britain in 1939 is to see another country and, indeed, another world. Americans in their twenties and thirties will find it difficult to realize how long a shadow Britain then cast across the globe. Aloof, imperial, her governments and policies alike were the target for that constant and vicious criticism which is always the lot of great Western powers. Economists and staff officers could discern cracks in the imperial façade. But the sum of the British impression on the rest of the world was one of immense and experienced military and economic strength and infinite political wisdom.

Although for the purposes of this book the comparison

is between 1939 and 1960, it is generally accepted that the decline of British power began much earlier. The zenith of that power was probably attained between 1815, when the Napoleonic wars ended, and 1880, when the industrial strength of the new German empire began to influence continental politics. During that period, in fact until the outbreak of World War I in 1914, Britain and the British achieved and largely maintained an unchallenged pre-eminence in world politics. So lasting was the impression made by this position on other nations that today, fifty years after the decline set in, there remains a tendency to ascribe to the United Kingdom and its official representatives wisdom and skill of an almost supernatural nature. Only a few years ago I talked with an Irish official of great experience who invariably referred to the government in London as "the government with the serpent's wisdom." He was an Irishman, and whatever successes the British have had in Nigeria or Malaya, they made a hash of Irish affairs. Yet he was apparently incapable of ridding himself of his exaggerated estimate of British political ability, an echo of the apparently unshakable position of the United Kingdom one hundred years ago.

If these memories are still important today, they were that much stronger in 1939 when the British government and people prepared to measure their mature strength against the bouncing bellicosity of the Third Reich. The perspicacious few were accurate in their diagnosis of British weaknesses. They erred, however, in their estimate that these weaknesses had irretrievably softened Britain. But to the world, including the German and Italian masses, Britain and the Empire still appeared very powerful. In 1939 no one could remember a time when the small island group off Europe's northwest coast had not been a great, and for long periods the greatest, world power. The economists might argue that the money power now resided in Wall Street. The staff officers might contend that militarily Britain was outclassed by Germany and Japan. All to no avail. The people, who were to fight the war that was coming, saw Britain, whether or not they liked the country and its people, and most of them didn't, as the nexus of a great combination of political, diplomatic, economic, and military power.

This flattering estimate of Britain's situation, oddly enough, took little account of the national characteristics that were to save the home islands and the Empire in the days ahead. These were the resiliency and courage of the British people. The world had become so accustomed to British triumphs, invariably exaggerated abroad and minimized by the British, that it was prone to overlook the morale on which they were based. More than anyone else, the Germans miscalculated. But the French and the Americans were not far behind.

The world of 1939 had been brought up in an atmosphere of British power, believing in British statesmanship and British craftsmanship. The ensuing six years were to show that the estimates formed before the war exaggerated the physical strength of the nation and were even inaccurate in terms of moral vigor.

One reason for exaggeration was that in 1939 Britain still stood at the head of a global Empire and Commonwealth, and, in those days, public speakers in Europe still thought first of the Empire. The shadows were lengthening. But the British writ still ran in Peshawar and Rangoon, the white ensign of the Royal Navy flew in the China Sea and the Caribbean, the products of Manchester and Birmingham flooded the markets of Sydney and Buluwayo. There were of course many, in Britain and elsewhere, who deplored this imperial domain. In Berlin, Rome, and Tokyo, able and active men labored to bring the whole edifice crashing down about the ears of the English, as they were still called. But the Empire was there. It was a fact. At two extremes, Mahatma Gandhi and William Randolph Hearst might assail it, but the Empire stood, impressing even iconoclasts like Adolf Hitler with its solidity.

The Empire and Commonwealth marched across seas and continents. But its influence was not confined to the great imperial holdings. The British writ ran, disputed by fervent nationalists, but still it ran, in Egypt and Palestine; it affected the affairs of princelings in Borneo and coral-fringed islands in the Pacific. The sum total of the Empire's influence was far greater than the colossal expanse of the Empire itself. To the outsider, Persia, as it was then called, and all of Arabia seemed fiefs of that Empire.

The Empire and Commonwealth in 1939 embraced 13,909,782 square miles of the earth's surface, and its population was approximately 500,870,000. But the populations of the four Dominions in which the political and racial ties were strongest were small by European standards. Canada was the largest, with 10,400,000, and South Africa was next, with 9,600,000. The population of Australia was 6,620,000, and that of New Zealand, 1,600,000.

This imperial presence was adorned by the imaginations of Europeans, particularly those of the Gott Strafe England and Perfide Albion schools, with an almost supernatural capacity for successful political intrigue and an enormous

appetite for other people's land. The beliefs lingered on, well
past mid-century; in the nineteen-fifties an American would
be seriously assured by Parisians that the Algerian rebellion
had been cooked up by those clever English who wanted
to grab the country themselves. This contrasted oddly with
a certain respect that the British had won for themselves in
World War I. Like the Almighty, the British appeared to
move in a mysterious way their wonders to perform; even the
Germans of pre-1939 days, happy in the joy of the Fuehrer's
revelation, spoke respectfully of that unseen, and hence mysterious, power exerted by the Royal Navy upon their efforts
in the conflict. The French would sometimes grudgingly admit that there had been a British Expeditionary Force. But
beyond popular prejudice one encountered among the educated a realistic view that Britain had contributed a great deal
to the Allied victory. The cost to Britain of that victory was
often advanced by Europeans as an argument why the British
would never fight again. There was also a strong belief, scarcely borne out by the facts of life in the United Kingdom, that the British had done very well out of the war and
everyone else had done badly. Paradoxically, the British at
about this time were dissecting their war effort with melancholy energy, proving to the satisfaction of many that they had
just muddled through, that Haig and his lieutenants were a
group of military bumblers unequalled in history, and that
the victory of 1918 was the surprising result of outrageous
military blundering.

Still the continental peoples, especially the old soldiers,
remained unconvinced. They ascribed to the sudden influx of
British manpower in 1915-1917 the frustration of the great
German offensives. Indeed, from the old soldiers one got the

impression that the addition of the British mass army to the
conflict was slightly unsporting. In 1945 and 1946 the same
feeling was evident about the Americans, who had, as had
the British thirty years earlier, provided the vital element of
victory. And, of course, beyond the memories of World War
I there existed a folk history of successful British intervention
in continental wars. "They are a very ignorant people," an
old Frenchman told me once in Arras, "but not so ignorant
as to miss any opportunities for engaging their strength in the
decisive battle and then taking the rewards for which better
people have died."

All this, the towering façade of Empire, the powerful and
possibly decisive intervention in the greatest of European conflicts, and a history of success in other wars, provided the
British with an unequalled base for the exercise of their political influence. We are accustomed now to believe that this
influence was at its nadir at the outbreak of World War II.
Yet the total impression in Europe of British strength enabled
politicians and diplomats in London to wield a great influence
upon international affairs. By the military standards of the
time, France was the greatest land power in Europe. Yet the
history of French policy-making from 1933 onwards records
successive surrenders of diplomatic and political initiative to
the British, especially in dealing with the Third Reich and its
unpredictable master.

This was not due entirely to the steady deterioration of
French political stability in the last years of the Third Republic. British statesmanship in some instances was almost
as bad as its detractors claimed, by turns arrogant and craven,
snobbish and ignorant, dilettante and unfeeling. Any late-
night conversation with Americans abroad would produce a

dozen examples of how "the goddam British" had insulted allies or alienated would-be friends. But these were the last years in which the British didn't care about the good opinion of anyone, including the Americans.

After all that has been said, it is worth remembering that British professional diplomacy in the years before the war was also in many instances far-sighted and resolute, more clear-eyed in its assessments of Hitler and Mussolini than its political masters, and, above all, far from hesitant in making its views known to the powers in Whitehall. In this period His Majesty's missions abroad housed such rising stars as Ivone Kirkpatrick, Roger Makins, Gladwyn Jebb, and a dozen others. The Foreign Office in London had men like Robert Vansittart and Alexander Cadogan. For part of the troubled thirties, their political boss was Anthony Eden, the ablest Foreign Secretary of his day. The high reputation enjoyed by British diplomacy today is rooted in that period as well as the more distant past.

British diplomacy did include some apostles of appeasement like Sir Nevile Henderson, the ambassador in Berlin at the outbreak of the war. But there is little substance to the legend, carefully exploited during the war years by the left, that the professional diplomatic service abroad and the Foreign Office at home were blind to German ambitions and indifferent to the terrible consequences of government policy. However, the professionals were not then able, nor are their successors today, effectively to challenge Cabinet decisions on policy. That limitation was understood in Europe in 1939, although there was a tendency then and later in Washington to lump the diplomats and the politicians together as fellow appeasers.

On the whole, however, British diplomacy benefited from the general impression of British global strength, invariably equated with the Empire, and of governmental stability. Neither allies nor enemies really understood the Empire and the Commonwealth—such understanding is still rather rare today —but it was recognized that in the event of war Britain would have the support of her extensive overseas territories. What was not understood, except by a few German staff officers, was that the Commonwealth and Empire were even less ready for the kind of war that was coming than was Britain.

Critics of British government and policy in that period have sustained the belief that 1939 found the United Kingdom entering a world war virtually unprepared. In some respects this was true. And, since a number of politicians of both the right and the left had seen the war approaching for at least three years, the lack of preparation was discreditable to Prime Minister Chamberlain's government. But any comparison of the military posture of Britain in 1939 and 1962 must lead to the conclusion that in weapons, and psychologically, the people governed by Neville Chamberlain were far better equipped to fight Hitler's Germany than those governed by Harold Macmillan would be for an encounter with Khrushchev's Russia. Indeed, Chamberlain himself powerfully supported rearmament in the last years before the war.

In 1939 Britain still possessed the largest navy in the world in number of available ships. This fleet, happily, had a tradition of victory that stretched back beyond Trafalgar into the eighteenth century. A combination of high professional competence and almost arrogant confidence enabled the Royal Navy in the next five and a half years to weather a series of disasters that would have broken a lesser force. The high estimate of the Royal Navy's capacities which friend and foe alike held in the last year of peace stood up under the strains of combat.

The presence of the fleet was of inestimable benefit to what we would now call the British image in the world. Sea power had not yet been effectively challenged by air power in battle, and although in 1939 there were airmen who believed that such a challenge could be made successfully, their views did not counteract the impression of power given by the fleet. Indeed, the numerical superiority of that fleet was the basis for one of the most marked differences between the British power status then and now; in 1939 the United Kingdom, through the possession of the 543 ships of the Royal Navy, and the additional 157 under construction, represented an independent strategic force of primary significance. The last hour might be about to strike for sea power. But in Scapa Flow, where the great ships swung to the northern tides, in the sunny harbors of Malta, Gibraltar, Trincomalee, Singapore, and Hong Kong, it was still high noon.

The superiority of the Royal Navy in 1939 overshadowed the two junior services, the Army and the Royal Air Force. Yet the quality of these two forces was excellent; it was quantity that was lacking. Nevertheless, Britain was able to send to France in 1939 and 1940 nine divisions which were better equipped than those of the French armies—this is not, of course, saying a great deal—and which were better led and better disciplined. The United Kingdom was also able to summon to its assistance in Europe, Africa, and Asia the forces of the Dominion and Empire. At the outset they lacked the modern equipment of the British Army. But when they got such equipment, and in some cases before they got it, they proved themselves formidable soldiers. The Germans were accurate in their analysis of the logistical weakness of the Commonwealth and Empire but wide of the mark in their estimate of the willingness and resolution of the troops it would send to battle.

The unknown element of Britain's military situation in 1939 was the Air Force, which consisted of 1,900 aircraft of all types, modern and obsolete. Here, as in the case of the Navy and the Army, a tradition of victory affected the view from the other side of the hill; at the end of World War I British military aviation was of a high standard. The British fighters and bombers were too few in 1939 and, in the case of the latter, outmoded. Yet in battle, first Fighter Command and then Bomber Command mastered the Luftwaffe, which at the start of the war was justly accounted the finest air force in the world.

The over-all impression of British military strength in 1939 was one of great, if unbalanced, power. In relative terms, however, it was clear that only at sea was Britain pre-eminent when compared with the forces of the Third Reich. Moreover, if we are to look realistically at Britain in 1939 and its position in the world, we must remember that in the eyes of foreign observers the quantitative inferiority of the British Army was more than compensated by the alliance with France, whose army was hailed, in one of the favorite clichés of the day, as "the finest standing army on the continent."

All this, the government at home, the Empire and the Commonwealth abroad, the diplomatic experience and influence, the fleets, divisions, and air squadrons, rested ultimately upon a basis of economic strength which the world considered, if not invulnerable, certainly strong enough to withstand the shocks of a second war against Germany. Indeed, the confi-

dence with which the government of that day went to war owed
a great deal to this assumption of economic superiority. "We
will win," ran one of the slogans of the day, "because we are
the stronger," and a government of businessmen regarded Britain's economic strength as an element which in the long run
would tip the scales in favor of the Western alliance.

The future being mercifully hidden, they could not even
glimpse, nor could their predecessors of 1914, the terrible toll
that war would take in the economy of Britain.

Again we note the influence of a century and more of
British industrial and commercial eminence upon the world's
view of Britain in 1939. In that century British inventions and
industrial techniques had established for Britain the world
reputation that the United States enjoys today. They had invented the industrial revolution and tutored the world in its
use. The Germans had made some dent in this reputation in
the years before 1914 and again between 1933 and 1939. But
in Europe, Africa, Asia, and some parts of South America,
British exports of machine tools and marine engines, woolens
and cottons, locomotives, hardware, and, equally important,
trained technicians—exports that had continued without successful challenge almost since the start of the industrial revolution—created an impression of industrial and commercial enterprise and sagacity that appeared to equip the home islands
for victory in any struggle in which their economy would be
pitted against that of Germany. There was, at the same time,
an almost pathetic underestimate in Europe, except in Britain
itself, of what the American economy could do if turned to
war.

When Britain entered World War II, she was the greatest
trading nation in the world. She had to be. A large proportion

of the home island's food supplies and most of the raw materials for industry had to be imported, and a high percentage of manufactured products had to be exported to pay for these imports. Only one important raw material was available in Britain: coal. The great imperial structure rested upon an industrial base dependent on imports and upon world trade dependent on exports, which meant the freedom of the seas for British ships.

In several industrial essentials Britain lagged behind the other great powers of the day. In 1939 she produced 13,434,-000 metric tons of steel, as compared with Germany's 23,208,-000 and the United States' 47,898,000. In the production of iron ore the British were second to France in Europe and about 500,000 metric tons better than Germany. But Britain's coal production was 235,050,000 metric tons, as compared with Germany's 174,698,000 and the United States' 402,156,-000. Britain was, however, producing more motor vehicles than Germany, and the machine-tool industry, which was to count for so much in the next five years, was recovering its vitality under the demands of rearmament.

These were the physical factors that contributed to Britain's position in 1939. It is more difficult to assess the morale of the country in that year and more difficult still to compare it with that of today. Oddly enough, although the morale of the British, along with inspired leadership, got them through the first terrible eighteen months of war, that morale was seriously questioned in the late nineteen-thirties. Those diplomats and commentators who were then busily weighing the assets of the two great antagonists believed for the most part that the dynamic character of the German regime, its ruthless modernity, its willingness to dare and risk, and the enthusiastic support of the German people gave the Third Reich a realistic advantage over the United Kingdom. The Germans are coming, the British are going—so ran another of the popular phrases of the time.

There were good reasons for doubting the psychological preparedness of the British for the kind of conflict that was brewing. The ten years before the outbreak of war had developed tendencies in life and thought that were unlikely to help Britain in a fight for survival. Some of these, such as the passage through the Oxford Union of a resolution "that this House refuses to fight for King and Country" and the endorsement of the Peace Ballot by 11,000,000 persons, created the impression abroad that the British were decadent and would refuse to fight for what their forefathers had won.

The British political ethos, however, was suffering from a situation a great deal more fundamental than the Oxford Resolution and the Peace Ballot, which were its manifestations. In no country, with the possible exception of Germany, had there been a greater revulsion from the horrors of the first war and a stronger resolution to avoid their renewal. To the shattering casualty lists that had swept away a generation were added the somber dissections of the military historians and the frank and horrible reminiscences of the survivors of that lost generation. As much as the Peace Ballot or the Oxford Resolution these conveyed to the world the impression of a Britain that would not fight again.

The scars left by World War I on public opinion were matched in the thirties by those left by the years of depression. Poverty, unemployment, and hardship inured the working class against any government but that of the Labor Party. Then the defection of Ramsay MacDonald from that party disillusioned many Labor voters. The feuds between classes which erupted under the Labor government of 1945 were fed by the bitter memories of those years.

Finally, the months preceding the outbreak of war in 1939 brought a general political disillusionment. Appeasement had clearly failed to satisfy Hitler, and the whole policy approach of Chamberlain and the Tories lay in ruins. The left, especially the articulate left of Westminster and Fleet Street, had watched with horror the fall of Austria and Czechoslovakia, the rape of Ethiopia, and the slow strangulation of the Spanish Republic. In increasing numbers and with increasing vehemence it had turned to the Soviet Union for salvation against Hitler and the Axis. Then its hopes were dashed when the Russians and the Germans became allies.

These were serious blows to a national morale already suffering from the effects of the blood-letting of 1914-1918. It is no wonder that observers underestimated the ability of the British to fight a war. Some believed that the social structure of the country was in such a parlous state that the government would have to abandon its last remaining positions in world politics and conduct an ignominious retreat. But there remained, in 1939, positive morale factors which do not exist today and which must be kept in perspective in any realistic analysis of Britain then and now.

The Empire existed. To it and to George VI, the King-Emperor, many millions were devoted. The middle class, which had benefited most from the Empire, invariably has been portrayed as the only class with a class interest in its survival. This is only part of the picture. The first forty years of this century developed an instinctive belief among ordinary people that, although they might not share in its financial rewards, the Empire belonged to them. This persisted far longer than some people would like to believe. When Britain got out of India in 1947, there was a deep if inarticulate sense of grievance among working-class people who had never directly got a sixpence out of the Indian Empire but who had spilled their blood all over the sub-continent. Aneurin Bevan once explained it to me with the phrase: "They didn't want it, they didn't understand it, but they felt it was theirs, part of their power. And people understand power."

The Britain of 1939 was in every way closer to the Britain of 1900 than to the Britain of today. The heroics of the late Victorian and Edwardian eras, the blind patriotism of the generation that died in 1914-1918, had some lingering influence. In the two or three years preceding the war, there had been a growing revulsion from the anti-national feelings of the immediate post-war years. This was accelerated by events abroad. It was seen, dimly by the mass and acutely by the few, that what had happened in Europe since 1933 had diminished Britain's position in the world. Neither the right's policy of appeasement nor the left's cult of internationalism, based on the League of Nations, had provided an emotionally satisfactory answer. The idea, so current today, that Britain must accept relegation to the status of a second-class power had very few adherents then. The issue rather was whether Britain should fight in defense of her position as a world power, to many the leading one, and how long it would take her to win if she did.

The concept of immediate and terrible punishment by the Luftwaffe in the event of war was accepted generally. But it was accepted as part of a war which most people wanted to avoid but which the majority believed would be won. There was not, as there is now, the conviction among a large part of

the population that war would write finis to the long story of
British history. The British, as always, had gone to great
lengths to avoid war—they are a sensible people—but they did
not doubt their ability to win it, no matter how flimsy the evidence on which their certainty of eventual victory seemed
based.

The morale of the British people in the twilight of their
world leadership was fundamentally strong. For proof, we have
only to look at the tremendous outpouring of national energy,
valor, and endurance that followed the defeats in Europe in the
spring and summer of 1940. And it is worth noting that the
middle and upper classes, which, on the whole, had been most
prepared to appease Hitler and Mussolini, provided in those
long, agonizing months the hard core of military leadership. In
the darkest hours it was the regular services, Army, Navy, and
Air Force, trained and led by young men of these classes,
which provided the strength which enabled Britain to survive.
History's final summation will find that their patriotism and
courage outweighed and erased the political aberrations of the
thirties.

But they were fighting for a Britain very different from
what it is today. Superficially, of course, many things are unchanged. Indeed, the sense of continuity, the changelessness of
much of British life, makes it difficult both for foreigners and
for the British themselves to grasp the alteration in the position
of the country. Ancient institutions and familiar rituals go on
from year to year. This, it sometimes seems, is almost as true of
the working class as of The Establishment, usually considered
the special custodian of ritual. In the north one meets working-
class families that for thirty years have taken their vacation at
a certain time in the summer and have returned, year after

year, to the same boarding house in the same seaside resort. The unspoken desire to cling to the familiar is just as strong in those families as it is in more fashionable ones in London for whom June means the Derby, Trooping the Color, and Ascot.

Yet, none of this should obscure the tremendous differences between Britain in 1939 and today. British power faded. Almost simultaneously, two and possibly three super-states, the United States, the Soviet Union, and China, emerged.

The Empire of 1939 has disappeared. The Indian Empire has become the Indian and Pakistan republics, both members of the Commonwealth and both independent. Burma is a sovereign nation outside the Commonwealth. Ceylon remains precariously inside. Two great British holdings in Africa, Nigeria and Ghana, formerly the Gold Coast, are now independent members of the Commonwealth. Tanganyika has become independent; Kenya is on the verge. The Federation of the Rhodesias and Nyasaland still includes Northern Rhodesia, a responsibility of the Colonial Office in London, but the Federation, too, is moving toward some form of independence. Of the great "white" dominions, one, South Africa, has left the Commonwealth. Another, Canada, has been drawn inexorably into the economic orbit of the United States. Australia and New Zealand remain loyal to a great extent to the United Kingdom. But that loyalty will be sorely tried after Britain enters Europe. For, as we shall see, the ties that bind the Commonwealth are tenuous and depend to a surprising degree on custom and habit arising from mutual trust, rather than on written rules.

It is this weakness of the Commonwealth ties that mocks the assertions of many Britons that the nation has lost an Empire but gained a Commonwealth. On the basis of reflected power and influence in the world, there is no comparison between Britain and the Empire and Britain and the Commonwealth. Consider what has happened in areas contiguous to parts of the Empire since it began to dissolve. As the imperial power decayed, Britain's influence in Egypt and the Middle East decayed with it. The peace that was kept from Suez to Singapore by the British-led Indian Army has been broken half a dozen times since India became independent.

All this meant the transfer, at a rather irregular tempo, of political and diplomatic leadership in the Western world across the Atlantic to Washington. The shift was not as rapid or as complete as might have been expected in the morning of victory in 1945. One reason, which Americans are prone to overlook, was that the British, even in their shaken state in the immediate post-war years, had a great reservoir of experience in the world's affairs. The British had the know-how. They lacked in those years, and still lack, the financial and economic strength that is the basis of international leadership. But they had emerged as victors in the war, they had been redoubtable allies in the fighting, and the world, even the hard-headed officials in Washington, tended to take them at something approximating their own valuation. The world had grown accustomed to British power; the idea was a long time dying. In this the United Kingdom was helped by the presence of Sir Winston Churchill, one of the outstanding personalities of the century. Even in his six years out of office, between 1945 and 1951, Sir Winston's presence on the international scene gave to Britain a certain authority in the world. Remarkably prescient in his forecasts of both the Nazi and the Communist dangers, he towered over his contemporaries on both sides of the Atlantic. The world's long memories and Sir Winston's long shadow helped obscure the realities of British power. It was probably not until Britain proved unable to implement Sir Anthony Eden's Suez plans in 1956 that the average citizen of the Western world understood how far that power had declined.

Oddly enough in one sense, the British were more powerful then than they had ever been. Except for the United States and the U.S.S.R., the United Kingdom was the only other nation to possess nuclear weapons. Possession of these weapons, carried by a small but highly efficient bombing fleet, was a positive advantage to the governments of the United Kingdom between 1950 and 1960, especially in their relationship with administrations in Washington. Even so, the tremendous growth of American and Russian military power in nuclear terms gradually reduced the importance of the British contribution to the West's nuclear deterrent. It became marginal, and, as the new decade dawned, it was highly unlikely that the Royal Air Force's V-bomber force was as important in the eyes of American strategists as the British Conservative government liked to believe.

The great armies and fleets that Britain had built at such great cost in World War II dwindled in the international military scale. By the end of the fifties the Soviet navy had far outstripped the fleet that once ruled the seas in numbers and tonnage. The army, rich in officers with successful war records, had been allowed by Conservative governments to run down to a point where it was inferior in armaments to the new German divisions taking over a share of the defense of Europe and, some observers thought, in dash and morale to the French forces at whose side it fought during the Suez adventure. From 1957 onward, this run-down of the so-called conventional forces was a planned aspect of defense. The White Paper on defense of that year, presented by the then Minister of Defense, Duncan Sandys, consciously diverted the weight of the British defense effort to the nuclear deterrent.

One reason advanced at the time by Mr. Sandys and others was that Britain could not invariably count on nuclear intervention by the United States in support of interests which might appear alien, i.e., British, to an administration in Washington. But, of course, the real reason the emphasis in defense was shifted to nuclear weapons was that the United Kingdom simply could not afford a balanced defense program that gave required strength to both conventional and nuclear forces. Here we approach the greatest difference between Britain today and Britain when she entered the last war: the difference in her financial, industrial, and commercial strength. The decline in the British economy in the years immediately after the war was not the sole cause for the disolution of the Empire, although of course it speeded the disintegration. Nor was the process by which the new nations broke away from the Empire, and in some cases from the Commonwealth, purely the consequence of economic conditions in the home islands.

Yet, the drastic change in Britain's comparative economic status altered her position more than any other factor. This change was one of the principal reasons for the United Kingdom's decision in 1961 to seek entry into the European Economic Community.

Here as elsewhere, in assessing contemporary Britain, it must be kept in mind that the change is comparative. Production has increased by over sixty per cent and exports by over one hundred per cent in volume since 1938. To meet the changed demands of world markets, engineering products and metals, motor vehicles and aircraft have replaced textiles and

coal as major items of export. Progress has been made—but it
is not enough. The world, especially the nearby world of continental Europe, has progressed even more rapidly. Ten years
ago, when British recovery began to take shape, the question
was whether the world could afford "three Britains," meaning
three comparatively small, highly industrialized nations dependent on exports: Britain, Japan, and Germany. The economic development of E.E.C. and Britain's subsequent attraction to it appear to indicate that both Britain and West
Germany have recognized membership in a larger economic
unit as the only economic course for them.

The British economy has in fact reshaped itself since the
war. But it has not been able to do so fast enough to keep pace
with the rest of the world.

The members of the Commonwealth, both the old white
dominions and the new Afro-Asian members, were turning at
varying rates into producers of some of the manufactured
goods that Britain had exported to them in the past or, equally
damaging to British trade, were buying these and other products from Britain's rivals in trade.

This situation was exacerbated much earlier than the British anticipated by the economic revival of the three great powers defeated in World War II: West Germany, Japan, and Italy.
Each has a large population, limited raw materials, and the
necessity to export. There is an obvious similarity between
their positions and that of Britain. Moreover, when the Germans entered the export race, they were spurred by a national
desire to erase some of the stigma of defeat, to show that their
undoubted intellectual resources and business energy could
outsell and often outmaneuver the slower British. Finally, in
the opening years of the competition between the two, West

Germany was not burdened, as Britain was, by a comparatively high arms budget.

By the end of 1960, therefore, the true dimensions of the changes in Britain's political, diplomatic, and economic stature were clear. But it is not enough to recognize the proportion of these changes or even to sense their effect on the country's fortunes. Of much more import with regard to what is happening in Britain now and what may happen to Europe and the United States tomorrow are the reasons for these changes. "It's the war" or "It's the trade unions" or, occasionally, "It's the Americans" are popular explanations among Britons. Each contains some grain of truth. But the over-all story of why it happened is far more complex and interesting.

· 3 ·

How It Happened . . . Defeat in Victory; the
Losses in Blood and Treasure . . . The Loss of
Influence in World Affairs . . . America Takes
Over . . . Britain Does a Lot with a Little

THE DECLINE and fall of the Roman Empire was a continuous process that lasted hundreds of years. Contemporary historians were able to describe limited periods, perhaps as long as twenty years, when they were prescient enough to understand what was happening to the Empire. The change in Britain's fortunes has been more swift. There are many people alive today who remember the might, majesty, and dominion of Victoria's Empire; more who enjoyed the Edwardian age; and still more who lived in the security of British power in the long weekend between the two wars with Germany. Mature observers, then, have been able to watch the entire process to date and to reach their own conclusions as to its origin.

Even so, any analysis made today is, like everything else, subject to the editing of time. The historian who writes fifty years hence, for instance, may regard the loss of British overseas investments between 1939 and 1945 as a less important factor in the decline of British power than the manner in which the grim memories of the nineteen-thirties led the British trades unions and a portion of the Labor Party to assume an aggressive suspicion of capitalism and its development which through strikes and restrictive practices slowed down post-war expansion of British industrial production.

Yet no historian of the present or the future can avoid the conclusion that a basic cause of the change in the position of the United Kingdom, both in relation to the Empire and Commonwealth and in relation to other powers, was the casualties suffered in the two world wars. These casualties must be considered in the light of the fact that, numerically, the British were always inferior to their great rivals for world dominion.

During the ten years preceding the outbreak of World War II, the United Kingdom, like most other advanced Western nations, faced the prospect of a declining population. There was good reason to believe, on the basis of the figures of births and deaths available in 1933, that by 1965 the population would drop from over forty million to under thirty-six million. No such decrease has taken place. On the contrary, the expectation is that by the end of this decade the total population of the United Kingdom will be about fifty-five million.

However, to keep this population increase in perspective, it must be balanced with the qualitative loss suffered by the country in the two world wars of this century. The changes that have overtaken Britain in the last fifty years may be said to have begun, from the demographic standpoint, on the battle-fields of Flanders nearly fifty years ago.

The troops of the British Empire, the majority of them contributed by the home islands, suffered 3,190,235 casualties in World War I: 908,371 killed, 2,090,212 wounded, and 191,652 missing or prisoners. The total was 35.8 per cent of the forces mobilized, and the population of the United Kingdom after the war was about forty-four million.

These losses were a good deal less, both absolutely and in percentage of men mobilized, than those of Imperial Russia, Germany, or France. But the British have argued that their losses bit deeper into the upper strata of society than the casualties of other countries and that this qualitative loss contributed to the poverty of industrial and political leadership by relatively young men in the decade before the second war. War, of course, kills noble and commoner, professor and moron alike. But a passionate burst of patriotic enthusiasm filled the ranks of Kitchener's "New Army" with young men from the middle and upper middle classes, where, due to the class system, the percentage of educated was highest. This was truly a lost generation in the sense that it was never replaced. Losses in the industrial working class were high. But the class of young men to whom English society traditionally looked for leadership in almost every field suffered appallingly. Twenty years later Winston Churchill was to see in Anthony Eden the "one, strong, young figure" capable of halting the drift toward disaster. Had it not been for the first war, Churchill might have seen twenty such figures.

The toll of casualties in World War II was considerably smaller, but this new drain was imposed upon a society not yet recovered from the earlier war. Between 1939 and 1945 Britain's armed forces suffered a total loss—both dead and missing, presumed dead—of 303,240, and the forces of the Commonwealth lost 109,000 more, a total of over 412,240. Air raids killed 60,500 civilians in the British Isles, and the Merchant Navy and the fishing fleet lost another 30,000, so the over-all figure is over 502,000. The military casualties represented a loss of one in every one hundred and fifty people. In the United States the ratio was one to four hundred and fifty.

The second war, moreover, involved material losses far greater than the first. When these are added to the cost in lives, the blow to the United Kingdom can be seen in all its staggering dimensions. The British, through their exertions and because of the folly of the German leaders, were able to escape invasion. It was about the only thing they did escape. Almost from the outset, industrial plants, shipping, housing, storage depots, ports, and railroads were under attack. As a result of shipping losses, bomb damage, and arrears of industrial maintenance and replacement, the run-down of British domestic capital was estimated at about £3,000,000,000.

Such gross figures mean little unless they are compared with the imperatives of the immediate post-war situation. During the conflict, exports had dropped because of the diversion of production for war purposes and because of the difficulties of obtaining materials needed for the export trade. By 1943 the volume of British exports was only one third of what it had been in 1938. To reactivate the export trade, ships were needed, and no section of the economy had been hit harder by the war than shipping.

The capital loss in shipping was tremendous. The total British-owned deadweight tonnage of general shipping and tankers fell from 22,100,000 in 1938 to 15,900,000 in 1945. Approximately 15,200,000 tons of general shipping and 2,800,000 tons of tankers had been lost; to some extent this loss had been replaced by new construction and acquisition, including ships obtained under Lease-Lend. Many of the new ships had been built under war conditions, when speed of construction, rather than quality and economic value, was paramount. Conditions, consequently, were not particularly favorable for an export drive. The ships needed to carry the exports were strewn across the bottom of the North Atlantic from the Clyde to Halifax; they lay along the sea lanes to Malta and in the shallow waters off the Libyan coast. The great ports that had serviced them, Liverpool, the Clyde, Southampton, London, were slowly recovering from the destruction and disorganization of nearly six years of war.

The people who were now to attempt to induce the world to "Buy British" were in a sorry state. The Labor government of the day spoke, as governments must, of the vigor and drive of the new egalitarian Britain, but the British were tired.

Although their government had organized the victorious coalition and they alone of the Allies had fought from the outset and had made a staggering contribution to the final triumph, the British and their shabby, weary country in the early post-war years had some of the aspects of defeat. The contrast between the magnitude of their achievements and the poverty of the results created popular attitudes that still exist today. Britain had won the war; very well, Britain must play the role of victor in world affairs. But Britain had suffered terribly in the cause, especially when she stood alone; therefore she was owed much by her allies. And, much later, when prosperity had made its belated reappearance: We've never had it so good, but why not, we've earned it. Please don't disturb.

These attitudes still affect much of British popular thinking. Few British politicians have successfully combated them, not because as leaders they lack perspicacity, but because they lack the courage to drive home the lesson that these attitudes are outmoded in the world of today.

The war, however, also undermined the financial position of Britain in the immediate post-war years in a manner not experienced after World War I. During the war the country had lived far beyond its national income. This was the only way in which, short of surrender, it could continue to live at all. Now the bill came in. It was a whopper.

First there was the loss of £1,118,000,000 through the sale of overseas investments. This figure does not include the holdings in the United States deposited as collateral for the loan made to the United Kingdom through the Reconstruction Finance Corporation. These overseas investments were requisitioned by the government and sold to pay for war supplies. They included investments of £428,000,000 in the United States and Canada. As a result of this capital loss, the net British revenue from overseas investments was reduced to less than £100,000,000, compared with approximately twice that amount before the war. While the shrewd investments of generations were going to feed the war, the United Kingdom also assumed new debts for the same purpose. By the summer of 1945 these stood at £3,355,000,000. Most of this debt was owed to sterling-area countries; the operation of Lease-Lend had restricted indebtedness to the United States. Finally, there was the loss of foreign gold and dollar reserves. These had stood at £864,000,000 in August 1938. By October 1945 they were down to £453,000,000. G. D. H. Cole estimated that, "in all, Great Britain had incurred a loss of overseas assets, including gold and dollar reserves held on behalf of the sterling area as a whole, amounting to about £4,200,000,000."

These losses were counted by Britain at about the same time that the statistics on war damage to housing were completed. It was found that about 4,000,000 homes had been damaged by enemy action; of these, 210,000 were totally destroyed and about 250,000 left uninhabitable. Here again was a development that, like the shipping losses, was bound to delay industrial recovery and the needed boom in exports.

Britain had emerged from the war much poorer than she went in. The arrears in investment had to be made up by production, which had been greatly reduced by the material losses. Borrowing was the answer if the necessary capital investment was to be made. In 1946 and 1947 the United Kingdom borrowed £856,000,000 from the United States and £235,000-000 from Canada. During this period the physical destruction of the war led Britain and other sterling-country areas to a new dependence on United States and Canadian products, just when their dollar earnings were inadequate to pay for such supplies.

These financial and material losses—indeed, the cost in casualties of two world wars—have largely been forgotten with the passage of time and the emergence in Britain of an affluent society. Yet they are pertinent to any examination of Britain's position today and her reasons for turning toward Europe. To some extent these losses explain the dissolution of the Empire and the more rapid change in the character of the Commonwealth than might have been expected on the morning of victory.

Although both world wars altered the status of Britain

within the Empire and Commonwealth and her relations with their members, the change was much more rapid in 1939-1945. One reason was that in Asia, specifically in Burma and Malaya, the British imperial realm was successfully attacked in 1941 and 1942 by another imperial power, Japan. The Japanese, at the outset at least, were clever enough to hide their imperialism behind such slogans as "Asia for the Asiatics" and to picture the war as a struggle, inevitably successful, waged by the indigenous inhabitants of Asia against the white imperialists from overseas. During the war this had an impact upon the more credulous members of the Congress party in India, who promptly expressed their devotion to the principles of Jefferson and Lincoln by burning policemen alive. Since the war the doctrine now known as "anti-imperialism" or "anti-colonialism" has been a potent factor in hastening the withdrawal of the British from India, Burma, Ceylon, and Malaya. These slogans also have been highly useful both to Russian and Chinese Communists, who have used them *ad nauseam* while imposing their own brand of imperialism wherever and whenever possible.

This political factor accelerated the British departure; but, we must remember, the British had made up their minds to a gradual surrender of control in India well before the opening of the war. Since the eighteen-eighties an element of trusteeship had been evident in British rule in India. The idea of home rule developed in a series of conferences between Indians and British in the inter-war years. For reasons of their own, the more extreme Indian politicians in the years since independence have created the impression that the British were "driven" from India. All the objective evidence is that both in London and in New Delhi the British officials understood that their work in India was done and that it was time to go. Their differences among themselves and with the Indians concerned the manner and timing of their departure, not whether they should go.

Even if the British had desired to retain their political hold on India, which they did not, this would have proved impossible. The United Kingdom lacked the economic and military resources required for such an operation. Moreover—and this may surprise many Americans—the British had no desire to stay. Just as many Britons cannot understand the American attitude toward Communist China, so the majority of Americans have misjudged the prevailing attitude of intelligent and knowledgeable Britons with regard to India. Among those who served there as soldiers or officials, one still encounters a sense of pride about the contribution they made to the building of a new nation. Their chief regret is that the national and racial hatreds that erupted with the partition of British India into Pakistan and India led to the loss of more lives in communal rioting and massacres than had been lost in the preceding century of British rule.

The political currents that affected the older members of the Commonwealth—Canada, New Zealand, Australia, and South Africa—during the war were of a different nature. These countries, largely colonized by Britons and in the case of South Africa also by the Dutch, had long before attained independence and sovereignty within the Commonwealth. Consequently, they were not moved by anti-colonialism. The development among their populations of a new attitude toward the mother country was guided by more subtle influences.

In these more sophisticated political societies the fumblings and follies of Britain's pre-war governments had lowered the reservoir of confidence in the political wisdom of the government in Whitehall. A new generation of political leaders developed who were loathe to rely too heavily on the guidance of London. The remarkable recovery of the United Kingdom from the disasters of 1940 under the coalition government of Winston Churchill did not completely wipe out the memories of the sloth of Stanley Baldwin, the futility of Neville Chamberlain, and the unpreparedness of their governments for the contest with Nazi Germany.

Parenthetically, it might be noted that the political and military events of the war had only a minor influence upon the Africans in Britain's colonies on that continent. The sleeping giant awoke in the fifties, with consequences to the United Kingdom which we will discuss later.

A final factor that affected the political development of the whole Empire and Commonwealth was the impact during the war of American military power. No overseas subjects of George VI were more loyal in 1942 than those of Australia and New Zealand. But it was painfully clear to them in that year, which began so disastrously for the Allied cause, that they would survive only through the use of American sea and air power in the South Pacific. Britain, still beleaguered, was far away. The British Army had been humiliated at Singapore, the Royal Navy disarmed by the loss of the *Prince of Wales* and the *Repulse*. Everything depended on "the Yanks."

Canada's case was different. Militarily she was never in so great a danger as the two Pacific dominions. But the tremendous development of industry in the United States during the war had a lasting influence on Canada. The co-ordination of the two economies developed rapidly. With Britain cut off by the submarine-infested North Atlantic, it was natural for Canadians to look south rather than east for aid and comfort.

The sharp reduction of British exports during the war weakened the economic ties that had bound colonies and dominions to the home islands. Some began to produce goods formerly bought in Britain. In the years immediately after the war, when the United Kingdom's ability to export was restricted, buyers turned increasingly to the United States. Economic nationalism became a factor in relations with Britain. The ideal of self-sufficiency inspired many who read the lessons of the war as a warning against too great a dependence on the mother country. India must have steel mills, Canada must make her own machine tools, Australia her own automobiles.

The growth of economic independence among Commonwealth nations may be exaggerated. Today the Commonwealth, excluding Canada, which is outside the sterling area, still purchases about thirty-five per cent of Britain's exports. This is about the same percentage as in 1938, although it is lower than the figure for the mid-fifties. A similar trend is seen in the United Kingdom's imports from the Commonwealth. There has been a fall in the last six or seven years, but the figure is slightly higher than that of the last pre-war year, just over thirty per cent. Australia and Canada, after the United States, are Britain's best customers, and India is the sixth largest purchaser.

The United States has emerged as the most powerful economic and military nation in the West since the war and consequently is the leader of the Atlantic powers, of their allies in antipodes, Australia and New Zealand, and of a number of client states in Asia. Yet, although American pre-eminence has been most striking since the immediate post-war years, the United States' progress toward that position began during the war itself. The starting point was the industrial mobilization,

which had begun in a comparatively small way before Pearl
Harbor to provide war material first for Britain and later for
the Soviet Union. American military involvement in Europe
against Germany and Italy developed at a slower pace. El Alamein, which was the turning point of the war in Africa, was a
British victory in terms of troops, and even the final African
triumph in Tunisia in May 1943 was largely won by the divisions of the First and Eighth British Armies.

Winston Churchill points out in *The Second World War*
that until July 1944, when the flood of American reinforcements began to reach France, Britain and the Empire and
Commonwealth "had a substantially larger number of divisions *in contact with the enemy* than the United States." This
applies both to the European and African theaters and to the
war in Asia against Japan.

Yet throughout 1943 and the first half of 1944 it became
apparent to the Allies in the European and Mediterranean
theaters of war that the war industry of the United States was
becoming a dominant factor in the Allied effort. Both America's allies and enemies abroad recognized the sheer industrial
wealth of the United States long before the end of the conflict
left Europe shattered and weary. The British, however, by their
early and continuous involvement in the Mediterranean and
Europe, were able to retain the position of almost an equal
partner with the United States in the alliance. In this they were
aided by the experience and skill of some military leaders. The
general officers of the United States Army, new to the conflict,
might find Field Marshal Montgomery intolerably arrogant
and condescending, just as many British officers did. But the
man had been victorious at Alamein, as he never tired of re-
minding them, and had not lost a battle since.

There were other generals, air marshals, and admirals who despite Britain's shrinking military resources managed to retain an honored and recognized voice in the war councils of the Atlantic allies. Field Marshal Sir John Dill in Washington, Field Marshal Sir Harold Alexander in the Mediterranean, Air Marshal Sir Arthur Tedder at Supreme Headquarters, and a host of brilliant and experienced staff officers, diligent in producing plans and persuasive in argument, exerted until the end a great and, in view of the American contribution in men, money, and material, a perhaps disproportionate share in the making of military decisions. Their influence might have been out of proportion to Britain's role in the latter years of the war. It is at least arguable, however, that had Montgomery, the least popular, been listened to in the summer of 1944, the war might have ended that winter, with the Russians still in Poland.

But Britain's greatest asset in maintaining her role as an equal in the alliance was Winston Churchill. Always careful to picture himself as Franklin D. Roosevelt's "ardent lieutenant," the great Englishman was not only the true father of Allied victory but the wisest councilor about the shape of the post-war world, especially about the intentions of the Russians. He was served moreover by a cabinet of distinction, including men like Clement Attlee, Ernest Bevin, Anthony Eden, Duff Cooper, Herbert Morrison, and Oliver Lyttelton, and by able ambassadors and pro-consuls abroad, including the Earl of Halifax and Harold Macmillan. British diplomacy, through industry and experience, managed to retain much of its old influence despite the difference in strength between Britain and the American giant. In the post-war years Britain's survival and hope for the future has often been explained to

Americans and the world in terms of character. Never was the influence of character, meaning resolution, skill, and industry, more apparent than during the war. Indeed, these men and their work contributed greatly to that exaggerated estimate of Britain's power and influence that some believe lingered on in the capitals of the West, certainly in Washington, until the disastrous fiasco of Suez in 1956.

Yet the years immediately after the war only emphasized what the war itself had foreshadowed about the power relationship between the United States and the United Kingdom. This country ended the war with its economy at full spate and at the zenith of its military power. Britain's comparative position declined. The old kingdom, as we have seen, faced the post-war world with a seriously weakened economy and its military and political resources stretched to the utmost. Moreover, the second war had forced upon Americans, as the first had not, the unpleasant fact that they must accept global responsibilities. Psychologically, perhaps, the people of the United States were not completely ready for the role their country was to play. A strong tendency to disengage, demonstrated by the premature demobilization of 1945, remained. But this was dissipated by events, chiefly the revelation between 1945 and 1947 of the Soviet Union's implacable hostility to the Western world and of the impossibility of working with the Russians to create that brave new world which is invariably glimpsed by optimists through the fog of war.

It was not long before economic weakness forced the new Labor government to abandon some of the more expensive politico-military British commitments. Early in 1947 President Truman's administration was informed that the United

Kingdom could no longer afford to provide military and economic aid to Greece and Turkey. The Greeks were fighting Communist-led forces in a civil war. The Turks were upset by ominous rumblings from Moscow about the Dardanelles. The administration, therefore, assumed responsibility for aid to these two countries. This act has rightly been cited as the starting point for that gradual extension of American strategic interests through military and economic aid to countries threatened by the Soviet Union or Communist China, a situation now commonplace. But it is also important as the first step in the progressive disengagement of the British in the Middle East, an area in which their influence was paramount in 1945.

During this period Ernest Bevin, the Foreign Secretary, tried to negotiate a withdrawal from Egypt. He also refused to enforce unilaterally upon Jews and Arabs a United Nations mandate for Palestine; rather, he withdrew the British troops and ended the mandate. These developments took place against the epochal drama of the liquidation of the Indian Empire, in which Britain abandoned another commitment, although not, as we have seen, because she could not afford it but as the natural consequence of the previous sixty years of British rule in the sub-continent. In Europe, too, the diminution of British power, and hence British influence, was apparent. Military and financial contributions in Germany and Austria were scaled down. To the French or Italians or Dutch of that time, the British might appear to be a victorious power. The diplomats from Whitehall, although they presented a confident face to the world, knew full well that their country was fighting a desperate economic battle. In retrospect, the surprising thing is not that at this period Britain appeared so weak, but that she managed to retain considerable influence around the world.

Meanwhile, each passing year saw the United States assuming new global commitments. The European Recovery Program took shape in 1948. A year later, after the Soviet coup in Czechoslovakia and the blockade of West Berlin, the North Atlantic Treaty Organization was established. The United States threw the full weight of its economic wealth and military power, then including a monopoly on atomic weapons, behind these developments. Historians will note, however, that in each instance the British government offered instant support. Some politicians of foresight, like Ernest Bevin, were far ahead of governmental and public opinion in the United States in realizing the importance of the Marshall Plan and the necessity of NATO. And on one occasion, when France's rejection of the European Defense Community appeared to block the integration of a rearmed West Germany in the Alliance, it was a British Prime Minister, Anthony Eden, who took the initiative and found the means of rearming Germany through the Atlantic Alliance.

The memory of her exertions in the war and of past imperial grandeur, vigorous leadership, and intelligent diplomacy brought Britain through the nineteen-fifties slightly larger than life-size in the eyes of many people. Abroad, especially in the United States, there had developed a contradictory picture of a country which to many Americans seemed old-fashioned but which still managed to retain a surprising amount of authority in the world. The British, they said in Washington in the last days of the Eisenhower administration, were trying to do too much with too little. But, some would add in a surprised tone, they were getting away with it.

In some cases the sheer effrontery of the British in maintaining so bold a face to the modern world takes the breath
away. Sterling carries nearly half the world's trade on less than
four per cent of the world's exchange reserves. As the leaders
of a nuclear power, Prime Ministers and Foreign Ministers of
the United Kingdom confer on apparently equal terms with
the President of the United States and his Secretary of State,
even though many of their nuclear weapons are "Made in
America," and the importance of the British contribution to
the over-all nuclear strength of the West is marginal. But Britain has her own bombs and her own aircraft to carry them.
In comparison with the nuclear armories of the United States
and the Soviet Union she is weak. And her large population
compressed into a tiny island makes her extremely vulnerable.

We have reviewed the various developments, demographic, political, economic, and military, which led to this
change in Britain's situation. And we find Britain once again
at the crossroads. This is not the Britain of 1914 or 1939,
however. The habits, the social outlook, the standard of living of the British have been changing since 1945 and never
more rapidly than in the last seventeen years. The British
who may become part of Europe are a far different people
from those who set sail for Utopia in 1945 or even those
who cheered the coronation of Queen Elizabeth II eight years
later. The magnitude of this change has not been understood
in the United States; yet Americans, often instinctively, understand the British better than their neighbors in Europe. The
changes are only dimly understood in the great European nations who may well be Britain's partners in the future.

· 4 ·

The Affluent Age . . . New Patterns in Living and the American Invasion . . . The Expanding Middle Class . . . Youth, Affluence, and Crime . . . Trade Unions and the Imbalance in Society

FOR THE great majority of her people, Britain's decline as a world power has been accompanied by an unprecedented rise in the material standard of living. Just as the period from 1945 to 1951 embraced a social and political revolution that produced the welfare state, so the years 1955-1961 brought a revolution in the material standards of the average person which has had a profound effect upon social relationships and politics. If this is decline, the average man may well say, let's have more of it. Nothing like this was experienced in the Victorian high noon or the Edwardian and Georgian twilights. Indeed, it was one of the weaknesses of Britain that at the zenith of her power the condition of the industrial working class upon which that power was ultimately based was infamous.

The millions packed in the industrial cities and towns were badly housed, poorly fed, subject to the vagaries of an economic system that ruthlessly passed on to them the penalties imposed by the laws of supply and demand. This was true, too, of the other great industrial nations at the end of the last century and well into this one. But nowhere else did poverty appear so grim and sordid. I can remember the shock that I, a boy born in New York and familiar with its seamy side, experienced when I first saw the slums of Liverpool in the mid-twenties. Fifteen years later, they seemed little changed. Few people who are familiar with the condition of Britain in the first forty years of this century can be surprised at the rise to unprecedented power of the Labor Party in 1945. The surprise comes from the fact that the industrial proletariat, once it had a grip on power, proceeded with so much restraint. Disraeli wrote that the world of his youth was for the few, the very few. The situation changed little in a century. But it has changed very rapidly since 1955.

The closest parallel to what has happened to British life since then is probably the change that American life underwent in the ten years between 1919 and 1929. That, too, was a period in which prosperity spread to income groups which had never enjoyed it before, starting a buying spree which was ended only by the depression. A similar spree has continued in Britain for seven years of almost full employment and steadily rising wages. Little wonder that the politician's sermons against inflation fail to deter the average man or woman from periodic bouts of buying.

Just as in the United States in the twenties, the automobile is the most visible sign of Britain's new prosperity. Possibly it will have an even greater long-term effect upon the national mode of living than television has had. The impact of the automobile on Britain this late in the motor age tells us a great deal about the country. Long after a car appeared to be the birthright of every American, anything more expensive than a motorcycle remained outside the financial grasp of the majority of Britons. In 1948 there were only 1,961,000 licensed private cars in the United Kingdom, compared with 1,944,000 in 1938. Perhaps the most exciting and revolutionary statistic in contemporary Britain is that by 1961 the number of licensed automobiles was about six and one quarter million and the total of all types of vehicles had more than doubled since 1948.

The phenomenon of working-men's cars parked outside a factory or a building site, which alarmed American Tories in the twenties, has become commonplace in Britain and has created similar alarm in those on the right who see it, incorrectly, as one of the rewards of "all this socialism." Cars have carried the British around their own island and onto the Continent. "The people you see touring nowadays," said a man in Oxfordshire, "are a great deal different from those we once saw." They certainly are. The butcher, the baker, and the lathe operator have packed Mum and the kids into the car and gone off to see their country or venture as far afield as Italy and Spain.

The spate of automobiles caught the Tory government by surprise. Road construction has lagged behind automobile production. The government spent £67,900,000 on roads in 1948 and £166,000,000 in 1959. Yet the streets of London remain clogged and highways are a nightmare on Saturdays, Sundays, and holidays. The old-fashioned complain of the invasion and desecration of rural Britain; the proletariat makes rude noises in return.

The automobile and the sustained progress in housing—one family in four lives in a home built since 1945—are what the stranger sees from the outside. But the revolution in living habits has kept pace inside the home. Television, of course, is a familiar story. There are about twelve million sets in the Kingdom. But television viewing is only one aspect of the changes inside "the Englishman's castle." First the middle class, then the lower middle class, and finally the industrial working class have taken to mechanical devices many of which have been common in American homes for a generation: electric washing machines, dish washers, food mixers. Their appeal to the middle class, which could not afford or find servants in the post-war world, was obvious. But it was equally strong for the other two classes, which have a high percentage of women workers.

The advent of the electric refrigerator has speeded the spread of new eating habits. The British are a conservative people with regard to food. The "cut off the joint and two veg" probably remains the national favorite, but prosperity has enabled the adventurous of all classes to try out the novel. While I talked one day to a mill worker in his Lancashire home, I was offered a slice of pizza. "It's Eyetalian, lad, but none the worse for that," he said. "Comes frozen and we keep it in fridge."

Britain has some of the finest raw material in the world for cooking and some of the worst cooks. But with prosperity, the Briton is becoming more demanding outside his home.

Consequently the quality of restaurant and hotel food is slowly improving. Home cooking in the country, especially in the north and west, was always good, if the visitor was prepared for a diet planned for people living in a damp, chill climate where central heating remained a novelty well into the nineteen-fifties. The new restaurants springing up in the cities, in market towns, and along country roads, many of them in pubs, fill the gap that once existed between the expensive hotel or restaurant and the sleazy café known to the *cognoscenti* as the "caff" or "cafe." Their clients range from the well-to-do, who a generation ago would have dined at home, being able to afford a cook and a maid, to the newly prosperous, who are tasting and liking dishes such as scampi and Wiener schnitzel, which to them are as exotic as nectar and ambrosia.

The old pattern of life of factory, pub, and bed has been smashed. Millions of young working people now "eat out." Often they go on to one of the nation's dance halls. The term itself is misleading. Dancing is a serious national pastime, more so than in the United States, and the preserve of the working and lower middle classes. Anxious Mums stitch elaborate ball gowns for daughter to wear when she appears with her formation dancing team at the local Palais de Danse, known universally as "the Pally." And young workmen and clerks buy dress suits on the installment plan to squire the young ladies. By a somersault of social graces, those who wish to see the formal dances of Queen Victoria's day done well must watch them done by the grandsons and granddaughters of the submerged proletariat of the nineties.

To the superficial, the hamburgers and the jukeboxes, the flood of cars and the flow of well-made, stylish cheap clothes spell "Americanization." In one sense this is true. Most of these symptoms of modern industrial societies appeared first in America. But their popularization in Britain would have occurred in any event. Great industrial societies, like the United States and the United Kingdom, tend to produce the same desires and the same means of fulfillment. The young clerk from the City, London's financial center, who gobbles a hamburger and a cup of coffee for dinner on his way to a date at the Pally with the girl from files dressed in her new, cheap dress only six weeks behind Paris differs little from his opposite number in a Wall Street brokerage house. The war, which hit Britain's economy very hard, and the post-war period of austerity and recovery delayed a natural development. But it is important to our understanding of modern Britain to remember that affluence has arrived with relative speed. It has flowered in less than ten years, and its effect on a society emerging from a long period of privation and danger has been startling even to those who thought they knew Britain and the British.

No one except their own prophets has ever thought the islanders a particularly spiritual people. Napoleon called them a nation of shopkeepers, and subject peoples like the Indians and the Irish have invariably regarded them as grossly commercial. Yet even their sharpest critics abroad would have been unprepared for the apparent emphasis on the material side of life in Britain today. Americans alone may find it unremarkable—a black mark for the United States in the record books of the British intellectuals.

The flow of cheap manufactured goods for the entire population has been fostered by advertising. This art or business in Britain owes much to American models; "Madison Avenue technique" is a term of reproach among "progressive" social critics in London as well as New York. The public-relations man is another product of the new prosperity, and he, too, receives many a hiding from the embattled, self-appointed keepers of the British spiritual heritage. As a corollary to the spread of advertising and the growth of commercial tub-thumping, there have developed, as there did in the United States of a generation ago, groups devoted to the good of the ultimate consumer, ready with statistics to prove that Brand A doesn't really wash whiter or smoke cooler than Brand B. Although manufacturers protest that this isn't really cricket and the ad men assert that they are really high-minded public servants, neither group loses much sleep over the activities of the various consumer-research organizations. They have a nice, concentrated market of 50,000,000 people, most of them with money to spend, so why worry?

The evolution of the urban British masses into mass-producing, mass-consuming citizenry, although natural among contemporary industrial societies, has been accelerated by the extensive movement of American business into Britain. Francis Williams, long one of the Labor Party's foremost publicists, and by no means anti-American, has described this as "the biggest economic invasion in our history," an invasion which, he points out, is being carried out not by small firms but by the colossi of American industry—General Motors, Standard Oil of New Jersey, Ford Motors, Procter and Gamble, to name only a few.

The United States Department of Commerce estimates that nearly eight hundred British industrial and business firms are already under American control. Dr. John H. Dunning, author of *American Investment in British Manufacturing Industry,* has estimated that the total net assets of the firms engaged in manufacturing alone were valued at £120,000,000,-

000 at the end of 1960. One twentieth of all the goods produced by British workers comes from plants owned by Americans, and one of every twenty British workers in the manufacturing industries is employed by an American firm.

Informed critics make three points about this wholesale take-over of vast areas of the British economy. First, the investment is in growth industries. Second, it has concentrated on industries that cater directly to the consumer and consequently plays an important role in what Mr. Williams regards as the reshaping of Britain into a shoddy imitation of the United States. Third, American industrial expansion in Britain, and elsewhere, carries with it the "vision of planned obsolescence"—the deliberate outdating of products by the introduction of new models in a wide variety of articles from television sets to girdles.

The factories that turn out products identical with or similar to those made in the United States, whether they are owned by Americans or Britons, are meeting a demand for such products, which is largely the consequence of another phase of the American invasion—that in the field of communications. Until the middle of the nineteen-fifties this took place chiefly through the motion pictures. But since then, it has spread as a result of the introduction of American programs into the television channels of the British Broadcasting Corporation and the Independent Television Authority. At the same time, popular records and cheap magazines, or their even cheaper British imitations, have professed to supply "the latest hits in the States." All these stimulate the demand for "American" products.

Much of it, from the movies to the magazines is, God help us all, pretty terrible stuff. It is terrible to me not because it emphasizes, or at least invariably includes, large helpings of sex and violence. These, after all, have been the staples of folk entertainment since Rome. What this export of commercial drivel really stresses is the conformism which is one of the worst aspects of American life, that conformism which, with its ridiculous antagonism toward erudition and education, notable especially in the Eisenhower era, has done so much to weaken the position of the United States in the scientific contest with the Soviet Union. We are, in fact, exporting to our closest ally and firmest friend those sloppy habits of thought, that ready substitution of glamorous unreality for the harsher facts of life which certainly will lay us open to defeat and conquest unless we reassess the values by which the people of the United States now live. The British, indeed, have something to worry about. But they are receiving only a portion of these elements. It is the Americans who ought to be frightened by this monstrous perversion of our political and intellectual heritage.

Unprecedented affluence has not developed uncriticized. Just as Mr. Coolidge's America aroused the scorn of social critics for its "Babbitry," so Mr. Macmillan's Britain is the target for attack by two important groups, each of which seeks to lead the country back to what it regards as the nation's true identity. The smaller, less vocal of these groups represents the conservative upper class. Its basic doctrine is nationalist, exalting service to the state and a settled system in which the classes know their place and in which social stability is as important as material gain in national development.

The concept is dying, of course. But it has been dying for so long and yet survives unchanged in so many places that one must grant it an amazing virility. Its spiritual home is rural, aristocratic Britain, its theme "the old ways are the best ways," meaning the old ways of society. Those who hold these views are not opposed either to the industrial revolution, as is sometimes said, or to the post-war technical revolution. From James Watt to Sir Frank Whittle they contributed quite a bit to both. They represent that section of the Establishment, the complex of economic, political, and social power that rules Britain, which still clings to what it regards as the traditional values of British life.

In theory, many of these critics have been impoverished by the two wars and their aftermaths. In fact, they manage, despite constant complaints of poverty, to send their sons to public schools, and their daughters to the better schools abroad, to shoot and hunt, and to accept, with an air of casual competence, top jobs in the City, the government, the services, and even in the mushrooming "new" industries that have developed since the war. Although often accused of anti-Americanism, they know more about the United States than most Britons. What they dislike about the United States is what many Americans dislike: the cheapness and vulgarity of contemporary society. Since much of this comes from, or is advertised as coming from, the United States, they deplore the source. They will say that they know the United States stands for something better than pop records and bingo and ask why "the other America" isn't as well known in Britain. These people don't object to the cheerful rudeness of the London cockney or the dour brusqueness of a Scots gillie. Indeed, they often seem to get along better with the working class than the brash young men of the new generation of Labor politicians. But they are irritated by the glib smoothness coupled with treacly sentiment which is the stock-in-trade of the young men and women who promote new products or who present the entertainment industry's view of what Americans are like.

The basic objection, then, is that the affluent society is imposing on British habits of living and thinking foreign modes which are alien and unsuitable. Fundamentally, they believe that Britain has a greater destiny than becoming the fifty-first state of the American union; they want her to remain British.

In this, they are at one with another group of critics which occupies a different sector of British life and which differs from the first group in its interpretation of the ultimate values of British life.

Those who hold the second concept have just as long a history in the life of the people. They are in fact members in good standing of the Establishment of Dissent. They are as willing to move with the times as any brash salesman of Hollywood clothes or "American-type" bikinis. But they move in a different direction. Theirs is the world of Blake, of the old British evangelical spirit that dreamed of Jerusalem not only in England's green and pleasant land but throughout the world. They agonize over Angola or the Congo; they demonstrate for nuclear disarmament. The long black stockings of the girls may be torn and the hairy young men may smoke villainous pipes, but their eyes are on the stars.

Although theirs is a world vision, their emphasis, no less than that of the well-heeled folk in county towns, is on Britain. Their antipathy toward the affluent society is more political in tone. To them, that society encourages apathy and is too ready to accept the soothing pronouncements of the government. The people in this group are not so much dis-

tressed at the spread of transatlantic living habits as they are at
the American political influence upon Whitehall. They see
British political independence smothered by Washington.
They are the apostles of change, but not this kind of change.
Usually, but not always, on the political left they find the
citizenry reluctant to stir from the television set or give up a
day in the country to march and demonstrate for the old
causes. They, too, find the affluent society at odds with the
British genius as they understand it.

In the last seven years, neither concept has had any great
influence upon the mass of the population. The people have
been told by Harold Macmillan, the great prophet of the affluent society, that they have never had it so good, and, looking
about them, a good many have decided that this is true. The
delights of full employment and prosperity have not silenced
the persistent grumblings of a notoriously contentious race. A
considerable part of British political life is devoted to answer-
ing those who each year claim a larger slice of the national
cake and who are increasingly unsympathetic to the broader
issues of national or international life. In the Parliamentary
by-elections early in 1962, it was not nuclear disarmament or
Berlin or even Britain's proposed entry into the European Economic Community that aroused the attention of voters, but
housing, municipal taxes, food costs, and highways. This
tendency of the electorate to concentrate on the everyday business of living is not confined to Britain. But when one con-
templates the tragically vulnerable position of Britain, the
continued precariousness of her economic position, and the
ghastly imperatives of the duel between East and West, then
this parochialism is a damning indictment of the complacency
of those who should rule the country.

It may be, of course, that this eagerness to savor the good life and this preoccupation with its minor difficulties reflects a hardy skepticism about the ability of the people or their masters to influence any longer the course of world events. Conservative ministers are quick to remind their countrymen that although Britain's power is not what it was she still retains vast influence that can be used for good by a forceful government supported by a vigorous electorate. In most instances, since 1956, when the Suez crisis provoked the last outpouring of genuine partisan political feeling, the electorate has acted as though it didn't believe this at all.

There may be another explanation. Although the leaders of Britain and the newspapers and television would deny the very suggestion, it may be that the mood of the British at the moment reflects a subconscious desire to divest themselves of international responsibilities, to forget the imperial past, and to live, in affluence, naturally, as an island Switzerland or Sweden. This is not the sort of idea which is aired at political meetings or even in pubs among a people who, on the whole, still cling to the big-power complex. Yet it contributes to the present tendency to turn away from the world and concentrate on domestic problems. Some great challenge may be required to divert the British from their own back yards and overcome their self-indulgence. The European Economic Community, which, with Britain's entry, will be one of the most powerful groupings in the world, should provide this challenge.

Britain is affluent. Britain, on the whole, is indifferent to critics demanding other less materialistic concepts of social development. But this society is far from static. The mobility among the classes that began in the war continues. From 1945 until 1955 its salient feature was the movement out of the industrial working class and into the expanded middle class of large numbers of men and women, then in their late twenties and early thirties, who embraced the patterns of life which, before the war, had been enjoyed only by the smaller, professional middle class.

This trend continues. But there is a difference in outlook among those moving upward in the social scale. The young marrieds now moving into the dormitory suburbs or into new apartment houses have lived all their lives in a Britain that has been prosperous, with full employment. They take for granted the new amenities of middle-class living—frozen foods, electric kitchen equipment, cheap, good, well-styled clothes—which still strike their elders by only ten or fifteen years as almost miraculous. To them, the affluent society is not something new to be thankful for but a settled way of life. As this group expands, it will have an important effect on Britain's economic and political development. We shall examine its political attitudes in a later chapter.

Another striking development since 1955, when the Tories took a firm grip on British politics, has been the consolidation of the position of the rich; I do not mean the well-to-do or the comfortably off, but the rich. Wealth does not offend by its singularity in Britain, as it does in Italy and Spain; but certainly here riches, whether based on land filched from the Church at the time of the Reformation or on quick and sometimes shady deals involving war-surplus materials fifteen years ago, has re-established itself as a normal part of national life. It no longer embarrasses the rich to display wealth as it did in the first ten years after the war. On the contrary, the young peer who loses £10,000 in an evening at one of London's flourishing gambling clubs, the millionaire who delights in special bodies for his fleet of cars, the young woman who appears every day in a different costly fur coat are now unabashedly part of British life. London is less visibly an expensive city than New York. But it is a wealthy city, and the rich are very rich, although probably less conspicuously so than their American counterparts.

Another development within the affluent society has been the flow of cash into the hands of young people. Young adults, that is, from fifteen to twenty-five, now earn 8.5 per cent of the national income. Many of them live at home, and, once they have made their contribution to the rent, what is left of their pay is theirs to spend. This can amount in some cases to £10 or £12 a week. By American standards this isn't a great deal, $28. But prices are lower in Britain, and the young find the world of cheap but flashy clothing, junk jewelry, coffee bars, and dance halls at their feet. Spending by this age group has doubled since before the war. The teen-age market is now as much a fact of British economic life as it is of American life.

Critics of the age of affluence on the left and on the right often blame it for encouraging a breakdown in manners and morals. The prophet of national decadence is no newcomer to British life. Unfortunately, in contemporary Britain he is supported to some extent by statistics.

There has been a very serious increase in crime. The number of indictable major offenses in England and Wales in 1960 was 188,396, the highest in British history. Compare this with the 1938 figure of 95,280. Worse still from the standpoint of the future, juvenile delinquency is on the increase. Young males from seventeen to twenty-one were responsible for 20 per cent of all crimes of violence in the peak year 1960, for 21.6 per cent of "breakings," that is, breaking and entering a property, and for 35.9 per cent of auto thefts. Paradoxically, these crimes occur in an age group that has more money than ever before.

No two authorities agree on the reason. Some are still inclined to blame the war, and the accompanying dispersal of families, forgetting that the youngest, and often the most vicious of the offenders, were born after the war. A more tenable theory is that the breakdown of parental discipline is responsible. Here, the child of working-class parents generally received and still receives more coddling than middle-class or upper-class offspring. The latter, if boys, are shipped off to school early in life and there endure the double discipline of their own kind and of the teachers. Corporal punishment is frequent and sometimes savage. Even the girls' schools impose a discipline that working-class parents would find intolerable in a state institution.

If the working class has had less to give materially, it lavishes affection and sometimes spoils its children. "It's the children from the East End who get bad teeth from eating too many sweets," a dentist said. "Their parents just can't say no." When the British Army contained a high percentage of conscripts, officers remarked on the care and attention that had been lavished on the Rons and Berts from working-class homes. It was the stern parents of the middle class who wanted their boys worked hard.

There is plenty of encouragement in Britain for delinquents, whether adult or juvenile. Legislation has forced the prostitutes off the streets, but London in many ways is a wide-open town. Nude shows and movies, night clubs that feature

strip tease and salacious dances give a lie to the city's old
reputation for staidness. Beer remains the favorite tipple of
Britains, but more money has enabled the adventurous to
tackle Scotch, gin, and brandy. One still sees less drunkenness
on the streets of London than in New York, but more than
before or just after the war.

Tolerance has always been a British virtue. In recent
years, however, tolerance of homosexuality has seemed to
many Britons to have outstripped propriety. There is no objective evidence that a greater proportion of homosexuals live
in London than in Paris or New York or Berlin. There is
plenty of evidence, however, that perversion is acknowledged
more openly in the British metropolis than elsewhere, and
there is certainly more discussion of it on all levels of society.
The Jeremiahs quote Gibbon's celebrated passage relating
sexual license to the decline of Rome. The optimists believe
that frank discussion of perversion and its cure will ultimately promote a healthier society. The ordinary man or
woman sometimes feels a bit sick.

But if affluent Britain is tolerant, it also has a large number of outspoken and able critics. Indeed, the foreigner in
London often feels that the British are too critical of themselves, that criticism tends to enforce a lack of confidence
upon a population that will need every ounce of self-
confidence to surmount the problems ahead. Certainly many
aspects of the affluent society in Britain, such as the complacency and indifference of the masses and the occasional
arrogance of their masters, deserve criticism. But criticism is
often destructive, even nihilistic, and sometimes altogether unrealistic. In politics the critics devote a disproportionate
amount of energy to attacks upon a Conservative government

because it refuses to follow a socialist policy, and in their general approach to the political situation they often forget that politics is about power, not about differing interpretations of sacred socialist texts. The Conservatives, often so much less admirable than their critics, have not forgotten what they want in politics: power.

Possibly because The Establishment in the last five years has steadily increased its influence, the critics have had a wonderful time attacking it.

An impudently witty revue *Beyond the Fringe* turned The Establishment inside out, poked fun at it, scoffed at its most hallowed memories, such as the Battle of Britain, and kidded the pants off its great heroes. As anyone who knows the British could have foreseen, The Establishment, headed by the Queen, attended the revue and roared with laughter. There are, naturally, more trenchant and perhaps more lasting critics of contemporary British society plunging their verbal daggers into The Establishment's broad back. Much of what men like John Osborne have to say is to the point. Yet the effect of this criticism on the great mass is negligible and will continue to be so as long as there is no issue on the horizon of the average man more important than which program to watch on television.

The Conservative government's long tenure of office—it celebrated its tenth year in power late in 1961—has tended to exacerbate political criticism from the left to the point where it is sometimes difficult to differentiate between the polemics of experienced and responsible Labor Party politicians and those of the Angry Young Men. This may be taken as a democratic phenomenon which occurs wherever one political party retains office for a long period. The Republican Party, after sixteen years of Democratic rule, did not particularly distinguish itself for moderate, responsible, and constructive criticism during the Truman administration. The left wing in British politics is often splendidly splenetic about the Tories. But the presence of moderate trade-union leaders and former ministers on the Labor front bench suffices to restrain the majority of the Parliamentary Labor Party from wild abuse.

For years, roughly perhaps since 1920, critics from abroad, both friendly and unfriendly, have seen Britain as a tired nation. She is, of course, an old nation. But so is France. So is Sweden. I have never been able to accept the easy belief that what is wrong with Britain and the British can be explained by a mysterious mental and physical fatigue. But I suggest that the country and the people have suffered intermittently from a periodic lack of balance within the society in times when one class or one institution exerted undue influence over the course of national development. In the past, the monarchy, Parliament, and the middle class have all exerted such influence, and almost invariably to the detriment of the country.

Over the last eight years, the trades unions seem to me to have imposed a similar imbalance upon British life. Paradoxically, their power has reached its zenith at the moment when there is full employment, when wages—and prices—have risen steadily, and the old, very real grievances built into the economic autocracy of Victorian Britain have been forgotten by all save a few members of the Labor Party's left wing.

No sane person can doubt the desperate need for industrial democracy which inspired the growth of the trades unions in Britain. Nor can it be denied that the movement has produced, and still produces, men of high caliber, passionately

devoted to what they conceive to be the interests of the workers. Clearly, many of the improvements in working conditions
and consequently in industrial efficiency would not have been
attained without steady pressure from the unions. At their
best, and their best has been very good, the unions have been
moved by the spiritual essence of Britain, the fierce ruggedness
of soul coupled with an evangelical desire for reform and
progress.

Yet any contemporary examination of the trades-union
movement must conclude that what Sir Winston Churchill
once called a new power in the British democracy must shoul-
der its share of blame for those areas of stagnation in the
economy which have weakened the country's export position.

Quite obviously, the Trades Union Congress and the
leaders of individual unions do not completely control large
sections of the movement. Naturally enough, the growth of
the unions to their present position of power and responsibility
has created vested interests, safe and, for the working class,
relatively well-paid jobs. But this has been accompanied by
the development within unions of Communist pressure groups,
like the one that held Electrical Trades Union in thrall, or the
many others that frequently paralyze great industries with unofficial or wildcat strikes. Many union leaders following in
the footsteps of the great Ernest Bevin have a notable fighting
record against Communism in the unions. But too many
others are either apathetic about Communist infiltration or,
goaded by fellow travelers, too ready to label all reports of
such infiltration, no matter how well documented, as attempts
to smear the particular union and the whole labor movement.

At the very time when some union leaders have been
challenged, often successfully, in their own unions and in the

labor movement by the radicals of the far left, many, instead of putting the union house in order, have ranged far
afield seeking and often attaining inordinate political influence. The skeptics might find the spectacle of Frank Cousins, General Secretary of the huge Transport and General
Workers Union, agitating for Britain's unilateral nuclear disarmament ludicrous. After all, Mr. Cousins once defended his
stand with the comment that Britain didn't need nuclear
arms: she won the last war without them. Yet the advent of
the union leaders in politics—men like Ernest Bevin, Sir Tom
O'Brien, and Charles Pannell—on the whole must be considered a good thing, if the country can be sure that they are
what they say they are, that is, the leaders of a united movement. But recent industrial history has shown that they do not
represent the beliefs or ideology of more than a small but
increasingly powerful section of their membership.

This exertion of power without representative authority
is one aspect of the imbalance that the unions have forced
upon British society. It affects the whole power structure in
politics. But the unions, through their power to halt production by strikes, also seriously affect the ability of the country
to compete in the world's markets. To a penchant for unofficial strikes must be coupled the extreme reaction of a large
section of the movement to any change in established industrial procedures.

Adherence to the known and the traditional is a strong
trait in the British character. In some sections of industry, it
has run wild. Innovation, even when it will lead to more jobs,
is fiercely opposed. Methods that waste time and money are
enforced upon industry. This may be explained as the result
of those fearful days before World War II when poverty and

unemployment stalked the land. But to explain is not to condone. The present trend in social and industrial development in Britain may, in time, reduce the power of the unions. Entry into the European Common Market will certainly force adjustments upon them. Meanwhile, the imbalance remains.

How much has it cost the country? Statistics show that the amount of time lost in strikes and lockouts has been decreasing since the war. The average time lost annually in Britain from 1933 to 1960 was 2,750,000 man-days, or about one eighth of a day per employee per year. Compared with the average of 21,000,000 man-days from 1910 through 1932, this is a striking improvement. But the effect on Britain's export trade of time lost from strikes, lockouts, and jurisdictional disputes within the unions cannot be measured. In Canada, the United States, Central Africa, and Europe, the traveler hears the same story: "We want British products, but we can't be sure about delivery dates."

Trade unionists retort that this is more the fault of lazy and archaic managements and inefficient sales techniques than of the workers. But the overseas buyer, who keeps Britain alive, believes the fault rests with the working class. A young Englishman trying to sell a superb British product in Canada said: "Whenever I go home, I despair; our workers just don't realize what has happened to our industry and our country since the war." In Britain, one often gets the impression that they do realize—and don't care a damn.

Early in February 1961, the ferry "Free Enterprise," which will carry passengers and automobiles from Dover to Calais, was launched in Rotterdam. She cost £1,000,000. As she slipped into the water, her Dutch builder raised his champagne glass in a toast: "To our best friend—the British trade-union worker." Twenty-two British shipbuilders had the opportunity to build the "Free Enterprise." Not one could guarantee a delivery date or meet the quotation of the Dutch firm. The Dutch, however, noted: "We are rarely bothered by strikes, so we can guarantee delivery."

This has been a brief glimpse of Britain as she prepared to move closer to Europe. Here was a prosperous society, troubled by some consequences of prosperity, uneasily sensing changes in the world, inattentive to prophets and critics. Neither Berlin nor Laos, nuclear tests or Central Africa have been able to divert the British public for long from its primary interests: television, football and the football pools, bingo and racing, and the getting and spending of money. Psychologically, Britain is ill-equipped to venture into the fierce competition of Europe. Yet the British have a genius for politics. Let us examine their political preparation for what may be the nation's last great attempt to lead the nations of Europe.

Britain Looks at Europe . . . Dr. Adenauer,
Germany, and the Psychological Scars of the
War . . . The German Reaction . . . France's
Future Stability and the Succession to de Gaulle

THE BRITISH approached Europe under one obvious disadvantage. They were late. Edward Heath, the Lord Privy Seal, who conducted the negotiations, and his staff of gifted civil servants sought entry into an organization that was already established. In the initial stages of these negotiations France was the dominant figure on the Common Market side. And France in turn was dominated by the austere intellect of President Charles de Gaulle. The British sometimes felt that the President wanted to make them pay for their tardiness and perhaps for fancied slights and insults of twenty years before, when he existed on the bounty of Winston Churchill's government. Imagination? Perhaps, but great men have their petty sides. Yet de Gaulle himself has recognized and recorded those national characteristics which will be of positive advantage to the British in their relations with Europe when and if they enter the European Economic Community.

First of these is political stability. In one sense this means continuity. This can be measured by the fact that when British politicians sought in history for a decision in public affairs comparable to the decision to become part of Europe, they had to go back to the Reform Bill of 1832. In that seminal year of British politics, two of the United Kingdom's prospective partners in Europe, Italy and Germany, did not exist as national states. But for three hundred years and more before that date, Parliaments had sat in Westminister, and British law, politics, and constitution had slowly developed. This is as important a factor in British stability as the Kingdom's antiquity as a nation, free for nearly nine hundred years from invasion and conquest.

The British are also fortunate in approaching union with the continent unimpeded by any serious internal geographical divisions. Scots and Welsh nationalists, to be sure, make their appearance in general elections. They have a high old time invoking the ghosts of Robert the Bruce and Owen Glendower and a glorious, parochial past. But in the end the British continue to be ruled from London, often by Scots or Welshmen. In a very real sense a British Prime Minister speaks for one people and for a country where sectional differences are more apparent than real.

Nor is British political life plagued by pressing geographical issues that create strains for her neighbors and exacerbate ordinary domestic questions. No problem facing Britain strikes as deeply into the heart of the national ethos as Algeria did in France or the nagging problem of reunification still does in Germany. The future of the Commonwealth is a problem for the British whether or not they become part of Europe. But it is not the sort of issue that would divert a government of the United Kingdom from basic policies in Europe if Britain joins. In fact, union with Europe will probably decide future relations with the Commonwealth. But in their future negotiations with Europe the older members, Canada, Australia, and New Zealand, all independent, will play the role to which independence entitles them. The British speak primarily for themselves.

British policy-making is not plagued by the importunities of special national groups. Neither the West Indian and African Negroes who have streamed into Britain in the last decade nor the Irish who have crossed the sea to enjoy the ancient enemy's hospitality and prosperity pose a political problem in the sense of a corporate body that must be accounted for in political calculations. France will have this problem in the future when right-wing Algerians are resettled in metropolitan France. Germany has had it in the refugees from East Germany. The British apparently are immune.

The British, we know, are a homogeneous people with a strong corporate sense who have an instinctive loyalty to the concept of the state, whatever party rules in Westminster. What will this mean in the future should Britain finally join E.E.C.? Primarily it will mean national support for policies within Europe which assert, protect, or advance British interests. The British talked of "entering" Europe, and the verb is important. Psychologically they were outsiders coming late into an organization composed of people with whom they have less in common than with Americans, Australians, Canadians, or New Zealanders. They have never considered themselves part of Europe, and it is highly unlikely that adherence to the Treaty of Rome will alter that. Should Britain join the E.E.C., the other members will have to cope with, in the first years of her membership, vigorous and strident assertions of national interests based on a politically stable and homogeneous populace.

It is useful to compare this political position with those of Britain's three principal partners in Europe: Germany, France, and Italy. When we do, we see that there is some substance to the complaint of those who have campaigned in the United Kingdom against E.E.C. Britain was being asked to join an organization whose political foundations are fragile, even unsafe. Advocates of entry replied that Britain's entry would make them safe.

The Federal Republic of Germany, that is, West Germany, is politically the creation of one outstanding man, Chancellor Konrad Adenauer. The measure of his achievement is that since 1949 this iron Rhinelander has imposed political stability on his country when it was faced with an issue that could easily have destroyed him and his country. The issue was, and is, reunification. Dr. Adenauer has now been in power for fourteen years, and we are apt to forget how important an issue reunification was in the first years of his Chancellorship. Here was a cause that appealed emotionally to all those millions in West Germany who had been driven from their homes by the advancing Russian armies or who had fled westward when the Communists clamped their grip on East Germany. A proud and vigorous nation-state was split in two. Millions of its people recalled, all too vividly, the glories of ten years before. The old radical nationalism survived among the curiously named neo-Nazis, who were, in fact, the old Nazis. The Communist bloc offered an enormous market for German products. Russia and the West had begun the cold war. A united Germany might ask her own price for alliance. From 1949 until 1954, when Germany's entry into NATO was negotiated, the issue was in the balance, far more so than those in authority in the West cared to admit.

But in the end, and perhaps only temporarily, the balance tipped in favor of the West. For one thing, the diplomacy of the Soviet Union under Stalin lacked the flexibility necessary to woo the Germans away from the West. Stalin believed war was coming and wanted his bridgehead in Europe located as far west as possible on the Elbe. But the probity and vision of Dr. Adenauer were more important factors. Almost single-handed he built the Federal Republic into the structure of modern Europe, overcoming both the prejudices against Germany among her new partners and the attraction of unity among his own countrymen. Compared to this political feat, the German economic miracle was child's play.

Facing unity with Europe, the British are entitled to ask whether the structure built by Konrad Adenauer will endure. The question is posed by serious students of European politics as well as by those politicians and newspapers in the United Kingdom who find it profitable to encourage hostility toward Germany.

The activities of the latter have played an important and deplorable role in forming British public opinion toward Germany since the West German state painfully rebuilt itself from the ruins. The resulting compound of suspicion, hostility, and envy felt by a considerable proportion of the British people toward Germany is a significant factor in the attitude toward Europe. It is folly to exaggerate it, but it is even worse to say that it does not exist.

The starting point is the fact that Britain has fought two long, exhausting, and costly wars with Germany in this century. Everyone over sixty remembers both wars, and everyone over thirty remembers World War II. In theory, those between eighteen and thirty should be immune to special hostility toward the Germans. But in fact young people, principally but not exclusively those on the left, have been infected as well.

One summer evening in London a group of American tourists stood in Carlos Place watching a torch-light procession of the Campaign for Nuclear Disarmanent and the Committee of 100, a more militant group pledged to the same cause. A youth of eighteen hurried over and handed out handbills clamoring for action against the war-makers. Not unnaturally, one of the tourists asked: "Why don't you do this in Moscow?"

"Ah," said the youngster, "they haven't got Germans quartered on them there." He referred to one battalion of German troops which had spent a few weeks training in Wales. And Germany is just as much an ally of Britain as she is an ally of the United States.

To a large proportion of Britons, the years between 1939 and 1945 represent a great emotional experience. Their country held aloft a bright image to the admiration of the free. Few lived through those years, especially the months between June 1940 and June 1941, without being touched to some extent by the glow of exultant national pride that bathed these islands. And the war is remembered also as the last period in which Britain led the West. Consequently, the conflict with Germany and the final victory retain, for those who lived through both, a strong psychological attraction.

This is understandable. What is neither understandable nor commendable is that the old enmity has been kept alive by a careful tending and exploiting of the emotions aroused by both wars. When, as in the United Kingdom, a fairly large number of people believe Germany is a greater danger to the British than the Soviet Union, the anti-German pressure groups have abundant material at hand. They have been helped, too, by the popularity of motion pictures and books about war. Since any kind of fiction oriented toward the masses deals in black and white, the Germans in these were almost invariably "black" and the British and their allies "white." The flow of both movies and books appears to be abating at last. But for years they kept the war alive, and those who, for their own reasons, foment distrust of the Germans profited from them.

Among these the Communists are the most blatant. Obviously, the North Atlantic Alliance, in which Britain, West Germany, and France are the most powerful allies on this side of the Atlantic, is a target for Moscow's propaganda. In the United Kingdom the comrades have directed their fire at the Germans. This is true of Communist tactics throughout NATO. After many visits to other members of the Alliance, my impression is that hostility toward the Germans is strongest in Britain, and certainly more public. Yet Britain was not occupied by the Third Reich, as were France, Belgium, and Denmark. The Communists have done well. But they probably would not have attained this measure of success without the assistance of other forces.

The left wing of the Labor Party is especially venomous in its approach to Germany. Some of its members are fellow travelers, some are in the great tradition of British dissent, men who would be the first to face a firing squad if the Russians ever took over in Britain. To them must be added those on the right wing of the Conservative Party who see in the alliance with Germany and in the whole program for closer association with Europe the sinister hand of Washington, where, they are convinced, a plot has long existed to reduce Britain to the status of a minor power.

These groups are encouraged and occasionally inflamed by various sections of the national press. Lord Beaverbrook's three newspapers, the *Daily Express,* the *Sunday Express,* and the *Evening Standard,* have long been notable for the vigor of their anti-German views. Letters to their editors indicate a warm response to these views. They are also the three newspapers most wholly committed to opposition to Britain's union with Europe. But although they have the largest total circulation of any of the press groups openly suspicious and critical of Germany, they are not alone. A vein of hostility toward the Federal Republic and its people runs through the editorials and affects the handling of news on a number of other daily and Sunday newspapers.

Parenthetically, it should be noted that hostility toward the British is almost non-existent in Germany. The less inhibited German dailies are occasionally stung to rage by some especially wounding slur on Germany in the British press, and Dr. Adenauer and some of his advisors nurse the belief that Prime Minister Macmillan and the Foreign Office would sell

Germany down the Elbe tomorrow, if given half a chance. But of enmity and hostility rooted in the war—and it is well to remember that the R.A.F.'s Bomber Command repaid the debts of London, Coventry, and other British cities tenfold —there is very little evidence.

Occasionally one encounters a German businessman who, more in sorrow than in anger, criticizes the lack of enterprise among British exporters or a union leader who doubts the wisdom of the tactics of his opposite numbers in the unions in the United Kingdom. The idea that Britain is old, which she is, is common currency. But there is a good deal of grudging respect for British political acumen. About the war and its scars, little or nothing.

Post-war Anglo-German hostility, then, travels a one-way street. It must be recognized as a factor of importance in the British attitude toward their new associates in Europe. But it will also affect seriously the process of establishing a pool of nuclear weapons, based largely on British and American contributions for the NATO forces, and indeed every international grouping that includes West Germany. Finally, it has diluted in the past, and will do so again in the future, the British sense of urgency in any crisis with the Soviet Union with regard to Berlin or a German settlement.

"People in this country won't risk a war to save the Jerries," a remark frequently heard in Britain in every crisis over Berlin, may be a generality. But, like most generalities, it contains a great deal of solid truth.

This digression will, I hope, emphasize the importance to any British government of the question of future German political stability. The question would be asked in any case. And it is asked of other future partners, often with an arrogance that puts their teeth on edge. But in Germany's case, it has a special importance.

British doubts start with Chancellor Adenauer. Strange as it may seem to a generation accustomed to seeing at the German helm that changeless face, so like that of a Sioux chief—largely rebuilt after an automobile accident long ago —the old man grows older. Like most masterful men, he has neglected to select and train a successor. Yet the next Chancellor of the Federal Republic will take office in a time of transition, when the Europe that has developed since 1945 may be able to reach out to grasp and exercise new powers as a more or less united entity.

This alone will present a problem requiring German and European statesmanship of the highest order. At the same time, however, the new Chancellor and his government will have to deal, as Dr. Adenauer has had to do, with the problem of East Germany and national reunification. No special prescience is required to see that, once Chancellor Adenauer has departed, the Soviet Union will make new approaches with regard to German unity, hoping with some justification that a new Chancellor may be ultimately more malleable than the old.

Under Dr. Adenauer, the Germans have almost forgotten their old image as a "weltgeschichtliche nation," that is, a nation with an historic role. There is a general understanding that in the age of nuclear weapons and international colossi like the United States and the Soviet Union Germany has little or no prospect of becoming a great power in the sense that she was a great power between 1870 and 1945. The German people are wedded to Europe with bonds that have grown tighter year by year.

None of this, however, is a convincing argument against future West German willingness to consider reuniting the country if the Soviet Union lowers her price for unification. The memory of a German entity, of one Germany, is far from dead in the Federal Republic. What happens to Germany, in fact what happens to the E.E.C., to NATO, to all the other European organizations of which Germany is a member, if the Russian price on unity is right? No government contemplating union with Europe can afford to blink this question.

The Federal Republic, more than most states, is shadowed by the past. Dr. Adenauer and his moderate, sober regime could not entirely eliminate from men's minds the sorry history of the Weimar Republic and its destruction by Adolf Hitler. Democracy as it is practiced in the United States and in the United Kingdom has never flourished for long in Germany. Its present health in the Federal Republic is largely due, as I have emphasized before, to the personality of Dr. Adenauer. So we come back to the question of what happens when he goes.

There is one other aspect of West Germany's development that gives pause for thought in London. Despite President de Gaulle's trumpetings about France and "la gloire," there is very little doubt that Germany, not France, is economically the strongest power in Western Europe and that in the foreseeable future she will be the strongest military power in terms of conventional armaments. The British must look beyond the Mussolini-like posturings of the French President to the reality of German power. Of all the European powers, the Germany that Chancellor Adenauer's heirs will inherit will have the best prospect of living in robust independence. This would be even more so if, through some bargain with the

Kremlin, unity could be restored. What then would be the attraction to Germany of remaining in united Europe? Would Germans willingly accept national political and military sublimation in E.E.C. and NATO? These questions cannot be answered now. But any government looking at Europe and remembering the German past must ask them.

One of the melancholy facts of international life for British planners is that in France as well as West Germany one man has dominated the recent development of the country. Those who chart the future course of the United Kingdom in Europe must look beyond that aloof and towering figure to estimate what sort of a partner France will be in the post-de Gaulle period. They must ask themselves with which France will they be dealing.

Will it be the prosperous France whose rising productivity, improved living standards, and fiscal stability have been an example to Europe since 1958? Or will it be the France which has difficulty in keeping order in the streets of the loveliest of European capitals, which must mount machine guns on the Arc de Triomphe because of a few thousand fascist fanatics, which muzzles a free press and allows its police to beat people to death in the streets?

The future, mercifully, is hidden from men. But there is nothing in the political experience of the Fourth Republic and there is nothing in the minor figures who squabble around the feet of the Gaullist idol to create confidence in future French stability.

France clearly is vulnerable today to the spread of a political attitude very like fascism. Indeed, the international prestige of the President, the admiration for his lofty and noble character have obscured the brutal aspects of his regime. No colonial war, even one so bitter as that in Algeria, excuses the excesses of the government in Paris. The maintenance of law and order is the first duty of government. But torture, police brutality, and censorship are not indispensable to their enforcement elsewhere.

This successful establishment of a form of government approaching right-wing totalitarianism surely will incur a terrible reaction. Every tyrannical action taken in the name of President de Gaulle in the long run will strengthen the left, led by the Communists. The inevitability of a powerful movement from the left, once de Gaulle leaves the scene, must be recognized. France today is not so prosperous that its people will accept forever the domination of a right-wing minority. The British are not alone when they ask themselves which France they will be dealing with in the future.

Naturally, the popular attitude toward France in the United Kingdom has little to do with these long-term considerations which influence government thinking and planning. The British probably know and like the French better now than they did in the palmy days of the Entente. More Britons of every class visit France each year than ever before, and as they explore the country, their old musical-comedy conception of France as a restaurant with a brothel upstairs has gradually disappeared. Britain recognizes a strong, reinvigorated France. But General de Gaulle is blamed for wrecking Britain's first attempt to join Europe and for assuming authoritarian airs. French support of the General underlines for Britons a fundamental weakness of French democracy. Relations are bound to worsen in the next twelve months.

De Gaulle's arrogant dismissal of Britain's entry, of course, was hotly resented by his partners in the European community.

Incidentally, the French leader's attitude toward the United States and Britain in the years since he took power is a shining example of how to achieve at least the façade of national greatness by sheer unadulterated rudeness and arrogance. President de Gaulle treated NATO with contempt, refused to attend the meetings of a United Nations Disarmament Committee at Geneva, and remained coldly aloof from the long and tedious talks on Berlin carried on in Moscow and Geneva. Did this weaken his position with the American and British governments or their people? Not at all. The two governments, smothering their anger at the great Frenchman's intransigence, fell over themselves to keep him informed about the doings of NATO and the discussions at Geneva and to ask his views. The two peoples, far from considering him an abrasive force dangerous to Western unity, applauded him as a man who knew his own mind and was devoted to the national interests of France. The General showed the Western world that independence pays. It will be instructive to see who follows his example. The next German Chancellor? Or perhaps the next British Prime Minister?

Yet, having paid all possible tribute to the leader of the French for his courage and independence, how can anyone who surveys the political state of France regard continued French stability as probable? In the next ten years France, already harboring an increasingly vocal and powerful right wing, will assimilate several hundred thousand Algerian French. Under Vichy, under the Fourth Republic, and under de Gaulle, the French of Algeria stood resolutely for reaction. Events since 1958 have only intensified their right-wing views. Once settled in France, they will reinforce vigorously all the groups on the right, which have become more daring and influential since the return of de Gaulle.

They will be opposed by all the republican elements in France, which constitute a large but temporarily leaderless section of the population. Each decade seems to emphasize the truth of the saying that France suffers from her failure to complete the Revolution of 1789. The sixties appear almost certain to reopen the bitter struggle between left and right which has been waged in 1848, 1870, 1940, and 1958. There is no guarantee that this time it will not go beyond political warfare. So, although Britons may see in France's prospective political instability an opportunity for leadership by their own country in Europe, they also discern the first distant muttering of a storm which, should it break, could shake a united Europe to bits.

To the British assessing Europe, the future of France and Germany represents the biggest question marks. But they have not forgotten that Italy, too, has a legacy of political instability, that the Communist party there is powerful and that the economic and political differences between the rich and booming north and the poverty-stricken south could promote internal political convulsions. On the whole, however, this was not regarded as a serious danger to the continued stability of a united Europe.

France was the original political leader of the six powers of the Community. Britain's admission challenged that leadership. The challenge in part is the result of Britain's extensive overseas relationships with Commonwealth countries, even though these have been reduced by entry into Europe. In part it comes from the peculiar and intimate relationship between the United States and the United Kingdom, a relationship which President de Gaulle and other patriotic Frenchmen have always suspected is an instrument for relegating France to an inferior role in the Atlantic Alliance.

It is highly probable, then, that the first years of British membership in E.E.C. will see a brisk conflict between the United Kingdom and France within the councils of Europe. This is not the best start for the Community. But, taking the long view, such a conflict is better if it is confined within the boundaries of a European community rather than taking place between Britain outside and France inside E.E.C.

· 6 ·

British Politics and Europe . . . Macmillan's
Leadership toward E.E.C. . . . The Breakdown
of Political Patterns . . . Tory, Labor, and Lib-
eral Prospects and the Struggle for Power . . .
Opportunities in Europe and the Civil Service
and the Crown

THE BREAKDOWN of the first round of negotiations between
Britain and Europe, while a disastrous setback to the
movement for unity, had several beneficial results. One was
that it forced the British to re-examine their economic position
in relation to the Continent. The second, and perhaps more
important, was that the differences between the two kinds of
Europe, the de Gaulle Europe and the Kennedy-Macmillan
Europe, were more clearly defined after the breakdown. The
British automatically became the chief European advocates of
the latter.

General de Gaulle made it clear that he had kept the British out of Europe because he did not want the sort of Europe that would develop once Britain was a member of the European Economic Community. This presents a real challenge to British statecraft. If the movement toward Europe is to continue, the Macmillan concept of Europe will have to be sold both to future partners on the Continent and to voters at home. Can this be done?

The British begin with more political experience than their continental associates. They are a political people—by turns traditionalists and innovators. Basically conservative, perhaps more so than any major people except the Americans, the British have avoided conformism in politics. Their conservatism has not prevented British pioneering in social legislation before World War I or the evolution of the welfare state after World War II.

The approach to European unity broke with centuries in which Britain had looked outward to the Empire and Commonwealth and to global economic interests. From the standpoint of their position in the world the British were asked to give up more than any other member of the Community in sublimating a large measure of their sovereignty in a united Europe.

Because the break with the political past was so serious, the Macmillan government, at the start of its attempt to bring Britain into Europe, laid more emphasis upon the economic commitments and rewards of joining Europe than upon political obligations. The negotiations, however, stressed the importance of the Community's political aims. This was minimized in London, where the government realized that the political aspects of entry would excite the loudest and most vigorous opposition.

"Some believe," wrote William Pickles of the London School of Economics, in a Fabian Society pamphlet, "that, after a friendly gesture toward the foreigners' quaint political dream, we can safely look only at present facts which are indeed wholly economic, and trust to British influence from inside to prevent future political folly." This belief does not square with what the founders of E.E.C. sought. For, as Mr. Pickles also pointed out, "the most important fact about the E.E.C. is that its ultimate purpose is wholly political."

Originally the Conservative government based its case for union with Europe almost entirely on economic considerations, discounting both political risks and opportunities. The well-advertised attitudes of European and Commonwealth leaders, however, soon made discussion in purely economic terms impossible. E.E.C. became a political issue, and it did so exactly when the patterns of British politics, established since the Conservative Party returned to power in 1951, began to dissolve.

The triumphant Labor Party of 1945 established the pattern for the immediate post-war years; it developed the welfare state and carried out extensive nationalization. Since 1951, however, British social democracy, which finds its political expression in the Labor Party, has fallen on evil days. The party's share of the popular vote has decreased in three successive general elections won by the Tories: 1951, 1955, and 1959. The great socialist leaders of the immediate post-war era have either died or withdrawn from active politics. Repeatedly, the Labor movement has been convulsed by protracted and bitter quarrels with regard to nuclear defense and nationalization, quarrels invariably exacerbated by personal vanities, jealousies, and ambitions. These disputes have arrayed an articulate and vigorous left wing against a moderate center and a right wing whose lethargy has often been its undoing.

In passing, it might be noted that these quarrels have often seemed fiercer than they actually were because of the uninhibited language used by the protagonists in referring to one another. The top in politics is clearly not the place to look for deep and abiding friendships. But the Labor politicians in the last ten years have seemed to glory in unbridled criticism of one another on personal as well as political grounds.

The nineteen-fifties, as Iain Macleod is fond of saying, belong to the Tories. Will this be true of the nineteen-sixties? It seems less likely now than it did two years ago. Until the end of 1961, although even then there were some signs of dissatisfaction, the Conservatives appeared to be safe in office for at least another eight years. But curious currents run beneath the surface of British politics. It may be that the sixties, the era in which Britain approached Europe and in which she faced new political challenges and opportunities in Europe, will be a period of continuous and largely indecisive political strife, with no one dominant party.

This is not only because the Liberal revival of 1962 threatens to destroy the two-party system of government that has prevailed in the United Kingdom since the election of 1945, when the Liberal Party succeeded in electing only twelve members to the House of Commons. The Liberals express and benefit from the discontent of a new political group that has emerged in British society since the Tory triumph of 1951. We shall examine this political group later. For the present, it is sufficient to note that, significantly, the Liberals have been the only party wholeheartedly to embrace entry into Europe from the moment Prime Minister Macmillan announced the government's decision in the House of Commons.

The Conservatives, who in politics have turned flexibility into a fine art, can argue, and some of them do, that the first initiative toward European unity came from Winston Churchill, then leader of the Conservative Opposition in the House of Commons. Speaking in Zurich in September 1946, the father of victory said that the "sovereign remedy" for the ills of an exhausted and shattered Europe was "to re-create the European family, or as much of it as we can, and provide it with a structure under which it can dwell in peace, in safety and in freedom. We must build a kind of United States of Europe."

Sir Winston was not alone in this feeling. Out of the Congress of Europe evolved the Council of Europe, which first met at Strasbourg in August 1949. The Council was patronized by the Conservative Party and by some members of the Parliamentary Labor Party. Its object was what was called "Big Europe," a larger grouping than that envisaged by the founders of E.E.C. But the first real supra-national authority was the European Coal and Steel Community, which was cautiously received by the Labor government of Clement Attlee when it took shape. The Conservatives, when they took office in 1951, were somewhat more friendly to this group, but until the Macmillan government took the plunge in 1961, neither the Conservative Party nor the Labor Party, as parties,

showed much enthusiasm for any purely European grouping, although the Tories in office were enthusiastic supporters,
vocally at least, of the North Atlantic Treaty Organization.

To ardent advocates of European unity on the Continent,
the British attitude was both confusing and irritating. Cabinet
ministers and opposition leaders visited Strasbourg, Luxembourg, and Brussels to make high-minded speeches lauding
unity. But British governments did nothing. They remained
aloof while the Treaty of Rome was being negotiated, drafted,
and signed. From Europe's standpoint, they did worse than
nothing; they took an actively hostile step.

In 1959 the United Kingdom organized the European
Free Trade Area as a counter-balance to the European Economic Community. In retrospect, the importance of E.F.T.A.
seems to have been the emphasis its presence placed upon the
folly of two "economic Europes." When the Conservative
government applied for membership in E.E.C. in 1961, it
committed itself to stay out of Europe unless the other members of E.F.T.A., Sweden, Norway, Denmark, Austria, Switzerland, and Portugal, were able to obtain satisfactory terms
for entry.

These vagaries in British policy toward Europe between
1945 and 1960 insured a frosty welcome for the United Kingdom when she applied for entry. Smaller powers, such as
Belgium and the Netherlands, were able to overlook the past
in their eagerness to get Britain in as a brake on French and
German power. But the British record predisposed Paris and
Bonn against concessions that would ease the islanders' entry.

The Conservative government's change of attitude in
1960 and 1961 about joining Europe has never been completely explained by the party leaders. The rapid growth of

E.E.C., the failure of E.F.T.A. to establish itself as a going
concern, the dangers of European economic and possibly
political division, the promptings of the administration in
Washington all played their part. But when fifty years hence
the Cabinet papers of the time are made available to historians,
it will be found that the movement toward Europe was inspired and led by Harold Macmillan. Without Macmillan, the
Tories would never have approached Europe. To him must
go the lion's share of the credit for forcing Britain to face the
realities of Europe's challenge and building support for eventual union with E.E.C.

What moved the Prime Minister is uncertain. He is a
complex mixture of wily politician with a well-developed
sense of timing, intellectual with a historian's view of the
day-to-day development of international affairs, and highly
sophisticated man of the world. The first two probably dominated his thoughts with regard to Britain's union with Europe.
Here, said the philosopher, is a historic movement that appears
to be attuned to the trend of the era toward greater concentration of power. Once a part of Europe, Britain may influence the direction of this mighty force and lead it toward an
even greater amalgamation of power with the United States,
Canada, and perhaps Australia and New Zealand in a great
community of the free. And, said the politician, here is a great
issue to awaken the British people, one which promises great
rewards and great prizes and which will establish the Tories as
a party wholly in accord with the most significant movement
of the era. The man and the party who bring Britain into the
European Economic Community will deserve well of their
country, establishing themselves, if all goes well, as far-sighted
patriots.

I would not suggest that Harold Macmillan was unmoved by other factors. He was also aware that competition within the Community could bring the trades unions to heel. His deep desire to remain on the best of terms with successive American administrations must have made him responsive to the urgings of both the Eisenhower and the Kennedy administrations that Britain join the E.E.C. Indeed, it is my belief that the most formidable problem which faced the Prime Minister and his government in deciding whether or not to approach the Community was whether the intimate relationship between the United States and the United Kingdom would survive Britain's entry. In the end, this was outweighed by Europe's opportunities and American pressure.

My own conclusion is that it was decided that the transatlantic relationship, inevitably, would be weakened at the outset but that this would be offset by an increase in British influence within Europe and a later restoration of her position vis-à-vis the United States as the power within E.E.C. with whom America had most in common and the closest economic, cultural, and political ties.

Finally, of course, there was the realization that the Europe of the Community was developing an economic and political dynamism which was absent from British society and which threatened the economic position of the United Kingdom. If you can't beat 'em, join 'em.

The role of Harold Macmillan in this great decision has been stressed intentionally. Although by constitutional tradition Britain is still ruled by the Prime Minister and the Cabinet, with the former as *primus inter pares,* in fact the most important development of Cabinet government since the war has been the mounting authority of successive premiers within the Cabinet. The decision to seek union with Europe was Macmillan's, just as the decision to launch the Suez operation was Anthony Eden's, in the sense that the will of the Prime Minister dominated the Cabinet. It is also interesting to note that in each case some members of the Cabinet had grave reservations about the wisdom of the step, yet no one resigned. This, too, appears to be a break with the traditional conventions of Cabinet government.

Mr. Macmillan is not only Prime Minister but leader of the Conservative Party. At the time his decision was taken, his personal ascendency over the party was probably even greater than his influence in the Cabinet. Since then, the Conservatives have entered a new and more dangerous political period. They are making, through the government, a major alteration in the British scheme of things. What sort of a party is it, after eleven years of rule?

British political parties, including the Labor Party, tend to be more united than their counterparts in the United States. The Tories' habit of burying their differences at the slightest sign that these imperil their parliamentary majority, which gives them an advantage over the Socialists, is frequently cited as an example of this unity.

The party's record on Africa, particularly the future of the Central African Federation and of Kenya, in 1961 offers abundant evidence that Conservatives can harbor internal differences as deep as those of the Labor Party, although Tory politicians usually express themselves in more moderate terms. The division between those who believe the Macmillan government has gone too fast in granting independence in Africa and those who support its policy is only one of the many differences within the party. There is, for instance, a segment of the party, not important in size, which is sincerely opposed to the government's invariable acceptance of policies advocated by the United States. This group, incidentally, almost automatically aligned itself with opponents of E.E.C., excited by the evidence that successive administrations in Washington have supported Britain's entry.

Since Labor's landslide victory in 1945, the great divide of partisan politics in Britain, a new concept of Toryism has evolved. Its leaders conceive of the Conservative Party as a party of the whole people rather than of the right wing in industry, commerce, and agriculture. Evolved during the years of opposition, this concept has been preached by R. A. Butler, Iain Macleod, Reginald Maudling, Enoch Powell, and, not least, Harold Macmillan. It has dominated party policy since 1951. But it is not unopposed.

There has always been a group that hankered for the old-time religion of right-wing conservatism opposed to any appeasement of the trades unions, to the surrender of the Empire and Commonwealth, and to the adoption of quasi-socialist policies by governments understandably anxious to continue to attract a sizeable portion of the industrial working-class vote.

Since the departure of Lord Salisbury from the Cabinet, this group has been handicapped by the absence of a leader of national stature and of an issue with a wide enough appeal to win the support of the entire party. The issue appeared to be at hand when the government decided to approach Europe.

Here was an issue that aroused the basic emotions of Conservatives, touching, as it did, the Commonwealth, long the party's special preserve; the farmers, most of them Conservative supporters; and, most important of all, Britain's status in the world. Those who took up the cudgels against the policy were undeterred by the fact that Britain's trade with the Commonwealth was no longer as important as it had been or by the changing character of the Commonwealth itself. Nor did they pay much attention to the fact that the farmers represent a very small segment of the electorate; one far less important, for instance, to Tory election hopes than the four million or so trade unionists who have voted for the Conservatives in recent elections.

The Conservative Party thus faced the task of shepherding the British people through a major change, with grave differences within the party. These were exacerbated at a time when other political developments had weakened the party's hold on the electorate.

It does not take long for age to wither or custom to stale a political party. In 1962 the Tories faced a dilemma familiar to all parties which have enjoyed a long spell in office; the public found them unexciting and uninspiring. The critics charged that the electorate was offered only the old familiar faces. The Tories presented two defenses. One, accurate but not particularly impressive, was that the Cabinet and the ministers were not those which took office in 1951. To some extent this is true. R. A. Butler was the sole survivor of the government leaders of twelve years before. But in the sense that the critics meant, that is, that they, and presumably the electorate, were tired of seeing Harold Macmillan, Mr. Butler, and even Iain Macleod, Reginald Maudling, and Duncan Sandys, the defense was not effective.

The more valid argument was that, although the government did include many ministers who had been in office for much of the party's tenure, it was offering a new and vital program in the approach to E.E.C. and that it still included men of great skill in politics. This was true. But it had little effect upon the tide that set in against the Conservatives in the series of parliamentary by-elections held in the first half of 1962. *La France s'ennui;* so apparently, was Britain.

The government's political problem with regard to E.E.C. was complicated by one of those uncomfortable political situations that cause ulcers in Whitehall. It was manifestly impossible to fight a general election on the single issue of entry into E.E.C. The country might support the Conservative initiative in this, but there was no certainty that the campaign itself would not revolve around less important issues such as restraint on wages, the shortages of housing, and the cost of living. The great issue might be submerged by these homely problems, which, in the majority of cases, have a dominant effect on popular thinking.

The Tories were also aware that there was in certain sections of the population a groundswell of discontent against the government based largely but not entirely on such down-to-earth issues. At the end of the first quarter of 1962, the Conservatives' prospects were poorer than they had been since the late forties.

In these circumstances, two things appeared necessary to a Tory victory in the next general election. The first, fairly obviously, is the restoration of party unity. This, as I have indicated, is going to be a much more difficult problem than it has been at any time in the past ten years because of the emotive effects of the central issue of entry into Europe. The second is to effect Britain's union with Europe, that is, to follow the policy adopted in 1961 to a successful conclusion. Here it must be re-emphasized that, although from the outset

Mr. Macmillan and his colleagues stressed the importance of gaining from the six members of E.E.C. the necessary safeguards for the Commonwealth, agriculture, and Britain's partners in the European Free Trade Area, there was never any doubt in the minds of responsible politicians that the government's policy was to negotiate entry. This was the overriding factor. In the long run it proved more important than Commonwealth ties, the welfare of the E.F.T.A. partners, and the many alternative schemes for reinvigorating the British economy.

The Tories thus entered a critical political period with one advantage. They had a policy. The Labor Party was at a disadvantage. They were not committed to Europe. And the longer they remained uncommitted, the fiercer became the intra-party disputes over joining Europe. These had a direct bearing on the future of the party. For the need for unity within the Labor Party is paramount. Without it, the party seems unlikely to win another general election on its own. And a fourth successive defeat in a general election may well finish Labor as a major force in British politics for years to come.

The most active force against unity in the Labor Party as it is now organized, that is, with the moderates, representing the trade unions, retaining a somewhat precarious control, is the militant left wing, which is violently opposed to the leader for both his policies and his personality. Some of its members flirt with the Communist party line. Others like Michael Foot are in the great tradition of political dissent. Still others shun the regularity of party life; they find more self-expression and, it is just possible, more headlines in an erratic course of opposition to the moderate political center. This group, when it is broken down, includes some members of the national executive of the party, such as Tony Greenwood and Mrs. Barbara Castle. Its strength within the Labor movement lies with the Constituency Labor Parties, which are so often well to the left of the Parliamentary Labor Party in their outlook, especially in international affairs.

The radical left is noisy, dedicated, and entertaining; more so on the whole than the radical right, which runs to some very dull fellows indeed. Its fellow-traveling component naturally is a danger to British democracy, although, in Parliament at least, it is less strong than it was a decade ago. But its existence is not the main reason for questioning the continuation of Labor as a great force in British politics. Time has hurt the Tories. And it has worked upon Labor, too.

The coming of the affluent society has not eliminated the industrial working class. That remains. But it has altered the thinking of its members. One night in 1961 I asked a young mechanic and his wife how they had voted in 1959. "Labor" was the reply. But in the course of the conversation it developed that the wife certainly would not and the husband probably would not vote Labor again. They were, she said, living in a new flat in a new town and they had new interests. In other words, they no longer considered themselves "working class." To generalize is dangerous in politics. But so many other voters have gone through the same social transformation that I think we can expect the same political consequences.

The Labor Party's base, the great solid working-class vote that combined with the dissatisfied members of the professional middle class to win the triumph of 1945, has been slowly eroded by prosperity. In its new guise, this section of the electorate is bored by the trumpet calls of the thirties. It has, for instance, never known unemployment. To its younger members, who are in the majority, the occasional parliamentary outbursts by Labor members against Franco's Spain are incomprehensible. Why, Spain is where Ron and Rene went for their honeymoon. They loved it. Definitely.

Thus the children of the worn, strong souls who saw Britain's great cities and industries through the war. Can Labor appeal to them? It can. But not by endlessly repeating the oracular sayings of Keir Hardie or Ernie Bevin. In the lean years since 1951 only one Labor leader of stature has understood that the party's appeal, but not its fundamental convictions, must be altered. The historian of the future will record that Hugh Gaitskell consistently tried to lead the Labor movement into the second half of the twentieth century and was kicked in the teeth for his pains.

Hugh Gaitskell's death, early this year, robbed Britain, and the Labor Party, of a potentially great Prime Minister. At the time of his death he had united and invigorated his party. Labor's problem is not the choice of another leader, but his development in the movement and in the country as a truly national figure.

Even in the age of mass communication by television and national newspapers, this is a great problem. To project the man, alone, is difficult. To project the man and his policies together takes years. This is especially true when the movement is as diverse as the Labor movement. Gaitskell's heirs, George Brown, Harold Wilson, Jim Callaghan, may be able to win party support after a struggle. Can they achieve Gaitskell's American and European reputation?

Unless one of them can impress his personality on the country through one key issue, as Gaitskell did on armaments, I think it extremely unlikely.

Hugh Gaitskell had preached the need to revise and revitalize the sacred canons of the Labor movement. The Labor
Party was penalized in both the 1955 and the 1959 general
elections because it was addressing Britain in terms suitable to
1935. The campaign to oust Gaitskell from the leadership of
the party reached its climax, oddly enough, immediately after
the 1959 defeat, when he was vainly trying to modify the constitution and modernize the party's appeal. The fury that his
efforts aroused established an interesting political fact: there
are many zealots in the Labor Party who prefer wearing a hair
shirt and wandering in the wilderness to winning an election
and exercising power. Administering a government in Westminster would bring them up against the harsh facts of modern
life, and there the pious sayings of the sainted Keir Hardie are
of little value.

Modern leadership of the party is based on a rather
curious coalition of intellectuals, trades-union leaders and
members, and a large section of the party that is moderate,
even reactionary, in its approach to economic policies. This
last group often seems a greater handicap than anything else,
for, although it dislikes the idea of attacks on the leader and
applauds him as a man, it is basically opposed to the kind of
change he believes necessary to revitalize the party. This section of the party tended to support the left-wing rebels in
opposing union with Europe, not because it had anything
fundamental in common with them, but because the question
of joining E.E.C. arouses its deep resistance to changes that
might diminish its share of the affluent society.

Labor waited a long time before taking a firm stand
against British entry on the terms offered by E.E.C. Clearly
the fear that any firm decision would create yet another divi-

sion within the party was one reason for the delay. Some of the reasons advanced by opponents of the move may have appeared capricious to continental members, but these were the reactions that could have been anticipated in a party which has always been a little insular in outlook. "Internationalism," as far as the rank and file of the party is concerned, means "socialist internationalism": be friendly with Social Democratic governments or parties abroad, but brothers, keep a wary eye out for the capitalists; they're after your watch.

The fact that the six powers of the E.E.C. are major capitalist states in which the socialist political content was negligible, as in France, or perennially unsuccessful in winning a national election, as in West Germany, has argued strongly against Labor's enthusiasm for the Community. Whereas some of the more extreme opponents on the right thought the United Kingdom was entering a union vulnerable to Communism, British socialists saw the danger of fascism, especially in France and Germany.

An equally important factor in socialist thinking was the belief that E.E.C., with or without Britain, was simply another Western weapon, supported by the United States, for use in the cold war with the Communist bloc. This touches a sensitive nerve in the Labor movement.

Although the North Atlantic Alliance has few more devoted supporters in Britain than the Labor center, there still exists within the movement a strong current of opinion which favors an accommodation with the Soviet Union. Those who hold this view are not to be confused with the fellow-travelers on the party's extreme left. Rather, they are people who, in common with a great many Britons, have never seen the contest with the Russians in the same stark terms as the majority of Americans see it. They contend that it is possible —indeed, that it must be possible for the future existence of Britain—to get along with the U.S.S.R. and its allies. Some, perhaps forty, members of the Parlimentary Labor Party are convinced pacifists, and their sentiments have a wide appeal in the entire movement.

This group accepted NATO, which Britain joined under the aegis of a Labor government, at a moment when the affairs of the West were far more desperate than they are today. They still support it. But they found the concept of a European bloc dominated by strongly anti-Communist powers —de Gaulle's France and Adenauer's Germany—vaguely distasteful. They feared that with British entry the gap between East and West would be unbridgeable. While that gap remains, while Europe is divided, there is always the chance of war. To them, and to most thinking Britons, war means extinction.

A more parochial Labor argument against the E.E.C. was that acceptance of the Treaty of Rome and Britain's merger with an economic community would raise a barrier against future extensions of socialism under a Labor government. National economic planning and the nationalization of industry would be impossible under the Treaty, Labor feared. This is an important argument because it leads back to the cause which nearly unseated Gaitskell in 1959-1960, the sanctity of the original provision of the party's constitution, which demands public ownership of the means of production, distribution, and exchange.

The first approaches to the Community made a favorable impression on some of the leaders of the trades unions. But here again we encounter that crippling disability within the union movement that arises from the differences between the policies and outlook of the leaders and the policies and outlook of union officials at lower levels. On those levels, the fear that entry into Europe would mean an influx of "cheap labor" from the Continent was strong. So was the bias against British membership in a predominantly capitalist, right-wing community. In the future union leaders will have to be very persuasive if there is to be any support in union ranks for joining Europe. Their recent record is hardly a picture of either conviction or fervor on behalf of any dogma newer than that of 1945.

Finally, attention must be paid to the "Little Englander" concept among working-class people who are still largely Labor in their political sympathies. The concept of Britain playing a major role in the new Europe has made very little impact on them, possibly because the government was so cautious in its first presentations of the case for entry.

A more important situation in the long run will result from the complacent satisfaction which this section of society now feels. There was jam yesterday, there's jam today, and there will be jam tomorrow. Why risk losing it for an alliance with foreigners? The working class is much more knowledgeable about Europe than it was—thanks to prosperity and travel—but it is highly doubtful that this new familiarity will overcome the insularity of this class and the unions' hostility to foreign labor and industrial change.

Until 1962 it was possible to discuss British political currents purely on a basis of what the Tories and Socialists would or would not do. But 1962 has seen the re-emergence of the Liberal Party as a force in British politics. The strength of the Liberal revival undoubtedly has been exaggerated by some of its followers and by the more excitable political commentators. Yet those Tories who regard this revival as simply another mid-term aberration of the electorate comparable to that in 1958 seem to be oversimplifying the political situation. In that year, the Liberals won a by-election at Torrington from the Tories only to lose that seat and all but six others they contested in the decisive Conservative triumph eighteen months later.

The Liberal Party's situation differed materially in 1962 for two reasons. The first of these could be demonstrated statistically. For thirty years after 1929 the Liberals have returned to Parliament after a general election with fewer than or with the same number of seats they had when the campaign began. But against this melancholy statistic must be set the fact that in the last general election in 1959 the Liberal vote, in the ninety-one constituencies where the party had candidates, increased by 22.6 per cent over the figures in 1955. The national Tory vote was up about 3.4 per cent and the Labor vote fell by 1.8 per cent.

In that general election, another Liberal development went almost unnoticed. The Liberals pushed Tory or Labor candidates into third place in thirteen constituencies, gained votes in a hundred and sixty-four constituencies, and lost them in only thirty-eight. So, the strength shown by Liberal nominees in the by-elections early in 1962 was not a sudden phenomenon but the result of a steady growth stretching back before the last national election. The Liberal victory in a by-election at Orpington and the strength shown by Liberal candidates elsewhere can be interpreted as a trend toward the return of the three-party system to British politics and the recreation of a new political situation that should continue even if the Conservatives or the Socialists win the next general election.

The second reason for this change in the Liberals' position is much more difficult to pinpoint. Iain Macleod, that astute Tory politico, contributed one clue when he noted that the British "are not, as a nation, confident of our future; we have not, as a nation, been ready to face the reappraisal that must follow the closing of the chapter of imperial power." Incidentally, it is interesting to note that Macleod believed from the outset that entry into Europe would restore confidence and direction to the British political ethos.

A great many voters, despite the impact of the affluent society, felt that time and change had robbed them and their country of international purpose. This feeling was found more among young people in their late twenties and early thirties than elsewhere; people, it should be noted, who are not frightened by the idea of a Labor government—they scarcely remember the last one—and who see no reason to be grateful to the Conservatives for a prosperity they take as a matter of course.

They wanted something different, and they found it in the Liberal Party. In the by-elections, they deserted both major parties in droves, but, and this was probably the most significant fact in the by-elections, more of them deserted the Tory standard.

There is very little evidence that any single aspect of the Liberal Party program, which was somewhat vague on many issues, attracted these voters. The Liberals were the first political party to advocate British membership in E.E.C., including political integration. But entry into the Community was not an important talking point in any of the by-election campaigns

in early 1962. The interpretation of the Liberal vote as a protest vote based on anything from boredom with an over-
familiar Tory government to anxiety on the part of home-
owners over constant fluctuation in the bank rate seems much
nearer the truth. It would be dangerous, however, to discount
protest votes. When the protest is strong enough, as it was in
the United States in 1932 or in Britain in 1945, the election
result can change the course of history.

No summary of the three political parties and their attitude toward Europe would be complete without a closer examination of nationalism as a component of British politics. There
was a tendency to discount this factor when the question of
entry into E.E.C. was first raised, largely because its manifestations appeared on the left of the Labor Party and on the
right of the Conservative Party. Once the government was in a
position to reveal the conditions under which the United Kingdom was to enter Europe, however, nationalism began to influence public discussion. The anxiety aroused because acceptance of the Treaty of Rome imposed serious restrictions on
British sovereignty, especially the sovereignty of Parliament,
was not overcome by the evidence that the United Kingdom
already had abandoned sovereignty, in varying measures, to
the United Nations, the North Atlantic Alliance, and to other
international organizations to which Britain belongs.

This is a reasonable enough argument, but I doubt if it
ever will overcome the complex mixture of nationalism, insularity, and chauvinism which will influence public attitudes
in the future. All the other surrenders of sovereignty were
made either in moments of grave national danger (the establishment of NATO, for instance, occurred the year after the
Communist *putsch* in Czechoslovakia and the Soviet blockade

of Berlin) or to organizations which were far away, such as the U.N. in San Francisco, or which were shadowy in the public mind. To enter E.E.C. would mean a clear surrender of sovereignty to an existing group of other nations. It will mean the abandonment of the unique position Britain salvaged from the wreckage of World War II: center of a global Commonwealth; a member of NATO, the Southeast Asia Treaty Organization, and the Central Treaty Organization; and the most intimate ally of the United States.

During the first twelve months of negotiations with Europe the Conservative government found itself caught in a dilemma of public relations of its own making. It could not arouse the British people to enthusiastic support of entry into the Community without appearing, in the negotiations at Brussels, as too eager to join Europe. At the same time, its delegation to the Brussels talks had to refrain from too many concessions to The Six lest these nourish the already vigorous opposition to the move.

Ministers of the Crown were curiously contradictory. Edward Heath, the Lord Privy Seal, who was in charge of negotiations, extolled the political purposes of the Community in Brussels but at the Conservative Party conference referred to E.E.C. as an "economic enterprise." Prime Minister Macmillan was wildly enthusiastic about the move into Europe at a speech in Stockton-on-Tees. But Duncan Sandys, then Secretary of State for Commonwealth Affairs, went out of his way in several speeches to emphasize the importance to him and to the party of obtaining the maximum safeguards for Commonwealth trade and left the impression that if these were not obtainable Britain would remain outside Europe.

Above all, there was a lack of information from a party

which, under Winston Churchill, had followed his father's precept, "trust the people." This could be explained, although the government seldom did so, by a desire not to prejudice the negotiations. This was especially true of the opportunities for political leadership offered Britain by membership in E.E.C.

These opportunities can be grasped by a people who have enjoyed a long period of political stability and who cherish a national belief in the importance of the state. Now, these characteristics also exist in other members of the Community. What the British had available to exploit the opportunities to a greater degree than any other member was a large body of competent professional civil servants. Although lately industry has won away some of the best—Sir Leslie Rowan is an example—there is still a steady flow of intelligent and well-educated young men and women from the great universities into the civil service.

The professional civil service also is reinforced by a group of men and women who, because of service during the war or special qualifications that have brought them into public life in the past, are familiar with the workings of government and the civil service.

Centuries of involvement in the world overseas have created in the civil service, and in its auxiliaries in the universities, a reservoir of knowledge and a fund of confidence in Britain's ability to cope with just such problems as those raised by union with Europe. Well-prepared arguments, well-documented briefs, careful, precise presentation seem to the civil service to promise the establishment of British influence in E.E.C., just as they have in so many other international organizations.

It is often claimed that the British civil service, especially in the Treasury, the Foreign Office, the Ministry of Defense, and the Board of Trade, all departments that deal with Britain's relationships with the rest of the world, is the best educated, hardest working, and most accomplished of all. This is an exaggeration. But the British civil service and the auxiliaries it can summon from Oxford and Cambridge or the House of Commons or the City or from quiet retirement are generally united and loyal. They are unaffected by deep political divisions; they serve the state rather than a party. They have been trained to think globally. They are unambitious in a strictly political sense. There is very little corruption.

The weakness of this admirable group seems to be that the economic pinch of the last fifteen years in Britain has inhibited many civil servants from taking a broad view. The unification of Europe is an opportunity for "thinking big." The British have been forced by their purse to think small, to weigh the priorities of more pay for university professors against those of more highways to accommodate the flow of new cars. If Britain ever leads Europe politically, the civil service will have to accustom itself to playing a role in an enormously wealthy and powerful economic grouping. It is the adaptability of the civil service that will be tested, more than its industry or foresight.

Moreover, the majority of civil servants, if Britain ever joins the union, will be dealing with political attitudes, theories of democracy, and constitutional issues which will be utterly foreign to most of them. The Europeans who hold these views will be in power within the E.E.C.'s Establishment. Some critics of Britain's entry into Europe at this time—for example, the distinguished William Pickles—believe that this situation disproves "the new imperialism of some politicians and civil servants, the belief that we can walk into Europe now and run the show. . . ." This, he claims, is an "empty dream. It would be folly to count on our influence to change either the purpose or the methods of the Community. We must see these as they are and accept them as they are, or stay out."

This is not the place for a discussion of the position of the monarchy in modern British society, but since the prestige and influence of the Crown has some relevance to Britain's union with Europe, a few points about it are worth noting.

First, although the monarchy is, and should be, under constant criticism—some of it irresponsible, some of it responsible—the Crown's role as a focus for national patriotism in Britain and as a symbol of alliance among Commonwealth nations remains a practical political fact. The influence of this royal link between nations clearly is more powerful in the old, predominantly white and Anglo-Saxon countries, Australia, New Zealand, and Canada, than in the newer states, such as Ghana and Nigeria.

So many other links with the Commonwealth will be weakened by Britain's entry into Europe that the Crown is not perhaps of paramount importance in this context. But it is the decrease in importance of the Crown in Britain that worries traditionalists—a worry which surprises many Americans but which should not be discounted. The Crown was a part of British government long before Parliament. Touch it, criticize it, reduce its admittedly theoretical authority, blur the mystique, and something stirs deep in the British soul. The argument, frequently heard on the left, that for a large percentage of Britons the Crown in the person of Queen Elizabeth II has no importance, is really no argument. There has not been a period in British history when *all* the people were fervent monarchists. Queen Victoria, now accepted as representing the apogee of monarchial popularity, was, compared to her contemporary successor, highly unpopular through much of her reign. Criticism of the monarchy for its cost, for the occasional folly of some members of the Royal family, must be distinguished from criticism of the Queen herself, which is almost non-existent.

The question of the monarchy inside a united Europe would not have arisen if there was any prospect that the Queen would assume a special position in Europe. This is out of the question. But the situation will be a new one for the Crown. The British isles have entered an alliance that will be intimate, powerful, and, above all, big, even by today's global standards. But Britain will not be the center of the community, as she has been in the Empire and Commonwealth, but one among many. Britain will surrender some of her sovereignty. Consequently, the unique position of the Crown in the world will be altered. This is sometimes exaggerated as a factor in British thinking with regard to Europe; but it cannot be ignored.

Oddly enough, this occurence is likely to be accompanied by an increase in the Crown's influence in Britain. No one who has watched the process of British government is likely to believe that the Crown has any tangible power over affairs of state. But it would be unwise to say that it has no influence. In the opinion of many politicians, hard-headed, proletarian fellows some of them, this influence will grow.

Elizabeth II is an intelligent and industrious woman. Her sense of history and of the Crown's place in history, especially British history, is profound. She has an accurate and retentive mind. Suppose she reigns for another thirty years. By the

1980's, she will have accumulated a store of experience and knowledge no minister will be able to match. If she retains her present interest in the business of government, as seems likely, the Queen's role in the guidance of government may increase, and, in the context of the times, this development may even be welcomed. The Western world is plunged into a long and savage contest with the Communist bloc which may grow more intense with the passage of time. In the circumstances, a fixed point of experience, knowledge, and detachment will be a welcome reinforcement for politicians. The Crown can play that role.

· 7 ·

Europe's Economic Challenge to Britain . . .
Stagnation in the U.K.'s Economy . . . The
Wages-Price Spiral and the Export Position
. . . Britain and Continental Industry . . . Pat-
terns of British Trade with Europe and the
Commonwealth . . . The City's Prospects in the .
Community . . . British Financial Policy in
Europe

HAROLD MACMILLAN compared Britain's entry into Europe to a cold shower rather than a warm bath. There are shocks in store for every section of the country's economy within the European Economic Community. The optimism with regard to the ability of the British to play a full, even a commanding, role in whatever form of political structure is

ultimately developed does not extend to the economic field.
Fortunately, perhaps, for the United Kingdom, the approach to
Europe forced the British to make a careful assessment of their
economy and its prospects within the Community.

Economists and politicians saw a good many weaknesses.
The problem was to bring these home to ordinary folk. In conditions of full employment, rising wages, and a buying spree,
it is difficult to make the majority believe that anything can be
wrong. Indeed, some of the skeptics feel that only competition
within the Community could force the British to recognize
their weaknesses and do something about them.

A primary factor was the stagnancy of the industrial economy. In 1960, 1961, and the first half of 1962, the economy
grew at one and a half per cent yearly. This is far below the
level of most other countries in Europe, including Britain's
rivals in E.E.C. Reviewing the whole economic field, the industrial correspondent of *The Statist* wrote: "We are inevitably
forced back to the point that only a much faster rate of wealth
creation can meet the need. If we do not achieve it, we shall
soon have to abandon the notion that Britain is still a leading
world power."

The rigidity of the British industrial structure is partly
political in origin, with both the major parties sharing the
blame. There is a surprising amount of subdivision and bad
location within industry; a multiplicity of everything from
steel works to automobile models. Declining industries are sub-
sidized, others are kept alive by protective tariffs—processes
which discourage movement to growth enterprises. A country
which is one of the manufacturing leaders in electronics and
automation too often leaves the industrial use of these to competitors in Europe and North America.

Some hard things have rightly been said about the refusal of the trades unions to accept labor-saving devices, automation, and other innovations. But many managements are equally reactionary. One of the country's major industrial figures is convinced that the refusal to use new methods is often due to the age of the employers involved. He had just revitalized two firms by pensioning off octogenarian managing directors and promoting much younger men keenly aware of the need for growth.

British efforts periodically to promote industrial growth have conflicted with the interest of succeeding Tory governments in halting inflation. The most favored method when a balance-of-payments crisis threatens is to introduce disinflationary measures, which have the effect of halting industrial expansion. Such measures are intended to restrict internal consumption and thus free goods for export. They do this. But they also limit growth. Under these conditions, industrialists and businessmen are reluctant to expand their capacity, for excess capacity adds to costs.

Costs and their effects permeate the industrialists' outlook on exports. An increase in average wages of four to five per cent in a normal year will mean an increase in consumer spending in Britain and an increase in the prices asked for British exports. The Federation of British Industries reports that prices are the main obstacle to an increase in exports. Wages contribute materially to these prices.

The British economy may benefit from the fact that wages, and consequently prices, are beginning to rise among some of the United Kingdom's chief competitors on the Continent. Workers' wages rose ten per cent in Germany in 1961, nine per cent in France, and seven per cent in Italy. In each case, wages rose faster than productivity. Some industrialists in Europe expressed the fear that the wages-restraint policy in the United Kingdom, popularly known as "the pay pause," might have put British industry into a better competitive position because continental industry was finally experiencing the inflationary consequences of its boom.

Prices and industrial stagnation probably are the basic illnesses of the British economy, especially in the export field. But there are many others, and critics, among them the Duke of Edinburgh, have drawn attention to them: slowness and delays in delivery due to strikes, a seeming indifference to foreign orders, the failure to provide spare parts—this originally was very damaging in the field of auto exports—and a tendency to think that because the customer had always been there, ready to "Buy British," he would continue to do so. Until quite recently advertising and packaging for overseas markets received far less attention than was necessary for competition with continental or American products. The entire attitude owed a good deal to the national refusal to believe that the good old days were over, to accept the nation's new status in the world. Clearly, changes are necessary throughout the sales structure.

Those who advise the government on economic policy believed that entry into Europe was the only means of imposing the discipline of effective competition on an economy which had grown deeply accustomed to and, to some extent, dependent on protection and feather-bedding. Obviously the economy is in for a shock, perhaps a bigger one than even the Prime Minister anticipates. Let us examine what entry into E.E.C. would mean to British industry.

One of the objectives of the European Economic Community, as laid down by the Treaty of Rome, is that "customs duties on importation in force between member states shall be progressively abolished." At the same time, external tariffs of member states are being adjusted at a common level in three stages. The Community will also reduce a number of institutional obstacles, such as customs declarations and inspections, which impede the free movement of goods; and end all restrictions on the movement of capital and labor within E.E.C. Europe, or at least the six countries now in the Community, intends to establish effective economic unity.

For the British this meant an increase in trade with Europe, more exports to the other members, and more of their goods in British shops. But the provisions of the Treaty of Rome raise difficulties that were at the bottom of the politico-economic opposition to entry in the United Kingdom. A common external tariff will mean duties on raw materials that now enter the United Kingdom duty free. There will be an end, too, to preferences for imports from Commonwealth countries. And those industries which now are protected by the highest tariffs will suffer. The recognition of these effects on the economy naturally is greatest in industries like aluminum, pulp, and leather, which will suffer the most. But all industry will be affected to some extent.

The outcry that arose in the United Kingdom sounded slightly unrealistic to many economists and industrialists in Europe. The British, they believe, are trying to create the impression, for reasons of their own—ah, perfidious Albion is at it again—of widespread dislocation as a consequence of entry. Europeans argue that, on the contrary, British industry is in a position to take care of itself in the new competition with Europe.

West German industry, despite minatory statements **by**

Dr. Ludwig Erhard that the boom is over, remains confident of its ability to compete with Britain inside or outside Europe. This is not true of France, Italy, the Netherlands, and Belgium. Industrialists in these countries do not fear British competition at present, given the state of the United Kingdom's economy. They are notably more apprehensive about the future, largely because they do not share the common West German distortion of the British situation.

"The Germans are making the same mistakes about the English now, in the economic and political field, that they have made in the past in military affairs," a French textile manufacturer has said. "As usual, they are underestimating the English and overestimating themselves. Whatever one may say about the General's [de Gaulle's] view of the English, evidently he does not undervalue them."

He and other continental industrialists believed then that, with the United Kingdom in Europe, Britain's entire economic outlook would undergo a rapid alteration fitting it for trade inside the Community. This belief rests, to some extent, on recollections of how continental economies, particularly those of France and Italy, were transformed by membership in E.E.C. Europeans were also impressed by the sheer size of many British industrial complexes. In many cases, especially in the automobile, chemical, and general manufacturing industries, these were larger and more efficient than their continental rivals. Such mammoth British organizations would be able to take care of themselves inside Europe better than their smaller continental competitors. Fear of such competition was a factor in French opposition to U.K. entry into Europe.

Europeans are also eying with some concern the presence in the United Kingdom of a large, highly skilled labor force. One of the advantages enjoyed by continental industry as a whole, and that in the Community in particular, in the last decade has been a reservoir of new industrial workers. This was most pronounced in West Germany, where the flow of refugees across the East-West boundary provided a continuous supply of labor; this factor enabled German employers to adopt a more forceful attitude toward the workers than would have been possible had there been a shortage of labor. The Russians, by building the Berlin wall, shut off that supply of labor. In consequence, West Germany is seeking and getting workers from as far away as Greece and Spain.

By early 1962 the labor shortage had spread elsewhere. In northern Italy, industry was advertising for skilled workers, taking peasants straight from the barren fields of Calabria, and offering inducements for the return of Italian industrial workers from Switzerland and West Germany. The French, Belgian, and Dutch economies were plagued by the same problem, and throughout E.E.C. wages rose as the supply of labor was reduced. The costs have been absorbed to some extent by the high rate of productivity in industry. But indications are that the spreading labor shortage and the resulting increase in wages may reduce the amount of industrial expansion this year.

Finally, European industrialists have noted a steady increase in the flow of British products into continental markets in the last five years. The expansion of continental exports to the British home market, so widely expected in Europe as a result of the United Kingdom's entry into the Community, cuts both ways as far as the European industrialist is concerned. Any resulting reduction in British internal consumption of home goods will, they reason, free more United Kingdom products for export to Europe.

There has been no shortage, in Britain or the Commonwealth, of prophets predicting calamity for British industry and exports should the country enter E.E.C. Yet the Continent's fears and the trade pattern in recent years furnish solid grounds for optimism. Granted a government policy that will put industrial expansion ahead of social security, something which no Conservative government has really attempted since 1951, the outlook is far from gloomy. The figures show that British exports established themselves among consumers in the Community well after E.E.C. came into being and before Britain's approaches to it had reached the stage of substantive negotiation.

Exports to Western Europe as a whole in 1961 were £163,000,000 above those of 1960, an increase of 16 per cent. Both 1959 (10 per cent) and 1960 (11 per cent) also showed increases, an indication that in the present world economic situation great industrial powers, Britain and West Germany, for example, tend to increase their trade with one another.

Trade with the members of the Community rose in 1961 by £94,000,000—an increase of 18 per cent over 1960. Trade with E.E.C. thus increased slightly more than trade with Western Europe as a whole. In the same year exports to France went up 28 per cent, to Italy 30 per cent, to the Netherlands 19 per cent, and to Belgium 19 per cent. The increase in exports to West Germany was less substantial, £8,000,-000, amounting to 5 per cent, but it followed increases of 15 and 12 per cent in 1959 and 1960.

There is an interesting comparison between these figures and those of exports to the members of the European Free Trade Area (Sweden, Switzerland, Austria, Norway, Denmark, and Portugal), which Britain organized as an answer to E.E.C. and Finland in the same year. Exports to these seven countries rose by £52,000,000—an increase of 12 per cent.

Significantly, these increases in exports to Europe have been accompanied in the past six years by a comparative reduction in exports to the sterling area overseas, including the Commonwealth countries. British sales to North America, principally Canada and the United States, and to the European Economic Community have risen from £344,000,000 and £420,000,000 in 1955 to £564,000,000 and £560,-000,000 in 1960. In 1955 the sterling area received nearly half of the total British exports, but five years later it received only slightly more than one third.

Australia was the most outspoken of the Commonwealth nations in its warnings about the consequences to that organization's economic and political ties of British union with Europe. But in 1961 exports to that country from Britain fell by £58,00,000, a drop of 22 per cent. There was also a reduction in exports to Nigeria (8 per cent), West Indies (9 per cent), British East Africa (2 per cent) and Ceylon (8 per cent). It is worth noting that in the preceding year exports to these countries had increased. There was also a decrease of 5 per cent in 1961 in exports to South Africa, which, although no longer a political member of the Commonwealth, still maintains close trade relations with Britain.

The pattern of Commonwealth trade was not entirely negative. Exports rose to Pakistan (10 per cent), to Malaya and Singapore (9 per cent), and to Ghana (10 per cent). But the reductions, and the fact that the increase in exports to New Zealand was only 3 per cent in 1961, point to the evolution of a pattern of British trade which varies from the traditional concept of an economic structure largely dependent on trade with the Commonwealth. The idea is hard to kill, however; two hundred years of what used to be called mercantile policy does not die overnight. Those who cling to this traditional attitude tend to overlook the development in Australia and Canada of secondary industries and the growth of exports to these and other Commonwealth countries from other European industrial nations.

These contemporary patterns of British trade should be considered in relation to two other significant economic and geographical factors: production and trade in Western Europe have been expanding more rapidly than in any other area in the world, including the United States, and from a geographical standpoint Britain can only become an economic partner in one large industrialized area, Western Europe.

When we discuss British exports in relation to the Community, it is worth remembering that they have undergone important changes in their character in the last twenty years. The popular view, in the United States, of British industry and exports is based, outside of certain specialized circles, on the economic geography of the twenties. Here again one encounters the sturdy refusal to believe that the British are anything but an old, unchanging people—a concept that the image projected by their own advertisers in the United States does little to belie. The trade figures, however, present a totally different picture.

A comparison of the figure for the period 1935-1938 and 1961 shows that the United Kingdom exports of engineering products are now 46 per cent of its total, as compared with 20 per cent before the war. Machine tools and special industrial instruments have risen from 13 to 31 per cent of all exports. The share of chemical products has risen from 6 per cent before the war to 9 per cent today.

Between 1935 and 1938, automotive vehicles constituted 4 per cent of the United Kingdom's exports. In 1961 they constituted 10.3 per cent of these exports. And exports from the industries which have developed fastest since the war have grown rapidly even after the Community came into being. For instance, exports of engineering products increased in 1961 by £102,000,000, 6 per cent over the previous year. But both 1960 and 1959 were growth years in this industry's exports, 6 per cent in 1959 and 7 per cent in 1960. The same pattern is evident in exports of machinery and instruments, which rose by 14 per cent, or £137,000,000, in 1961, as compared to the previous year. Larger exports of radio and electronic equipment, particularly valves and tubes, and of radio and radar communications and navigational equipment accounted for a third of the increase in this field.

During this period Britain's old export staples have declined in volume. Before the war, textiles amounted to 24 per cent of the country's exports, but in 1961 the figure was only 8 to less than 1 per cent.

Exporters who are now doing well in continental markets are confident they will continue to do so. They represent industries whose equipment is more modern and whose concentration and amalgamation are more advanced than in the members of E.E.C. except West Germany. This is particularly true of the consumer-goods industry; Britain has some of the largest manufacturing units in Europe producing vacuum cleaners, chemicals, and cars in the medium-price range. Management in these industries is aware that continued successful competition in a rapidly expanding European market will demand extreme flexibility in adjusting output to changing demands and, if necessary, in reducing or scrapping unproductive lines. Here, too, one finds the greatest emphasis on the introduction of labor-saving equipment and on the continuation of wage restraint. Talk of "industrial discipline" by employers invariably touches off trades-union explosions. But with Britain in the Community, successful competition will prove possible only if wages rise no more rapidly there than in the E.E.C. and if equipment is put to use imaginatively and efficiently.

The British believe the outlook is bright in at least twelve different export lines. These include chemical products, a branch of industry notably quick in adopting new techniques; electrical appliances, where British exports are already doing well despite the existing tariffs; television and radio and other electronics; commercial vehicles, sports cars, automobile accessories, and tractors; and wool textiles and man-made fibers. The last of these is a good example of an industry in which early research and development combined with concentration in major producers has given the United Kingdom a lead over European competitors.

Among the industries whose prospects in Europe are uncertain are paper, non-ferrous metals, machine tools, metal manufacturers, rubber, passenger vehicles, motorcycles, and heavy electrical engineering. The rubber industry is expected to increase its sale of tires but to lose exports of rubber footwear. Lower tariffs will scarcely affect exports of non-ferrous metals, but the demand for copper is expected to increase.

The outlook, in or out of Europe, is poor for another group of products, headed by cotton textiles. In the Community, Britain might get some protection from Asian competition, but many exporters are weak compared to their continental rivals. Leather goods, footwear, cameras, toys, carpets, and china would be hurt by European competition.

These forecasts of what would happen to Britain in Europe indicate a period of readjustment for British industry while she remains outside of Europe, competing with it and hoping eventually to enter. Everything will depend on the ability of industry to alter its outlook. That means co-operation by the trades unions and a more progressive approach by management to new techniques and new products.

Union with Europe or an intensified competition with E.E.C. while outside will affect the U.K.'s political ties with the Commonwealth. For these are based to a great degree on economic relationships, some of them well over a century old.

How important are Commonwealth preferences to British industry? In 1960, four fifths of Commonwealth imports into Britain, 38½ per cent of all imports, entered free of duty, and over forty per cent of Commonwealth products received preferential treatment. The same products imported from outside the Commonwealth were dutiable whereas those from the Commonwealth came in free or with a very low duty.

The same situation existed with regard to British exports to the Commonwealth. These, consisting almost entirely of manufactured products, usually enjoyed a tariff preference in the importing country. The system gives Britain extensive markets abroad and access to raw materials from Commonwealth countries.

The imposition of full duties on Commonwealth products

can be most serious with regard to food and raw materials. In most recent years, the United Kingdom bought roughly 50 per cent of its cereals, 69 per cent of its sugar, 56 per cent of its dairy products and eggs, 33 per cent of its meat, and 38 per cent of its fruits and vegetables from the Commonwealth. Of major raw materials, 62 per cent of non-ferrous metals, 25 per cent of wood and 25 per cent of paper and pulp came from Commonwealth sources. The rest of the world supplied Britain with the same percentage of meat and slightly more (41 per cent) fruit and vegetables. Of the three raw materials, the percentage imported from the remainder of the world is higher only in wood, and that by a margin of 1 per cent. Thus, the outlook for food producers in the temperate zone who now sell directly to Britain and in future would compete with the Community producers has worsened.

Canada is a good example of a Commonwealth country that would be harmed by British entry into Europe. A quarter of Canada's exports go to the United Kingdom, and about 95 per cent of these enter the British market duty free. Only about 33 per cent would come in duty free under the Community's tariff. Wheat, timber, and newsprint, dairy products, aluminium, and virtually all manufactured articles become dutiable. At the same time, wheat, dairy products, fruit, and manufactured goods would enter Britain from E.E.C. countries duty free. Should Norway and Denmark join the Community, as seems likely, their wood and paper products would also come in free of duty to compete with Canadian exports.

Australia's case, although serious, is not quite as bad as Canada's, largely because wool, which accounts for nearly half of her exports to Britain, is duty free under the Community's tariff. But other Australian exports to the home islands, roughly 28 per cent of the total, will suffer—particularly wheat, meat, butter, lead, and zinc.

New Zealand, British ministers have said, had to be taken care of in any agreement with the Community. Her economy is the most vulnerable of all. Parenthetically, New Zealand's traditional ethnic and social ties with the mother country are perhaps stronger than those of any other member of the "white" Commonwealth.

The small, robust country sends as much as 60 per cent of her total exports to Britain, and her main exports are those which will suffer most from the ultimate acceptance of the E.E.C. tariff: meat and dairy products. In recent years, out of a total annual export of about 155,000 tons of butter, 143,000 tons come to British tables: out of 345,000 tons of mutton and lamb, 310,000 are bought in the United Kingdom; and of 80,000 tons of cheese, the British used 74,000. New Zealand would go broke if it had to compete against Community shipments to Britain which entered duty free while her products faced a tariff barrier.

Problems arising from trade between Britain and the tropical and sub-tropical Commonwealth countries, although important, do not raise economic and political differences of the same severity. A number of their products—rubber, hemp, sisal, jute, oil seeds—will enter E.E.C. free of duty. Duties do exist on cocoa, coffee, and tea, but these are imposed for revenue rather than for protection. One difficulty is that some of these foods are produced by countries which were once French colonies or by Latin American recipients of United States aid. A convention and a special section of the Treaty of Rome give the former French colonies preferential treatment as associated territories.

Commonwealth trade has been discussed thus far chiefly in terms of foodstuffs and raw materials. But Britain's union with Europe will also raise the problem of Commonwealth exports of manufactured products. Canada is the country most deeply involved. However, its claims for easy entry of exports into Britain, and eventually the Community, are offset to some extent by the belief of many politicians and economists in the United Kingdom that Canada's brightest hope is membership in some form of North American economic community. Prime Minister Macmillan's government, naturally enough, has been reluctant to endorse or even echo this suggestion. But it is in line with the collective Cabinet vision of the creation in the future of a great Atlantic Economic Community including the United States and Canada.

Both Britain and the Community also had to study the question of imports into the United Kingdom of textiles from Hong Kong, India, and Pakistan.

These trade arrangements argued powerfully, in the view of the British government, for special guarantees for the import into the United Kingdom or into the Community of food products from the Commonwealth's temperate-zone countries, of foodstuffs from members of the Commonwealth's tropic or sub-tropic zones, where they compete with those of France's "associated territories," and of certain Commonwealth raw materials. Any other arrangement meant economic penalties for the Commonwealth and an inevitable and drastic adjustment of the political relations between the Commonwealth and the mother country.

The sales requirements of Commonwealth members in Britain must be considered against the background of general import patterns. One third of British imports in 1961 consisted of food, beverages, and tobacco. Slightly more than two fifths were industrial materials, and semi-manufactured goods amounted to nearly one fifth. Between one seventh and one eighth were finished manufactured goods and capital equipment. The expectation is that in the initial phase of membership in E.E.C. the imports of finished manufactured goods will rise.

The trade figures since 1945 show a steady increase in the import of manufactured and semi-manufactured goods. In general, the changing structure of British industry is reflected in the increased demand for semi-manufactured goods, such as metals, and the reduced demand for raw cotton and other basic materials. Britain has also been affected, as have been her rivals and partners in the Community, by the progressive removal of restrictions on trade and by increased industrialization abroad. These have resulted in rising figures for trade in partly finished products and in much greater industrial specialization.

Imports from the overseas sterling area, which includes the Commonwealth countries with the exception, an important one, of Canada, have not shown a consistent trend in recent years. In 1961 such imports on the whole were 2 per cent under the preceding year. Imports from Australia and New Zealand showed a general decline: 12 and 13 per cent less in 1961, respectively, than in 1960, largely as a result of lower prices for wool, meat, and butter. Imports from India fell sharply in comparison with the trade pattern of preceding years. Those from Pakistan fell by 14 per cent, but there was a considerable increase in 1960. British buying from Malaya and Singapore fell by 9 per cent, and imports from Ghana and Nigeria were down 8 and 4 per cent.

A comparison with the general situation shows that imports from Western Europe were only 1 per cent higher in 1961 than in 1960, although those from the Community rose by 2 per cent. Imports from Sweden, Denmark, Norway, and Finland were less than in 1960, but there were additional increases in purchases from France, West Germany, and Italy of 8, 7, and 4 per cent. The increases in the first two, however, were far lower than in the previous year.

Imports from the Soviet Union and its satellites were 12 per cent higher in 1961 than in 1960. However, these imports improved less rapidly in 1961 than in 1959 (14 per cent) or in 1960 (19 per cent).

Few can deny that Britain's entry into Europe without guarantees imposed severe initial penalties on the Commonwealth and on Britain. Most Commonwealth countries supported any agreement with Europe that would provide access to that market and to the capital investment and technical aid they need. But there was no willingness on the part of France, which dominated the discussions with the United Kingdom, to offer any comparable access to Europe to Canada, Australia, and New Zealand, or, in fact, to India, Pakistan, and Hong Kong.

The British, adopting the old tactics of appearing bloody, bold, and resolute, may have been out of line in the negotiations when they suggested, politely, that they be allowed to continue the free entry of Commonwealth produce into the home market. The brusque rejection of this proposal should not, however, divert attention from the fact that certain products of the Commonwealth are a speciality of the producing countries. What real, competitive economic reason is there for eliminating the duty-free import into the United

Kingdom of lamb, bacon, or tea? Britain herself might wish to impose a duty for revenue purposes, but there is little ground for the argument that free entry of these products would harm the producers of the Community.

Britain's second line of defense was a proposal that some products, which Commonwealth countries depend on for their livelihood, be allowed free entry into the Community. This might involve a change in the arrangements of the General Agreement on Tariffs and Trade allowing free entry from all members of GATT. At present, free entry into the United Kingdom market is provided for the Commonwealth by GATT, but not free entry for the rest of Europe. Final arrangements, therefore, would ultimately rest on those made between the Commonwealth and the enlarged E.E.C., including Britain and possibly Norway and Denmark.

The crux of the debate between Britain and her prospective partners concerned the products exported both by the Commonwealth and by members of the Community: wheat, butter, cheese, eggs, and fruit. At the outset of their negotiations, the British hoped that they would be able to make some special arrangement in keeping with the common policy of the Community with regard to each product. The rules of GATT and existing "most favored nation" agreements might bar preferential entry of Commonwealth products into Europe. The United Kingdom sought preferential entry of Commonwealth goods for Britain alone, but the first reactions of the Community members ranged from a flat refusal to consider any preferences between the U.K. and the Commonwealth to suggestions that a quota system be applied to such goods entering Britain.

The great issue that divided Britain from the members of

the Community in the first phase of negotiation was the extent to which preferential treatment for the Commonwealth, even under a quota system, would affect the fundamental character of the E.E.C. The British held that the concessions they sought would not alter the essential concept of E.E.C. The Europeans, particularly the French, held that they would. Although this, like all other issues, has its political aspects, the primary approach was commercial. Later we shall review political planning for Europe and the interplay of British and continental proposals in this field.

It is in the field of Commonwealth preferences, however, that continental criticism had the greatest application. The English, they said beyond Calais, wanted to join the club, but they sought to change the club's rules even before becoming members.

The prolonged international argument over the Commonwealth and its future relations with Britain and the Community was linked closely to the debates within E.E.C. with regard to agricultural policy and to the existing differences in price arrangements in Britain and the Community. In finding a solution, E.E.C. was guided by two salient principles: there must be a single price level for agricultural products throughout the Community, and there should be a common trade policy for agricultural products.

The Community was created on the assumption that it would provide new and increasing markets for the agricultural and horticultural products of three of the original members, France, Italy, and the Netherlands. All three welcomed Britain's entry, if she accepted the existing rules, because the United Kingdom is the largest importer of such products in

Europe. The Six understood that after a transitional period Britain would offer duty-free entry to farm products of E.E.C. members, accept common marketing and price arrangements, and restrict imports from non-member countries, including countries within the Commonwealth.

The situation was complicated by the differences between the British and continental systems of protecting the farmers. Most continental countries, including members of the Community, protect the farmer by import duties. France, for example, places an *ad valorem* duty of 30 per cent on wheat, 35 per cent on beef, 25 per cent on mutton, lamb, and butter, and 20 per cent on bacon. Britain, on the other hand, allows wheat, mutton, and lamb to enter without duty and beef to come in free from the Commonwealth, although the exporters pay about 3 per cent *ad valorem* duty. Butter from the Commonwealth enters free of duty; other exporters pay about 5 per cent. Commonwealth bacon bears no duty; other suppliers pay 10 per cent.

In Britain the market price paid the farmer for a number of products is ostensibly the result of free competition. When the average market prices fall below a guaranteed level fixed by the annual farm-prices review, they are brought up to this level by a deficiency payment, which is a state subsidy paid by the Exchequer out of taxes. Prices paid by the consumer for food in the United Kingdom, thus, often do not cover the full cost.

Support for farming in the United Kingdom has been added to a system that emphasized low food prices, which in turn were the result of free trade. Under this system the cost of support for home agriculture is perhaps clearer than under the continental system, but, in an economy perennially fearful of inflation, support also has the effect of overstimulating demand for some products.

In view of present views on support pricing in E.E.C., it is possible to envisage considerable changes for British agriculture. The most dangerous politically would be the end of guaranteed prices for major farm products after an annual review and the establishment of a price level by the Community. Some Britons have argued that it would be wiser for E.E.C. to accept the British system of agricultural protection, but this is highly unlikely. Moreover, although continental farmers find a good deal to admire in the United Kingdom arrangements, to their masters the suggestion is irritating and impractical.

In the Community, British products would have no tariff or quota protection against food imports from other members.

British agriculture, once the United Kingdom is in the Community, may have to pay levies to sustain European agricultural standards, and it is likely to find output of some products limited. But, on the whole, the outlook is not doleful. The level of agricultural prices established by E.E.C. will probably be higher than the present guaranteed prices in Britain and above the average of prices in the member countries. Comparative prices show that British beef cattle, sheep, and arable farming will do better in the Community than they do at present, whereas market gardens and poultry farms would do worse, and so, probably, would dairy farming.

The problems of establishing a common policy for the Community and then agreeing on some form of rational protection for Britain's farmers, at least for a time, are complicated by the global ramifications of the situation. Agricultural technology is progressing rapidly, acreage yields are rising to fantastic figures, European farming, especially in France, is rapidly being improved by the new techniques so that previous calculations of E.E.C.'s agricultural production will have to be jettisoned. United States farm production soars while the farm population falls. The hungry mouths multiply in Asia and Africa. All these point out the necessity for a global study and a global solution of the problem of agricultural production and distribution.

British trade and agriculture, if the country joins E.E.C., may well suffer some setbacks. Certainly there will have to be a long period of readjustment. There are opportunities for both the trader and the farmer in the Community, but no certainty of safety. Some judges of the United Kingdom's economy believe that the greatest economic opportunity for Britain lies in the field of international finance. "They may lose a bit on trade at the start," a distinguished American diplomat said early in 1962, "but you watch these boys in The City once they're in Europe. They've got the know-how and the experience and the guts to make something big out of it."

Were it not for the nationality of the speaker, this might be considered simply as another example of the chauvinism with which many of the British approached union with Europe. There is a great deal of optimism. But the best judges are still waiting for an answer to the question that faces the City. This is whether the amalgamation of banks, insurance firms, brokerage houses, commodity markets, and other financial organizations can give industry and commerce better

service than its continental counterparts and whether, ultimately, it will be able to compete successfully with the financial centers of Zurich, Milan, Frankfurt, Amsterdam, and
Paris.

To do so, the City will have to make a fast start. The establishment of E.E.C. stimulated financial activities in Europe; there has been a startling growth in cross-fertilization
among bankers and financiers from capital to capital. Most
continental bankers have a healthy respect for the abilities of
the British, especially with regard to transactions in dollars
and sterling held outside the United States and the United
Kingdom respectively. The City has the skill, the experience,
and a considerable number of well-staffed and well-directed
financial institutions. But the shortage of capital persists, and
trade finance is expensive. This situation contrasts sharply
with that in the European financial centers, where the volume
of capital grows yearly and trade credit is cheaper. Both Paris
and Amsterdam believe they will become the financial centers
of the new Europe because they have the financial organisms
best suited to the Community.

The City early recognized that should the Tories lead
Britain into E.E.C. certain aspects of British finance might
have to be altered to improve the competitive position vis-à-vis
continental rivals. For example, commercial banks in London
provide far less long-term capital than do their competitors in
Europe. The banks approved of this approach, and since the
capital market is well organized and experienced—some think
it is better than anything in Europe—the system has been held
to benefit industry as well as the banks. After watching the
new Europe in action, some British bankers and industrialists

have become convinced that the continental system provides better service to industry, especially in the fields of capital reorganization and mergers. On the whole, however, the City is confident that its arrangements are adequate to meet continental competition. The City might have been fitted by skill and experience to enter Europe. Is it as well equipped for a period outside Europe, resulting from France's rupture of the Brussels negotiations?

One obvious result is that continental industry will lose much of its present interest in the British economy. It is unlikely that existing ties between City and European banks will be strengthened. The connections of the great London financial institutions with the Commonwealth and the United States will argue powerfully for a greater interest in those countries and less in a self-sufficient, economically hostile Europe.

The City, like every other branch of the British economy, must prepare itself for a period of maximum pressure from Europe, one in which its flexibility will be tested to the utmost. The freer flow of continental funds into British securities, expected after entry, will not now develop, although there will always be some movement because of the higher yields on industrial shares in Britain compared to most European centers.

Like large sections of the economy, the City, on January 1, 1963, was prepared to switch its interest from the Commonwealth to Europe. Now it will have to go into reverse and nourish its ties with the Commonwealth and with E.F.T.A. and the United States during the period before the inevitable movement toward Europe gains new momentum. The change will be no easier to carry out because it will have to be done in the face of severe continental competition.

Such a change of attitude will have to effect others beyond the City. London's role as a shipping center is endangered by the recurrent strikes, whether official or unofficial,
which plague dockland. Foreign shipowners, like foreign shipbuilders, are frightened by the instability of British labor.
The expansion of port facilities in Rotterdam, the stability
of the labor force in the Dutch port, and that port's proximity
to continental sources of supply all argue powerfully for its establishment as the unloading center for E.E.C. Arrangements
for shipping may still be made in London by the insurance
firms, but the ships themselves may go to Rotterdam. The same
is true to a certain extent of London's commodity markets,
which would face severe rivalry should Rotterdam become the
Community's commodity center.

Rivalry with E.E.C. obviously raises more far-reaching
financial problems than whether the City is able at first to
compete with continental financial centers.

It was said that the government's budget of 1962 would
be the last British budget to be prepared completely independent of the European Economic Community. Critics added that
the entire intent of the budget should have been to prepare the
economy for entry. Those who assessed the strength of the
City of London also asked whether, in the event of Britain's entry, budget policy would be influenced by other members of the Community, how much the bank rate would
be affected by continental financial attitudes, and to what
extent sterling would be merged into a common European
currency.

These questions appear academic now in the light of
what has happened. But they still emphasize the fundamental

challenge presented to British finance and commerce by a prosperous, dynamic economic community. The relevant articles of the Treaty of Rome indicate the gravity of the E.E.C. challenge.

The reader should remember that these articles will be as important to American as to British interests, if the Community continues its present financial tendencies.

The Treaty states that the Community's aim is to coordinate the economic policies of the members and to "remedy disequilibria" in their balance of payments. Exchange rate is to be a matter of Community interest, and each member will establish an economic policy with three goals: a balance of overseas payments, confidence in its currency, and high employment and stable prices. Some European ministers sniffed at these rather grandiose objectives. How, they asked, is a high level of employment to be reconciled with a sound currency and stable prices? This is a problem, incidentally, that has baffled British governments since recovery began a decade ago.

Whether or not Britain is a part of Europe, the Monetary Committee established under Article 105 of the Treaty of Rome is one of the most important and controversial of its instruments. Here is where the joint financial policy of the Community will take shape. But a word of caution is necessary.

The French, West Germans, other members of the Community, and certainly the British, now on the outside, settle such important issues through financial or foreign ministers assisted by experts. Ardent pro-Europeans think that in future civil servants will assume this policy-making function. Here is the germ of a real conflict between politicians and bureaucrats.

It bears directly upon the question of a federal or confederal Europe. It has much to do with the authentic democracy of the future Community. It will plague Europe for years to come. The idea that "the man from Whitehall," that is, the government civil servant, knew best has always been heresy to most Britons. The initial impulse in Europe has been to trust the civil servants, but this attitude may alter as the stakes rise.

As it is now understood, the Monetary Committee is a consultative body empowered to review both the financial and monetary situations of members and the general pattern of payments within the Community, to report at regular intervals on its findings to the Council of Ministers, and to give its views on economic issues either on request or on its own initiative. When the British application for entry was under consideration, the Committee was mainly interested in the freezing of capital movements among the six members and in the broader problems of monetary policy, currency plans, and economic trends. These were all of vital importance to the United Kingdom.

For example, the existence of a Community policy on capital movements would present Britain with a major financial issue. As a member, the United Kingdom would find it necessary to remove a number of restrictions on the movement of capital in order to align its policy with that of the other members. Since Britain has not moved as fast as Community Europe in this respect, particularly in freeing the movement of stock-market securities, the process of alignment will be complex and perhaps painful.

Co-ordination of E.E.C. monetary policy in its initial stages was confined to a well-meaning insistence on intergovernmental consideration of the general impact of decisive changes in this field. The European Commission, which is the Community's watchdog over the whole field of E.E.C. interests, has kept an eye on this field as well as on other aspects of financial policy.

The British are skeptical, however. The government's experts, reviewing the early experiences of the Monetary Committee, got the impression that its proposals were liable to be limited by political influence within the member governments. They cited the revaluation of the mark in West Germany as an example. Here was an important change in the monetary policy of a major member government—one that had voiced through its politicians the importance of consultation. The assumption of the guileless would be that the whole thing would have been discussed, if not planned, by the Monetary Committee for at least six months. This was not the case. The Committee had talked about German revaluation in general terms without reference to specific dates and with no hint from the German representatives that the move was contemplated in the immediate future. When Dr. Adenauer's government decided to act in March 1961, the five other finance ministers in the Community were notified at midnight before revaluation.

The entry of Britain, with her global financial interests and the City's prestige and influence, was expected to expand co-operation in these areas. With Britain outside the Community and nationalism on the rise, led by France, the prospect is that the members will approach the Committee not as a policy-making body but as a forum for discussing, in the broadest terms, monetary policies and as a source of information about these policies. The trend is toward using the Committee as a sounding board for proposals concerning monetary policies to be applied in countries or groups of countries outside the Community, rather than as an executive for group decisions.

Nevertheless, the Committee will play an important role in decisions with regard to the removal of restrictions on the movement of capital. The Community has a timetable, which is being followed by most of its members.

Acceptance of this schedule would raise for the British government in the future the problem of security sterling: the blocked sterling payments made to aliens when they sell certain British securities. Another problem is that of hard and soft dollars, that is, currencies used by Britons to buy American or European securities. The British will have to solve these problems if they are to fit sterling, a world currency, into the narrower limits of the E.E.C., which seeks complete internal freedom for the movement of capital as well as for labor and services.

The Community already has taken steps to liberalize capital movements among its members. However, there is a proviso, in the case of movement of certain credits, that a country may reintroduce restrictions because of internal difficulties. But this move is subject to consultation with the Commission.

The liberalization of restrictions on the flow of capital has progressed much further in Europe than in Britain. If, to enter Europe on a sound basis, the government is to match this, then the United Kingdom will have to offer the Community some treatment comparable to that accorded members of the sterling area. This would involve discrimination against other areas, notably the United States. In British eyes the goal is a much wider liberalization.

The British financial community and the British government have a primary interest in keeping the pound strong enough to compete both with the Community and with the dollar. This is a fetish that sometimes diverts expert governmental attention from essential reforms. The pound is as strong as the British economy, no more and no less. When the economy is in difficulties, as it has been recently, the pound's position in the financial capitals of the Community will suffer. If and when Britain succeeds in joining Europe—perhaps over General de Gaulle's dead body—that reaction will be much more rapid because of the more intimate relations among the capitals.

As Jean Monnet, the father-figure of the Common Market, has said, many of these problems would be eliminated or reduced by the establishment of a common currency for the Community. To convinced Europeans, including some Britons, this seems a logical future consequence of the development of E.E.C. However, the growth of nationalism in France appears to preclude an early step toward a common currency and a common reserve fund. These problems also are related to those of world liquidity and of development funds for use outside Europe.

In this chapter we have seen the complexity and high emotional content of many of the economic problems that faced Britain and The Six in the negotiations at Brussels. One of the saddest aspects of the breakdown of these negotiations was that so many of these problems had been solved after months of patient negotiation and others were very near a solution.

Yet we know, after the French action, that the long-range difficulties of Britain and Europe are probably political rather than economic. The United Kingdom's entry would have been one of the great watersheds of European history. When it does come, it still will change the face of Europe.

· 8 ·

Origins of European Unity . . . Federal Union or Confederation? . . . Nationalism versus Unity . . . Danger from the East . . . Britain's Future Role in Europe

IN 1960 Professor Walter Hallstein, the German diplomat, remarked of the European Economic Community: "We are not in business, we are in politics." With these words he stated a simple truth discounted or avoided by many Americans and Britons.

From the outset, discussion of the Community in both countries has tended to center on its present economic arrangements and their effect upon economies outside Europe. The opening scenes of Britain's negotiations with E.E.C. dwelt largely upon economic considerations. Businessmen, quite naturally, have thought of the Community in terms of its effect on industry, commerce, and finance. Speculation and discussion have covered a wide range, from a common European currency to the prospects for the export of tulip bulbs from the Netherlands.

If this were the be-all and end-all of the Community, European unity would not have stirred the world. In fact, however, the possibility of union offers a great deal more than commercial arrangements. Something more was necessary to awaken the dreams of wise and experienced political leaders, to inspire men to leave high-paying posts or comfortable retirement to campaign for the Community. The source of these developments is European unity—a goal pursued by great men and great nations since the dissolution of the Roman Empire; sometimes a mirage just out of the reach of politicians, sometimes a prize about to be grasped by forceful leaders, who at the last moment found it dashed from their hands by pressure from outside.

Indeed, the historical fact that European political unity has so often been frustrated by the actions of non-continental powers—the Soviet Union, the United Kingdom, and the United States—provides part of the emotional stimulus for the movement. One encounters among "the Europeans" the deep-seated conviction that Europe will yet achieve the goal, despite her friends and enemies.

One night in the summer of 1945 I found myself talking to a young German ex-lieutenant in Hanover. He had been looking for his family in the ruins of that most German of cities and after two days of fruitless search was heading for the Ruhr, where, he thought, they might have found refuge with an uncle. I remember him well because, in that year and in that city, he was one of the few Germans who did not publicly deny admiration for Hitler.

"A bad wound gives you a chance to think," he said. "Much of what I saw to admire in the regime, much of what took me out of a schoolteacher's job and into the army, I now know was false. But one thing was real. Europe must be united. Whoever had the idea, Hitler or his lieutenants, was right. I knew they were right when I first went to Russia and saw that wide, unending land and its riches. I knew it again last summer when I saw your people pouring into France, rich in a way no army has ever been rich. How can we, the Germans, or the French or anyone be a power in the world unless we act together as Europeans?"

This, I am satisfied, is what lies behind the attitude of many Europeans toward the Community. Because this is Europe, very old, very cynical, and bedeviled by appallingly virile national interests, the idea has not taken definitive form outside the minds of the politico-intellectuals who never fail to produce a plan but who are invariably deficient in the political know-how necessary to make it acceptable to the masses. The absence of a clear political plan for the Europe of E.E.C. reflects a lack of agreement among Europe's leaders about what form political unity should take.

The debate about the most desirable form of political unity will continue whether or not Britain goes into Europe. And this debate is of maximum importance to the United States. Whether the outcome is a small, relatively compact Europe, little different from the original six-nation Community, or a larger Europe encompassing Britain and probably Norway and Denmark, with extensive global interests, the power situation in the West which has existed with very few alterations since 1950 is going to change. The political repercussions in a world in which for a decade and a half power has been polarized in Moscow and Washington will be incalculable.

Today the Community is fundamentally economic in outlook, and the Treaty of Rome substantiates this by emphasizing as the paramount aim of E.E.C the harmonious development of a full economic union through the establishment of a common market and a process of "progressively approximating the economic policies of member states." Yet the effect of advance toward this aim has been scarcely less political than economic. Every step taken toward economic unity has underscored the political issue. It is important to understand that no blueprint exists at the moment for political unity in Europe and that the Treaty of Rome, admirable as it is as groundwork for economic unity, is an insufficient guide to the planning of political union or even of political co-operation.

At this point the economists might point out, and several have, that if the economic groundwork is stable and efficient, the political superstructure will create no grave problems. This might be true of a single self-sufficient nation. It cannot be true of Europe, the oldest and most politically sophisticated of contemporary civilizations. It is very well to talk about what Europeans think and what Europeans do, as long as it is not forgotten that the "Europeans" are Frenchmen and Italians and Greeks and Danes.

Understandably, the movement toward political unity, although it had always been an objective of many of the Community's founders, had taken longer to get off the ground. During the winter of 1961-1962 a committee of the Community began to discuss the form of political association, at about the same time the British application for entry into E.E.C. was being developed in the Ministerial Council. Since the admission of the United Kingdom would alter the basis for a political union, little real progress was made.

The chief reason, which was related to the entry of Britain, was the dispute about the most desirable form of political unity: federalism or confederation. Definitions differ, as they must with regard to any political issue so deeply felt. However, federalism is generally thought to aim at a permanent union of states in which the government acts not only on the governments of member states but directly on all citizens. The central government of Europe thus would be the sovereign power, with its own civil service. This is the real "United States of Europe" idea, the dream of European thinkers since the war, a concept which most Americans have endorsed without knowing much about it—or about Europe.

A confederation, on the other hand, is a union of sovereign states prepared to align certain policies—defense and foreign policies are the most important—through regular and systematic consultation governed by decisions taken unanimously. There is no central, sovereign government, and the work of whatever civil service is established would be confined to matters of secondary importance. The Community at the moment has both a confederal aspect, since its powers extend over a limited but important area, trade and finance, and a federal one in the sense that its authority is applied directly, in some cases, to the citizens of member states.

The time factor is important in any comparison of these two possible political developments. As we shall see, a federal Europe may be out of the question for the moment because of what are now thought by their leaders to be the vital interests of nations. But the confederation that could arise as a compromise from the present conflict of national interests may well be the staging area for advance into federalism. Europa is an old lady now; she will not be hurried. It may be that despite the manifest difficulties confederation is the wisest first step.

There are, it seems to me, two basic forces at work in contemporary Europe which are in conflict. At the moment this conflict is unamenable to settlement by international agreement. It involves the United States, a great outside power deeply interested in Europe's development but faced with a reawakening of national independence which makes the task of American diplomacy vis-à-vis Europe far more difficult than it has been since the end of World War II.

The first basic force is one everyone talks about and almost everyone has written about. This is the movement toward European unity expressed largely through economic and cultural media. It existed long before the Treaty of Rome was written. It is an ill-defined movement, but a popular one.

One can trace the ramifications of European business and finance to prove its virility. But in everyday terms it means the jets flying across Europe to take Dutchmen to do business in Milan; the fast, comfortable new trains carrying Frenchmen to Frankfurt or Belgians to Vienna. This economic cross-fertilization means the breakdown, one hopes, of economic nationalism. But there are even stronger reasons for believing in the permanence of this basic drive toward the creation of a united Europe.

There is, for example, the mingling of the races. Each summer since about 1953, Europe has seen migrations of a size that in the past resulted only from wars. Out of the bleak north come the Germans, the British, the Scandinavians seeking the Mediterranean sun. Since they know a good thing when they have it, the southern Europeans are less likely to seek the holiday joys of London or Copenhagen or the Rhineland. But more and more of them come—even though some of the southern countries, notably Spain and Italy, are not prosperous enough to support a mass migration northwards. Even the middle-class French, despite their stout insistence that if one has France there is no sense in going elsewhere, are venturing beyond the borders of the motherland; possibly, as a Frenchman suggested, to get away from the English, the Germans, and the Americans at home.

Any one who has traveled through Europe can tell stories of how the Italians hate the Germans, how the Swedes return home vowing never to be cheated again by the French, of scottish behavior on the part of the British, the Dutch, and people of every other nationality. There's a good deal of truth in such reports. Foreign travel affects even the most conventional. The worthy, pious North Countryman from Manchester turns into a clumsy, drunken lady's man; the meek *hausfrau* from Württemberg shrills abuse at waiters and sasses strangers. They regret it when they get home. But it probably doesn't make a great deal of difference in the very important result of travel, which is the growth, subject to setbacks but steady and ever stronger, of knowledge about the other fellow and his way of life.

Youth has been the standard-bearer in this process, as it should be. Long before tourists began arranging their trips, the young people of Europe were on the road. The first genuine movements toward a new Europe were made, not by M. Schuman and Herr Adenauer in the late forties, but by groups of bronzed and tireless young people who tramped from France into Germany and from Germany into France. Polite, far more so than some of their elders who followed them, inquisitive and utterly devoid of that national pride which, in the stranger, makes the native's blood boil, they were the heralds of a new attitude toward Europe on the part of Europeans.

This intermingling has given Europeans a better idea of how they all live and has shown them how insignificant are the barriers that nationalism has raised between country and country. It has also revived and reinforced the old idea, never entirely dead, of a common stake in Europe, her treasures, natural and man-made, her past and her future. In Geneva I have been moved by good French Catholics admiring the memorial to the Reformation, not because they accepted its religious tenets but because here a great movement had been born in Europe, their Europe. In the long lines of people moving through the Louvre or the Vatican, in the crowds gazing at the miraculous beauty of St. George's Chapel at Windsor, there seems to be the bond of a common belief in the European cultural heritage. Surely this, too, must extend in time to the common historical experience. If the French and the British have forgotten "the old undying sin we shared in Rouen market place," cannot others forget the worst and remember the best of the years of European strife?

A continuation of the present dismantling of international barriers in Europe is vital. Before the old continent lies the gravest political test it has ever faced. Can Europe as a group of nations, without the leadership of a Charlemagne, a Napoleon, or a Hitler, resolve her difficulties and establish unity?

This is the essential question; and just as some forces are moving toward unity, so others have already delayed and may eventually frustrate its achievement.

By far the most important and familiar of these is nationalism. The national state, as we know it today, was born in Europe; it may well die there. But after outlining the forces now at work against nationalism in Europe, we must consider its present strength. No one should underestimate it—certainly no American. It sometimes seems, as one travels around the United States, that we have assimilated much of the worst of European nationalism, its parochialism, its intolerance, and its xenophobia, without adopting its virtues of dedication to the state and unwavering support of the ideal of a state above the bickering of political factions.

Nationalism in Europe today is most powerful and at the moment most dangerous to European unity in France. Potentially it is highly dangerous in Germany, and, should anything go awry, almost equally so in the United Kingdom. We may be witnessing the last gasp of national ambition in Europe. To the outsider, the conditions appear to be against a revival. But the strength and attractiveness of nationalism should not be discounted. Already it is playing a potent role in the decisions taken by continental governments with regard to the form European political unity should take.

Before we consider the role of nationalism in the great European debate about the future political form of the continent, let us discuss the major external unifying factor and place it in perspective. This factor is fear of Soviet aggression—military, political, and economic. Here a new perspective is necessary because of the changes in the attitude of the West toward Russia and in the Soviet posture in Europe.

It does not take a great effort of memory to recall the dismay and fright which overtook Western Europe in 1948 and 1949 after the Communist *putsch* in Czechoslovakia and the imposition of the blockade on West Berlin by the Soviet authorities in East Germany. In retrospect the scare may seem exaggerated to some. At that time the United States still had a monopoly on nuclear weapons; there is no evidence that the Soviet Union was prepared then to push any policy to the point of provoking war with America. But Europe, frightened, was willing to accept the need for some general form of military alignment and to welcome the North Atlantic Alliance when it was established.

NATO is now almost as familiar a piece of international furniture as the United Nations. It was not so then. The banding together in a defensive alliance of European powers, many, like Norway and Denmark and Portugal, with a long tradition of neutrality, without the emergency of military invasion was a great diplomatic feat. A combination of enlightened political leaders in the member nations and wise and flexible direction at supreme headquarters by men like General Eisenhower and Lord Ismay encouraged countries still suffering from the effects of war to devote considerable amounts of their gross national products, clearly needed for industrial and social rehabilitation, to reconstructing their military establishments. The threat itself was grave enough. The response, given the times and the conditions, was splendid.

Since then, the Alliance has grown slowly into a major military and, consequently, political force. Because its existence imposes a considerable burden on the economies of the members, there is always a tendency to trim the sails whenever the gales from Moscow abate. Politically, the Atlantic

Alliance is likely to be most united when Soviet pressure is directed, with all the sound effects employed by Communist propagandists, at some point along the long frontier that separates East and West in Europe. Berlin, guaranteed by a NATO pledge, is the most sensitive of these points.

In the present nuclear stalemate, pressure from the Russians is more likely to be political than military. In Moscow it is known that an era will end and political patterns alter when the aging men who have led most of the West's important states pass from the stage. Adenauer in Germany, de Gaulle in France, Macmillan in Britain, Salazar in Portugal, Franco in Spain—their deaths or retirement will offer the Russians the opportunity for a more subtle and possibly a more dangerous political strategy.

The Russians seem to have made up their minds that no one, Greeks or Norwegians, Germans or Danes, can be frightened out of the North Atlantic Alliance. Consequently, they have turned their diplomatic and political resources to the more difficult job of dividing the Alliance by other means.

Earlier I referred to the probability that immediately after Chancellor Adenauer's departure the Soviet Union will reopen its campaign to draw West Germany out of NATO by offering a promise of German reunification. It is in such a situation that the clash between nationalism and democracy will threaten the stability of Europe. The Russians will not expect in answer, at the outset, anything but an uncompromising negative. But they will leave the offer open and will renew it from time to time, adorned with new embellishments to poison German politics and seduce nationalist politicians.

In those circumstances the damage done by Dr. Adenauer in refusing to allow any of his lieutenants a hand in formulating high policy will become apparent. The situation in Central Europe five years hence will demand from the German Chancellor of the day political wisdom and diplomatic experience of the highest order. Has Dr. Adenauer enabled any of his possible successors to achieve these? The answer is no, and this failure will cost the German people and the whole Alliance a great deal.

We have come to regard the North Atlantic Alliance as an eternal verity. But usually alliances are casualties in any period of rampant nationalism. It is absurd now to think of any member of the Alliance making a bilateral treaty with the Soviet Union. But would it be so absurd if E.E.C. foundered and some great national state, France, Germany, or Britain, found itself in desperate need of economic outlets elsewhere?

This kind of question has not been asked for over a decade because the West generally has been sure of the Alliance. But if the period of military pressure from the Soviet Union has ended, if Russia finally realizes that she can create the chaos she desires only by an adroit combination of subversion and diplomacy, then we will not only have to ask these questions but find the answers as well.

In view of the present situation of Europe and of the renewal of national ambitions, these questions seem more important than those commonly associated with the Soviet Union and its manipulation of the Communist parties in Western Europe, particularly in France and Italy.

There is a tendency to confuse the strength of the party with its voting figures in elections. In the recent experiences of government in France and Italy, little exists to indicate that the Communist party in either country is in itself a powerful factor in political society. But there is a great deal of evidence that the principle of revolt which the party upholds has attracted masses of voters. Should European prosperity continue, this attraction will lessen, just as British prosperity between 1951 and 1959 dealt the Labor Party an all but mortal blow.

The Communist parties and their voters will always act as loyal allies to the Soviets. But the Russians are cynical enough to pay more attention to the interplay of national interests, the frictions within the Alliance, and the growing American doubts about Europe.

One reason for doubt, and a powerful argument for accelerating the creation of a united Europe, is the vigorous swing toward nationalism on the Continent, a swing that conflicts directly with the movement toward unity. One of the most remarkable features of this new nationalism is that it thrives despite the presence of a threat to Berlin so real that the United States reinforced its conventional forces in Europe by 50,000 men. Yet at the same time France, after withdrawing two divisions from Algeria, refused to assign them to NATO.

This did not mean that the French were unconcerned about the threat to Berlin, but it indicated that in the present, unlike the past, they retained the right to assess the strength and immediacy of this threat. This attitude may be short-sighted; it may represent an inflated idea of the importance of France in Europe. Or it may reflect General de Gaulle's belief that the Soviet Union is not going to fight over Berlin and that as long as allied garrisons remain in the city no reinforcement is necessary since any attack on these garrisons would involve the Soviet Union in a nuclear war. In this event, in the General's mordant phrase, "all the world will die," and the Russians know it as well as anyone.

This French attitude is echoed in some unlikely places.

Basically, it animates a good deal of high British strategic thinking on the dangers of war, and it has supporters in less important capitals than London and Paris.

Opposing it must be placed the strong belief of many powers, large and small, that the deterrence of some form of Soviet aggression into Western Europe rests almost as much on the conventional forces of the Atlantic Alliance as it does on the United States Air Force's Strategic Air Command or the Polaris missiles aboard the submarines of the United States Navy. Those who hold this view are ready to continue their sacrifices, sacrifices which, if small financially by Washington standards, nevertheless look pretty big in Oslo or the Hague, to maintain NATO.

The powers that remain faithful to the NATO ideal are also, however, the strongest supporters of any attempt to establish a basis of negotiations with the Soviet Union. There is one exception. The British, from the outset of the Berlin crisis of 1961-1962, showed themselves unwilling to make any important material contribution to the conventional defense of Western Europe. But they were most willing, indeed eager, to support any policy that sought negotiations with the Soviet Union on an interim settlement for Berlin.

For the moment it seems clear that Soviet threats no longer have the old power to nourish unity within the Alliance, although that unity may be stronger than it appears. But it was quite apparent at the NATO meetings in Paris in December 1961 and in Athens in 1962 that the sense of urgency reappears only fitfully, and then only when the United States reminds its allies of the harsh, brute facts of Soviet ambition.

Many countries are undecided about the form European unity should take, but not France. France is far more com-

mitted than any other member of E.E.C. to the pursuit of
national interests; she is enjoying a powerful resurgence of
national economic strength. Having lost her colonial empire,
often through humiliating defeats, in the seventeen years since
the war, France is looking around for an arena wherein she
can reassert her greatness. In these circumstances, she is
led by Charles de Gaulle, a strong, incisive, somewhat old-
fashioned chief, certainly the most impressive Frenchman of
his generation.

It is understandable, then, that France, which in this
context means de Gaulle, thinks of Europe in terms that offend
Americans, Britons, many Europeans, and quite a few Frenchmen, who have conceived a different course toward European
unity. The French President wants a Europe that will be
basically confederal in form. Above all, he would reject any
arrangement which would give the other members of a European political community, great or small, a veto on France's
independence of action. In the mind of this gifted septuagen-
arian there burns the dream of France as "the great nation" of
the past; he wants to re-create in the minds and hearts of
Frenchmen that burning belief in themselves and their country which marked the great epochs of French history. Studi-
ously contemptuous of republican political patterns—natural
enough in view of recent history—he both rules and reigns.

Charles de Gaulle has been compared to many great
Frenchmen of the past, and these comparisons are justified
by some of his qualities and acts. But is there not a basis for
comparison with a Frenchman not remarkable in history: the
Emperor Louis Napoleon? The reader of history will note a
resemblance between the lordly tours undertaken by de Gaulle
and those direct appeals to the French made by Bonaparte's

nephew on similar tours. There is the same recourse to porten-
tous but basically empty phrases to satisfy a public that asks
embarrassing questions about policy. France will be fortunate
if some of the phrases of the President do not turn as sour as
the Emperor's famous, "L'empire, c'est la paix."

De Gaulle and France have assumed the role of arbitra-
tors of Europe, a role, incidentally, which Louis Napoleon
played with some success until the advent of a Prussian named
Bismarck. France has firmly established policies on the future
political shape of the Community and on other topics, such
as the development of the North Atlantic Alliance negotiations
with the Soviet Union and the functions of the United Nations.
She has every right to establish such policies. But what are
her credentials for claiming the leadership of Europe?

Here is a great, rich, pleasant country. The year 1962
saw France enjoying a level of prosperity in all classes quite
unprecedented in her history. This also was true of her chief
associates, Britain, West Germany, Italy, and the Benelux
countries. But compared with Britain and Germany, the
French boom came rather late. And France, although undeniably prosperous, does not have the same resources for
continued basic prosperity as these two powers. The French
economy does not boast foundations in essential heavy industry comparable to those of Britain and Germany.

France's power status, like that of Britain, has undergone
a startling reversal in the last decade. Indochina is gone, Algeria is gone. The legions of France are withdrawing to the
motherland. In the midst of the bombast about the French
army and *la gloire,* one must remember that glory has been
rather rare. The French were beaten in Indochina, beaten in
Algeria, and most disastrously beaten in France in 1940. The

bitterness arising from these defeats has created a mood of chauvinism that de Gaulle has exploited. Listening to some Frenchmen, one gets the impression that the two terrible wars of this century did not occur, that one is back in the Edwardian era.

The President and his advisors see Europe in terms of French leadership of a confederation. They oppose federalism. But if we grant that the de Gaullist leadership is a temporary phenomenon, we must also grant that many intelligent and energetic Frenchmen do not see Europe developing that way. Most of the orthodox political parties, eclipsed since 1958 by Gaullism, are committed to some degree of federalism in future political organizations. They will undoubtedly pursue this aim after the President's departure, and they obviously will be in direct conflict with all those national elements, the armed services and the opportunist politicos of Gaullism, which have been encouraged by the President to believe in a national future for the country.

When de Gaulle was asked what would happen "when de Gaulle disappears," his answer was pregnant for the future of France, Europe, and the whole Atlantic Community.

"The danger," he said, "is not so much, in my view, that after the event . . . there would be a political void, but that there would be considerable overcrowding."

The absence from the scene of the man who has dominated French politics since 1958 is the first factor in the confused and dangerous political situation that is likely to arise in France when de Gaulle goes or, what could be much worse, if his powers begin to wane while he remains in office. France will then face a resumption of that old, never completely resolved conflict between the left and the right which has bedeviled her history since the Revolution. The greatness of the issue at stake—France's survival as an independent national power (the same issue, incidentally, which now faces Britain and West Germany)—is bound to exacerbate the conflict. Yet I believe we would be wrong to see the clash entirely in terms of the past.

The right will array the clerical, military, and bureaucratic interests which, supported by some but not all of the major industrial firms, have striven against republican, democratic France for a hundred and fifty years. Opposed to them we shall find the classic "left," anti-clerical, anti-militarist, imbued with an unyielding belief in French democracy—with one difference. As things stand now, the left is the more inclined toward a federal Europe. But one of the most important components of the left in its long conflict with the right is the French Communist party. And Communism, in France and elsewhere, opposes the political and economic unification of Europe.

It can be assumed that a Europe des patries, favored by de Gaulle, appears slightly less dangerous to the strategists in the Kremlin than a federal Europe, since the former, by preserving national identities almost intact, would offer the Russians only slightly reduced opportunities for their tactics of divide and defeat. However, the Communist party in France, like all others in Western Europe, will most likely oppose any form of European integration. Communism feeds on chaos, and the differences within the country with regard to the future organization of Europe will be exploited to the utmost.

France is never as powerful as she looks—or as unstable. But it is difficult to see the post-de Gaulle period in anything but the most somber tones. The nostalgia for past glories, the national egotism, the panache and bravura of the right are potent still. They survived the triumph of the left in 1945; there is no reason to believe they will not survive the settlement of the Algerian situation.

The end of that situation, which imposed on many Frenchmen the inhibitions common to all national emergencies, will release and encourage the furious energies of the French left. This will occur, it may be supposed, precisely at the time that de Gaulle's days in power are nearing their end. The British are right not to expect too much from France in the way of political stability when the dynamism of nationalism collides with the dynamism of federalism.

This collision will raise the question of the ability of the strangest alliance within the Western community to survive. This is the intimate relationship that has developed between the France of de Gaulle and the Germany of Dr. Adenauer.

The relationship is not new. The first stirrings toward European unity were powerfully supported by a desire in both France and West Germany for a *rapprochement* that would form the nexus of future continental solidarity. Robert Schuman, French Premier and later Minister of Foreign Affairs, and Dr. Adenauer made the first moves in this direction in the early fifties. But the motives that led the German Chancellor and the French President to stress the importance of the relationship in 1962 were the same.

Federal Germany, when it emerged as a nation in 1949, was still weak, although potentially powerful, and still regarded with the deepest suspicion by France, the least powerful of her Western conquerors and occupiers. The German republic's path in Europe would be smoothed if relations with France were improved; so reasoned Dr. Adenauer. Finding in M. Schuman a man who understood the folly and futility of division between the two countries—he had served in both the German and the French armies and spoke both languages— the Chancellor set to work to create cordial relations. He succeeded in so doing and in laying the foundations for European unity; a feat for which all Europeans must be grateful.

Several important factors were working for him. Europe in 1950 was only five years away from a war which had shaken its social, moral, and political foundations. There was an urge to find a better way of conducting European affairs, an urge which produced some zany proposals but which also supported the efforts of the Chancellor and the French statesman. There also existed, although the French like to overlook it, the memory of a myriad personal relationships, profitable to both sides, which had grown up during the occupation of France between 1940 and 1944.

This is not a slur on the French Resistance, which was maintained in the face of terrible odds and at the risk of torture and death by thousands of devoted men and women. The Resistance was not, perhaps, as important militarily as its veterans wish us to believe, but it provided considerable assistance, in espionage and sabotage, to the allied cause.

It is important to remember, however, that other Frenchmen, who considered themselves no less patriotic, established working arrangements with the German occupiers, that they co-operated industrially and commercially with them. The vision of a United Europe, even when put forward by Hitler's minions, is not ignoble, and many Frenchmen looked beyond the nightmare of the occupation to a time when France and Germany together could contribute to the restoration of Europe's old position in the world.

This last concept is a striking part of the Adenauer-de Gaulle relationship. The two men are Europeans; they speak to the Continent as Europeans and talk about Europe as an entity—whether a federation or a confederation is not particularly important here—with an existence outside the Communist bloc on the East and the United States and Britain on the West.

The Franco-German Treaty of Co-operation of January 21, 1963, was an expression of this relationship. And General de Gaulle's desire to keep the "Anglo-Saxons" out of Europe was the reason that he wrecked the negotiations between Britain and the E.E.C. Parenthetically, it might be noted that neither de Gaulle nor the French people oppose the entry of the Anglo-Saxons into Europe when, as in 1914-18 or in 1939-45, they come to save France from conquest. At other times, however, de Gaulle, with Adenauer following meekly behind, wants to dictate continental Europe's attitude toward the Communist bloc and maintain an illusory continental military strength.

The present amity between Paris and Bonn may be ephemeral. Dr. Adenauer needs it. Will his successor? The debate in West Germany on the future political organization of Europe is waged between those who believe the Paris-Bonn axis will endure and those who believe this relationship will dissolve soon after Chancellor Adenauer departs from the scene.

The Chancellor's grasp is perceptibly loosening, not through any evident public reduction of his powers or defiance of his authority. Rather, it is to be found in the more independent attitude of some West German ministers; Dr. Gerhard Schroeder, the present Foreign Minister, is a good example. The visitor in Bonn senses that the new men, tired of waiting in the wings, are gradually nibbling away at the Chancellor's authority within the government.

Dr. Adenauer has shown at times that he is as conscious of the situation as anyone in Bonn's busy diplomatic colony. His awareness of it explains his sudden explosions of energy and his bouts of diplomacy by press conference in which, either directly or by implication, he reverses the line his own government has already taken on major issues of policy, such as the discussions with the Soviet Union about Berlin.

Five, even three, years ago these incidents would have marked a turn in German policy. The most significant aspect of the Chancellor's bout of one-man policy-making in Berlin in May 1962 was that within two weeks almost everything he had said had been reversed by his subordinates in private discussions with American and British leaders. Since he is a proud and stubborn man, however, the West must expect periodic reassertions of his old authority as long as he is in power.

A Franco-German understanding as the basis of any European political community is certainly to the Chancellor's taste. But does this preference reflect the feelings of other German politicians and officials? Once Dr. Adenauer has left the scene, taking with him most of the sychophants who have surrounded him, there may be a rapid change of outlook in Bonn.

In the Adenauer-Schuman period the idea of a federal, supra-nationalist Europe was strong in Bonn and in West Germany generally. During that period Germans who knew almost nothing about America talked enthusiastically about creating a "United States of Europe" and were encouraged by Americans, in the High Commission at Bonn, who knew almost nothing about Europe. There was a great deal of popular interest in the idea, and, had it been presented as a tangible political policy, there would clearly have been strong political support for it. To some extent it has subsided, leaving behind firm supporters of the "Little Europe" idea such as Professor Hallstein.

Since then, Germany's position has changed. The economic miracle re-established national confidence and reduced enthusiasm for any proposal which arose primarily from the earlier belief that Germany needed Europe. By the end of the fifties Germany was arming again. This has not meant the reappearance of militarism as many feared. But it is another factor which leads Germans to think of their country as an independent unit rather than as a partner in a federal union. There has been nothing in Germany to equal the renaissance of French nationalism, nor has any German political leader exploited nationalism as de Gaulle has done. The net effect, however, has been away from federalism.

The early successes of the Community encouraged this trend, just as the failure of the earlier European Defense Community offered a warning against too rapid integration. E.E.C. has grown and prospered because it has moved step by step, pragmatically and functionally, toward economic unity. To the Germans, especially to the business community, this now appears a more reasonable road than the imposition of political or defense pacts like E.D.C. West Germany today is less fond of political blueprints than she was ten years ago.

However, despite the support given President de Gaulle's concept of a Europe of Fatherlands, that is, of national states, by the government, the idea seems to fall a good way short of what most Germans want from Europe. Opposition springs from two sources. One is the belief that de Gaulle's concept would mean in practice no more than a coalition of sovereign governments, which would not lead to the degree of economic unity established by the Treaty of Rome. The best its opponents can accord this plan is the status of a halfway stage leading, by cautious steps, toward European unity. Another group objects to the Europe des patries idea on the basis that it envisages a small compact Europe too narrowly based and too restrictive to take advantage of the Continent's political and economic diversity, which can be a source of strength as well as weakness.

This objection is particularly strong in northern Germany, which, unlike the Rhineland, Hesse, and Bavaria, looks northward to the Scandinavian countries and westward to Britain. Businessmen in Hamburg and Bremen concede that the united Europe they envisage—including Britain, Norway, Denmark, and perhaps Sweden—will be more loosely joined than the present alliance of six continental powers. But they maintain that this is acceptable since, in time, the larger Europe will be a far more powerful economic and political complex.

West Germany, thus, is subject to differences about the shape of Europe similar to those which affect France. On one hand is an aging but still influential Chancellor who favors the retention of a compact political and economic grouping; on the other, industrial and commercial interests which, primarily for economic reasons, want a wider association and are not immediately concerned with the exact nature of its political development. This latter group is much more influential in Germany than in France, and the Chancellor, although still politically powerful, lacks de Gaulle's pre-eminence in national affairs.

Earlier I touched on British suspicion of German political stability and direction as a factor in Britain's ultimate support of entry into Europe. So much has been made of this attitude in the United Kingdom that some attention should be paid to the other side of the coin.

On the whole, the Germans have borne with commendable patience attacks and criticisms from the British press and from politicians. However, they, too, find reason to doubt the political maturity the British claim for themselves. How is this maturity to be equated with ridiculous attacks by loud-mouthed agitators against Willy Brandt, the Mayor of Berlin, whose anti-Nazi record is a historical fact? The agitators represent the small but noisy Communist party in Britain, a party without influence at the polls. But why, when this fact is common knowledge, was there no defense of Herr Brandt by British politicians of comparable stature in the Conservative Party? A German newspaperman posed the question. No British leader provided an adequate answer.

The debate about federation versus confederation has less impact in West Germany than in France because the Germans are not now interested, as the French are, in the political consequences of a united Europe. The present generation of political and industrial leaders is not concerned with Germany's historic role as the leader of Central Europe. The scars left by the last attempt to play this part are still visible. The German of today, living as he does on the edge of the

Communist empire, is also more aware than a Frenchman or an Englishman of the resources of Russia. Consequently, he is more likely to think of world politics in terms of America and Russia, with Germany, like France and Britain, sheltered under the wings of the United States Air Force.

This outlook may alter with the emergence, five or six years hence, of a new group of leaders. But it is at the present time an important factor in European stability. When the Chancellor departs and a new figure moves into the seat of power, the expectation is that this attitude will still prevail. And, if Dr. Erhard succeeds Dr. Adenauer, those who have endorsed Britain's entry and the pragmatic development of European political unity will receive a significant reinforcement.

President de Gaulle made a psychological blunder when, in his series of pronouncements on the future political shape of Europe, he assumed that Italy would follow his lead. To begin with, he overlooked the atmosphere of contemporary Italy, which, in its bustling, buoyant economic optimism, is very similar to that of West Germany in the mid-fifties or France in 1960. Both General de Gaulle and Dr. Adenauer appeared to take Italian acquiescence to Franco-German leadership for granted. This was a mistake.

Contemporary Italy wants to co-operate in Europe; she doesn't want to be bossed. The Italians are far more aware of their own internal problems than their allies appear to be; they are also aware of their growing economic strength. There is very little ground for believing that either politics or business in Italy is prepared to accept an inferior role for that country in a severely circumscribed "little Europe" dominated politically by France and economically by West Germany.

A great many factors argue against such acceptance. Talking to Italian politicians, diplomats, editors, and businessmen, I have been struck by the significant difference between them and their French counterparts, who are only too willing to claim the leadership of "Latin Europe."

The Italians are able to restrain their enthusiasm for General de Gaulle and his nationalist aspirations, perhaps because they know to their cost the dangers of jingoistic ambitions ill-suited to national resources. I am not thinking here only in terms of Benito Mussolini, although he is the most recent and disastrous exponent of Italian jingoism. But for fifty years, from 1885 to 1935, Italy, newly united and poverty-stricken, indulged herself in a series of overseas adventures in pursuit of what politicians call glory and imperial status. The lesson finally taught Italy in the western desert between 1940 and 1943 has been learned.

It is not a question of distrusting de Gaulle. It is rather that the Italians, from their own experience, see his kind of nationalism as out of date. In this and in much else the Italians appear to have assimilated the lessons of World War II better than their northern allies.

For example, German domination before and during the war is too recent an experience to facilitate Italian acceptance of German leadership in economics or politics. There is a good deal of suspicion and even active dislike of the Germans in Italy. In that country, the cross-fertilization of tourism has not had positive results where the Germans are concerned. Never the most tactful of peoples, the Germans, who each summer go by tens of thousands to Italy, affront the Italians —although not to the extent that the latter reject their money.

Oddly enough, the British, who brought about the fall

of Mussolini's Italy, appear more popular than the Germans
or even the French. This may be rooted in the long history of
British interest in Italy and in the genuine admiration for its
people of Britons who have settled there.

But a considerably more solid basis exists for Italian
sympathy for Britain and support of her entry into the E.E.C.
There is in Italy a far greater appreciation of the stabilizing influence of Britain on the Community than there is in
Paris or Bonn. The Italians admire, in some cases even vener-
ate, British political experience in a working democracy. This
I have found to be as true of Italian socialists as of Italian conservatives. They feel that, with the British "in," Europe and
even Italy will benefit from the traditional *savoir-faire* they
ascribe, perhaps wrongly, to British democracy.

Among some Italians this concerns over-all European political balance as much as specific problems. Although a compact, Catholic, strongly anti-Communist Europe has advocates
in Rome, as it does in Bonn and Paris, many Italians on the
left believe that a more liberal and flexible approach to the
Soviet bloc is preferable for the Continent. Since there are
no outstanding differences between Italy and the United Kingdom, they believe that Italian governments will find themselves more attuned to British policies in this area, even if a
Conservative government was in power in Whitehall, than
they would with French or German political programs.

British flexibility on the Berlin issue and in regard to
other outstanding differences with the Soviet Union, which
raises hackles in Bonn and Paris, appears sound and logical
to many people in Rome. The possibility of a London-Rome
axis, once Britain enters Europe, is not to be discounted as a
balance to the combined influence of Bonn and Paris.

Support for Britain predisposes many Italians in favor of
a confederation as the preliminary political formula for the
continent. But it should be emphasized that the Italians think
of this as the preliminary form, one suitable to the initial years
of British membership. With the United Kingdom safely inside the Community, many Italians hope that Europe, politically, will move slowly and steadily toward federalism. Their
own national experience is not so long, or so happy, that they
are wedded to a confederal form for Europe. But the history
of the movement toward European economic unity has impressed them, as it has many Germans, with the wisdom of
moving step by step toward the political goal.

In Italy, as elsewhere on the Continent, the lessons of
the failure of the European Defense Community have been
learned. Unity, it is now accepted, cannot be imposed quickly
or by any single proposal. If, in the interval, the Community
accepts confederation, then Italy will be content. But the federalists there and in Germany and France obviously will return to the campaign once the formative period encompassing
the entry of the United Kingdom and perhaps Norway and
Denmark has been concluded.

Generally, the federalist idea is strongest in the smaller
members of the Community. In the Netherlands, Belgium,
and Luxembourg, a federal political union is the ideal. The
one transitory factor that adulterated this view was the anxiety
of the three countries for British entry. The drive for federalism among the Benelux powers abated considerably in the
spring of 1962 when it became known that Britain's progress
into the Community would be impeded should federalism
become the acknowledged, immediate political goal.

"I remain the supporter of a supra-national Europe," said

Paul-Henri Spaak, Belgium's Foreign Minister, "and shall continue to fight for that. But I know that at the present moment this supra-national Europe is impossible not only because of the British position but equally because of the French attitude. Thus I say that because I cannot get a supra-national Europe, and instead a Europe des patries is offered to me, I prefer to undertake that with Great Britain."

M. Spaak's comment reflected the desire to get Britain "in" shared by all but the most fanatic federalists. He was the most bitter critic of France for keeping her "out." The reason is clear. The Benelux countries fear that a restricted Europe, as planned by de Gaulle, would be dominated by France and Germany. Britain's entry, which they desired, would establish a powerful political and military counterweight to these two. Yet the Benelux countries did not fear that Britain's presence would operate to their disadvantage. On the contrary, Britain's historical record of support of Europe's smaller powers was regarded as a safeguard against French and German domination of the Community in the future.

This is an example of the benefits to Britain of her reputation for political maturity and diplomatic expertise. The French and Germans may not like it. But it's there.

The Dutch, in addition to their other preoccupations about the economic and political future of Europe, are more sensitive to memories of the German occupation of 1940-1944 than other European members of the Community. Such memories strengthen their suspicion of a restricted European alliance run by France and Germany and their desire to see Britain participating in the movement of European political evolution.

This emphasis on British membership, highly distressing

to those French and Germans and Italians who believe they
invented a united Europe, is equally strong among two members of the European Free Trade Area, Norway and Denmark.
The Norwegians, in fact, have made it clear that, although
they want to join E.E.C., they will not join until after the
British have done so. The Danes, affronted by de Gaulle's
stand on Britain, now agree. These attitudes emphasize the
fact that the admission of the British was the great divide
of the whole process. With the United Kingdom in, Europe
becomes quite different from the closed society of nations envisaged by General de Gaulle; this, of course, was one reason why he fought so hard to keep the British out or, alternatively, to admit them shorn of their global Commonwealth
connections and reduced to the status of a simple European
power.

In an earlier chapter we saw that the British, for various
reasons, doubt the stability of the Europe they are joining.
Many elements within E.E.C. members and some governments believe that the United Kingdom's entry will contribute
to stability. The reader, regarding the firmly established governments of the Six, may object that this is a lot of fuss over
nothing. There's France, firm as a rock. There's Germany,
the economic flywheel of Europe. There's Italy, changing
rapidly into a highly prosperous, modern state. All this is true.
But it is equally true that this old continent has in the past
been subject to violent and unexpected aberrations.

Contemporary Europe offers two developments potentially dangerous to continued stability. France and Germany,
the two most powerful and influential states in the European
Economic Community, are now in a position to pursue national policies to a degree unknown since 1945. Under Presi-

dent de Gaulle, the French have already traveled a long way along this road. There is a very strong possibility that the next German Chancellor but one may follow nationalist rather than internationalist patterns.

Nationalism is not always incompatible with democracy. But it can be argued that, historically speaking, democracy has suffered in both France and Germany when nationalism was in the saddle. The peoples of these two countries, and of Italy too, do not need reminders from London that parliamentary democracy has never been particularly successful in their countries. But their irritation with pompous British pronouncements on the point does not invalidate British concern. No one has yet answered the question: will democracy and unity survive a new upsurge of nationalism in Europe?

· 9 ·

Europe's Challenge to Russia . . . Big Europe the Danger . . . Communist Reactions to E.E.C. . . . COMECON and the Satellites . . . Economic and Political Stress in the Russian Empire

ONE OF THE nightmares that periodically haunts Western politicians and diplomats is the vision of Premier Khrushchev on a fine Monday morning looking around the table at his lieutenants and asking: "Well, where shall we raise hell for them this week?" The pessimist will suggest this is more fact than fancy, that the Western position provides the Soviet leadership with an infinite variety of opportunities for mischief: Laos today, Berlin tomorrow, Finland the day after, and Iran over the weekend.

Without discounting the Soviet Union's opportunities, two points should be made in the West's behalf. The first is that, although the Russians have raised hell on a global scale since 1945, the results to Moscow may appear somewhat meager in compensation for the time, money, and material spent to achieve them. In Europe, especially in Berlin and Germany, and in the Middle East and Asia the goals that must have seemed so near in the immediate post-war years have been denied the Russians.

The second, specific point is that the Atlantic Alliance in its slow, fumbling way has been able to frustrate Soviet aims, to bloc Soviet moves, and to produce in Europe plans and organizations such as the European Economic Community whose final development will be a direct defeat for the Russians. When it finally is established, with Britain and the Scandinavian democracies as members, the Commonwealth involved, and the United States more closely associated year by year, E.E.C. will terminate Soviet hopes in Western Europe, the area where its political strategists have always believed the cold war can be won or lost.

The big game has never been anything less than the establishment of Communist governments in Western Europe. To achieve this end, certain preliminary conditions had to be established. The first and probably the most important was the elimination of United States military power on the Continent.

This meant the withdrawal by the United States from the air and naval bases of Western Europe and the departure of the United States Army from Germany. The Soviets saw quite clearly that as long as the Americans were there any military incursion west of their present frontiers would involve them in war with the United States. Moreover, they believed that Western Europe was too weak to defend itself with either

conventional or nuclear weapons. Finally, it was highly doubtful whether the kind of political chaos which would promote
the advent of Communism in Western Europe could be created
as long as the Americans were there.

Because, like all imperialist powers, the Soviet Union is
moved by considerations other than long-term objectives such
as this, Russian policies often have followed contradictory
courses. Indeed, Soviet pressure on Western Europe not only
brought NATO into being but made it certain that the United
States would make a handsome investment in the defense of
the Continent. Moreover, the tendency of Premier Khrushchev and other Russian leaders to bluster and bully in international discourse prevented Western Europe from taking
seriously such proposals as the Rapacki Plan, which sought
demilitarization in Central Europe. This was the boldest and
most seductive proposition suggested by the Kremlin, in this
case through the Polish government, in the post-war era.

Initially, the plan made a good impression. Politicians in
and out of office, including many who could not be regarded
as either appeasers or neutralists, were encouraged. Yet the
Soviet record for double-dealing was so well known, the reality of Russian ambitions so evident, that the Western governments shied away. Moreover, John Foster Dulles, then Secretary of State, pointed out to the allies that any movement to
meet the Rapacki proposals would inevitably weaken the position of Dr. Adenauer's government in Germany and, consequently, the Federal Republic's role in the Atlantic Alliance.

Since the fall of Czechoslovakia, the Soviets have made
almost no progress toward their goals in Europe. And there
has sprung up in Europe a political and economic force that
will bar their way westward and more. Europe, as it de-

velops its political and economic potential to the utmost, not only will be impervious to Communism's military and diplomatic pressures but will, in the next decade, begin to exercise powerful political influence upon the periphery of the Communist empire.

To do this, the Community must develop as broadly as possible. This means a flexible, adventurous organization including not just Britain and the original Six, but, in the next phase, Norway and Denmark at one end of the continent and Greece at the other. In the next phase, close economic associations must be established with Sweden, Switzerland, and Austria, the Continent's three leading neutrals.

This kind of Europe, politically stable and with a booming economy, cannot help but have a powerful attraction for East Germany, Poland, and Czechoslovakia, nations that by historical development are European.

One argument against a smaller Europe, the Six as seen by President de Gaulle, has always been that it could not have generated the military strength to bar the Russians or exerted political influence on Eastern Europe.

The Russians would only take "Little Europe" seriously from the military standpoint if it were armed with its own nuclear weapons. These could be obtained in either of two ways. The United States would provide them; or the six nations, France, West Germany, Italy, Belgium, the Netherlands, and Luxembourg, would pool their resources and build them.

The first course runs counter to the American policy of restricting the possession of nuclear arms. The second would burden the Community with an enormous arms expenditure, even if the costs were distributed among the six members. When de Gaulle talks of building a French nuclear force, he is referring to a process that will cost well over $3,000,000,000. A nuclear armory for the Six would cost a great deal more.

Nothing would help the Communist parties in France and Italy, and perhaps elsewhere, more than an enormously costly nuclear program which would postpone those economic and social benefits that are impatiently expected by large sections of the European community.

From the military standpoint, it is clear that, if the program were carried out without the help of the United States, the weapons and delivery system would be obsolescent or obsolete by the time they were in service.

There are reasonable arguments against the program. There is a tendency to find comfort, however, in the fact that President de Gaulle is its principal advocate and the hope that, when the President goes, the project will be dropped. It would be reassuring to believe this. But I fear that the political and military policies which would be followed by a European Third Force would be nationalist and that de Gaulle's successors, unless of course they were Communists, would be almost as fervent in the pursuit of a nuclear force as he is.

The pursuit of this idea, then, adds very little to the balances of nuclear war which are held by the United States, with some assistance from the United Kingdom, and the Soviet Union. It does offer a prime source of political discord within the Community which the Soviets will be quick to exploit.

Indeed, the whole concept of a small, restricted Europe, the kind of thing President de Gaulle was talking about in 1961 and 1962, is shadowed with danger for the West. The creation of such a Europe, seeking to establish military and political independence from both America and Russia, could lead to a reduction of United States forces in Europe. The general subject of American reactions to the new Europe will be discussed in a later chapter. But here it should be noted that too much independence from the United States on the part of European leaders is as bad as too much dependence. Just as Americans should never take the fidelity of continental allies for granted, so Europeans, especially when they are brusquely rejecting Washington's advice and opposing its policies, should never take continued American military involvement for granted.

Soviet reaction to the creation of the E.E.C. in the field of political and economic policy was rather slow. One possibility foreseen by Western diplomats was an attempt to woo non-members of E.E.C., who might later join the Community, using the Russian home market as bait for increased trade relations. Another distinct possibility is that the Soviet Union might direct its efforts at the Community itself. The Community would be stoutly anti-Communist in ideology. But there is nothing in the Soviet record to indicate that this would be a barrier to some arrangement between the U.S.S.R. and the E.E.C. if the former believed that the exigencies of the world situation demanded it. To de Gaulle and others, United Europe represents a balance between the two great blocs of East and West. I suggest that Soviet leaders may not see it that way. They may see Europe as an alliance established outside the American orbit and, consequently, as a fortress to be undermined and stormed.

The Russians would be able to exert considerable pressure on that sort of European community. They might apply the same means used with non-members: advertising the value of Russian and East European markets to West European

exporters. They might also be influential through the two
large blocs of Communist voters in France and Italy. The
Russians would know, as everybody now knows but seldom
mentions, that at the outset a united Europe would contain
long-standing animosities and differences which could be exploited by clever Soviet diplomacy. This would be done more
easily if the political formula followed the confederal rather
than the federal pattern. But whichever shape was followed
by a "little Europe," the Russians would soon be at work.

The real danger to the Soviet Union lies not in "little
Europe" but in "big Europe." Its establishment would mean
greater political stability, partly as a consequence of Britain's
entry and the subsequent admission of Norway and Denmark,
and greater economic and diplomatic flexibility in dealing
with the Soviets. Big Europe, that is, the six original members
of E.E.C. plus Britain, Norway, Denmark, Greece, Sweden,
Switzerland, and Austria, will speak for 258,000,000 people
as compared with about 170,000,000 in the present six-nation
E.E.C. This is really Europe, with all the diversity of thought
and energy and culture that has enabled it to survive the
holocausts of the centuries and emerge from recurrent dark
ages stronger and more dynamic than before. If that Europe
comes into being, no one will have to refer to it as a Third
Force to impress the rest of the world. The world will understand without being told. And that Europe will have one inestimable advantage over the Gaullist conception: it will be
intimately linked with the United States.

No European would have to worry whether the Community was "in tow" to United States policies, as General de
Gaulle worries now about France. The association would be
one of equals. Although the United States would continue to

command the West's main nuclear forces, these would be un-alterably disposed to the defense of Europe because no American administration could do otherwise. The big Europe of the future will be as essential, politically and economically, to the United States as the United States will be to it militarily. And it will make an important contribution to conventional military forces.

The Soviet Union would thus face the linked strengths of Europe and the United States. It would have to contemplate the future growth of this giant community, with the Commonwealth countries cleaving to it as a matter of economic and ideological wisdom and loyalty. In two areas of high politics, China and Africa, the creation of this kind of Europe would confront the Russians with serious problems.

The Russians, consequently, must rethink their policies to meet the new situation that will emerge when Big Europe is organized economically and moving toward some form of political unity. They will have a choice of two policies, both expensive and potentially dangerous.

They can face the facts and admit the attraction of a booming, confident European community to their satellites on its periphery. They can even allow these satellites a slight increase in political independence and economic freedom. This is a course traditionally perilous to authoritarian regimes. And we should not let the changes in the Soviet Union lead us to the conclusion that the present regime is anything but authoritarian.

The alternative is to tighten the Soviet Union's economic and political grip on the satellite states. This seems the more likely course. It means a further reallocation of industry within the bloc. The Czechs, for example, will be allowed to make automobiles but the East Germans will not. This will involve a greater centralization of planning in Moscow, which Khrushchev found did not work in the Soviet Union itself, and new frictions between the Soviet government and its vassals.

Both courses will involve the Russians in difficulties. Any new course will have to be charted when the rule of the Kremlin over world Communism is being challenged by other Communist states. And, although it must be emphasized again that the Soviet Union remains an authoritarian state, the changes taking place within the country inevitably will alter some of its characteristics.

Since the late nineteen-fifties the Russian people have been able to enjoy a slightly improved standard of living. The improvement is small compared with that which has taken place in Western Europe since the war. But it is there, nevertheless, and it represents to the Russians, who have no means of comparison with standards of living abroad, a marked difference in their fortunes. During this period, the bureaucracy and the senior officers of the armed services have become entrenched in power and grown in numbers and importance. They, along with the intellectuals, amount to what in a Western society would be called a middle class.

Theoretically, of course, no classes exist. But I was struck on my last visit to Russia, after an absence of more than a decade, by the increasing stratification of Soviet society. A group has developed which is interested not just in enough food, enough clothes, and adequate housing, as all Russians were from 1917 until about 1956, but in better food, clothes, and housing, and the maintenance of the status quo. They are materialists, not revolutionaries.

Those who see in this change a benefit to the West theorize that this new class, this Communist bourgeoisie, will be loathe to risk their new and, God knows, hard-won comforts in pursuit of purely Communist objectives. This class, it is contended, wants peace, more trade with the West, and a continued improvement in standards of living. The old war cries of international Communism fail to affect it, and Lenin for them is as dead as Nero.

Comforting though this theory may be, a second interpretation of the changes in the Soviet Union must be considered. This begins with the historical fact that societies dominated by the bourgeoisie or a middle class are not necessarily peaceful. Germany and France in 1914 were the most bourgeois of societies; yet the French and Germans took to each other's throats without much prompting from political leaders.

Such societies also tend to be more nationalistic than others. I have always believed that love for Mother Russia was a far more potent factor in spurring the people to endeavor and sacrifice than the desire to spread Communism. The farm boys who went out to defend the motherland in 1941, often with one rifle to every four men, were only distantly acquainted with the ideology of their rulers. Twenty years later it seemed to me that the new class, although not wildly enthusiastic about Communism, was, if anything, more devoted to the Russian state than were the Russians of the immediate post-war years. This devotion to the state, the country, the very soil of Russia, coupled with the deep strain of fatalism in the Russian soul, is a powerful factor in Soviet thinking. The Russians might not be willing to dare and die for Communism. But it would be dangerous to proceed on the assumption that they would not risk what they have won and, if necessary, die for their motherland.

Nevertheless, these changes in the lives of millions of Russians must force some modifications in the character of the regime. The government of Premier Khrushchev is not as tyrannical as that of Stalin. From a number of meetings with the Premier, beginning in 1946 when he was liquidating the Communist apparatus in the Ukraine at Stalin's orders, I have concluded that although he would be as ruthless as his late master if the situation required it, he believes that flagrant imposition of the state's police power, still enormous, is not the way to run modern Russia.

He also recognizes, as Stalin was not required to, the existence in the Soviet Union of power groups which have developed in the years since the war. One of these is the new middle class, with its entrenched privileges, its power to ease or impede the workings of the state through its control of the bureaucracy. From the behavior of Soviet diplomats abroad, one gathers that this class is as powerful as the entrenched fighting services with which it is in general alliance.

The shooting down of the U-2 espionage plane in 1960 was far from a victory for Khrushchev. It was, in fact, a serious reverse, because it subjected his rule to the criticism, perhaps only whispered, of the armed services, whose leaders believed that one of the Soviet Union's most important weapons, secrecy, had been seriously compromised by this and other flights.

I do not believe that Marshal Malinovsky or any other military figure bosses Khrushchev. The Party remains supreme. I do believe that the Soviet leader must take the

wishes of the military, the middle class, and those party theo-
reticians who long for the old days when the Party line was as
clear and as hard as crystal into account when he formulates
policy. Khrushchev's ability to dictate the direction of the Soviet state at the moment is, I believe, less than that of Hitler
at the climax of his power.

Possibly the most interesting question that arises from
this situation concerns the policy to be followed by Khrushchev's successor toward these groupings of power within
modern Russia. There is certainly a probability that a new
Soviet leader would seek to reverse the trend toward a somewhat more liberal society and re-establish total dictatorship
by one man. Since the trend is not deeply established—essentially it is less than a decade old—the next Chairman of the
Council of Ministers might succeed in this. He will be faced,
doubtlessly, with mounting problems in the Far East and in
Europe.

The attitude of the U.S.S.R. to the establishment of the
European Economic Community, and all that it will mean to
the politics of Europe, inevitably will be affected by the growth
of Chinese power. The People's Republic of China already
constitutes a rival to the Soviet Union's ideological leadership
of the Communist world. This fact has been amply demonstrated since 1960, and many millions of words have been
devoted to the dissection of the ideological divisions between
the pope in Moscow and the pope in Peiping.

What is infinitely more important for the future is
whether these existing divisions are sharpened and widened
by the growth of Chinese economic and military power and
the consequent expansion of Chinese influence upon the
Communist parties of Asia and Africa. This growth will be

200 THE *Supreme Choice*

slow, although it would be foolish to fall into complacency about the strength of China as Europe and America did with regard to Russia thirty years ago. To judge the Chinese of five years hence on the obvious inadequacies and inefficiencies of today could be disastrous. The West and the Soviet Union must remember that in countries where there is an enormous expansion of population, such as that taking place in China, governments often cannot wait for the most favorable moment to use their new power. We may find Chinese imperialism on the march in Southeast Asia or in western China long before either the Western governments or the Soviet government believe it is prepared to take the offensive.

Any survey of the position of the U.S.S.R. at present must conclude, I believe, that the Russians are in trouble. They are challenged on the east by the painstaking rise to power of an ally infinitely more populous than the Soviet Union and equally imperialist in its ambitions. It is not enough to say, although this is accurate, that the Russians and the Chinese now act in rough accord on great issues presented them by the West. The problem, and it is as much ours as it is Russia's, is how the Chinese will act in the future.

"China is like Russia in 1935," a Pole remarked. So it may be. But six years after 1935, the Russians broke the finest army ever sent out of Germany in the climactic battles for Moscow.

To the west lies another challenge. A European union including Britain and some of the E.F.T.A. powers not only will bar the Soviets from further political or military ventures in Western Europe; it will create an industrial complex far more powerful than anything the new Russian empire can boast. Given these resources and wise statesmanship, the European Community of tomorrow can do more than the U.S.S.R. in areas like Africa and Asia where the Russian opportunity lies. Finally, it is going to be increasingly difficult to deny to the Soviet Union's European vassals the commercial opportunities of trade with the new Europe.

Khrushchev himself revealed Soviet concern about the creation of European unity. He spoke on May 30, 1962, when the European Economic Community still consisted of the original six powers and did not yet have the resources of Britain at its command. The speech, even for a man not given to moderation in his public utterances, revealed him as badly rattled. This was one of the times when his usual exaggerations were so out of line with the facts, as Europe knew them, that his words had very little impact outside the faithful of the Communist parties.

The E.E.C. was characterized as "a state-monopoly agreement of the finance oligarchy of Western Europe which threatens the vital interests of all peoples, the cause of universal peace, inasmuch as the aggressive quarters of imperialism use it with the object of strengthening NATO and stepping up the arms race." The Soviet leader was especially sensitive to the influence of a united Europe in the underdeveloped and undeveloped countries. He saw as one of the Common Market's principal aims the harnessing "of a number of liberated countries to the economy of imperialist states to keep them in bondage." "This aim is naturally camouflaged by high-sounding phrases about 'aid' to the peoples of backward countries, about the advantages of duty-free sales of their produce." Khrushchev added: "The imperialists want to use the Common Market to flood African countries with their industrial goods with which the just-emerging industry of these countries cannot compete as yet. Subordination of the young sovereign states of Africa to the Common Market would signify their consent to reconcile themselves to the role of agrarian and raw-material appendages of the former metropolitan countries."

Khrushchev's heated attack on the "collective colonialism" Africa might expect from a united Europe was the most definite disclosure of the Soviet attitude in the months when Britain was entering the difficult phase of her negotiations with the Community. Its historic importance lay in the reflection of the Soviet belief that the game would be lost in Africa if the Common Market developed as intended and in the confession that, beyond calling for an ill-defined world conference on trade arrangements, there was nothing Russia could do about it.

In Europe and Africa the Russians are entering into an industrial and commercial competition they are ill-prepared to wage, and, it is quite apparent, they know it. This accounted for Khrushchev's revival, in the speech quoted above, of his two-year-old proposal for a world-trade organization "without discrimination" and his announcement that the Soviet Union was prepared to conclude long-term trade agreements with the African countries, thus creating a stable market for their products.

Soviet concern about the growth of E.E.C. is probably generated more by political implications than by economic pressures. Russia's foreign trade amounts to only three per cent of the gross national product, and two thirds of this trade is carried on within the Communist bloc. The one per cent tied up in commerce with the West is manipulated to close gaps in domestic supplies and for the propaganda advantages which come from the exploitation of trade opportunities. But since agriculture in the bloc, particularly within the Soviet Union, is in a sorry state, imports of farm products are expected to increase in the immediate future. So when Khrushchev offers to purchase surplus farm products in underdeveloped countries, he is really seeking to appease the demands of his own people.

Poland, Czechoslovakia, and East Germany are three Communist states that have real grounds for uneasiness about the effect of the E.E.C. upon their economies. As much as five per cent of the total trade in each of these three countries is with capitalist countries. They fear that the increase in the Community's tariffs will hurt exports of farm products such as Polish bacon.

The Soviet government has available the mechanism that could enable it to appear to meet the challenge of the Common Market. This is the Council for Mutual Economic Assistance, which is the Communists' counterpart of E.E.C. With the development of E.E.C., the pressure on the Soviet government to improve COMECON, as the Council is called, has increased. It is far from the closely integrated and beneficial apparatus envisaged when it was founded in January 1949 by the Soviet Union, Poland, East Germany, Czechoslovakia, Hungary, Rumania, Bulgaria, and Albania. The Albanians, incidentally, did not attend the fifteenth session of COMECON in December 1961 because of their ideological dispute with Big Brother in the Kremlin.

The purpose of the Council is "to strengthen the economic collaboration of the socialist countries and to coordinate their economic development on the basis of all member states." Fine words, but their implementation has been curiously uneven. In December 1955 it was decided to begin five-year plans for economic development throughout the bloc in the following year. The only exception was backward Bulgaria.

The decision was modified in the eyes of some satellite regimes, although naturally they did not protest too loudly, by the refusal of the Soviet Union to share in the division of economic tasks and by its retention of full freedom of action in all economic matters.

The development of COMECON was also delayed by the shock waves that ran through the Communist bloc in the autumn of 1956 and in early 1957 as a consequence of the Hungarian revolution. However, by 1957 the Council was able to establish standing commissions, sub-committees, and working groups to increase co-ordination, specialization, and standardization in industry and agriculture. The heads of the Communist parties in the bloc met in 1958 and considered long-term planning and specialization.

By the time the Council held its tenth session in Prague in December 1958, it had developed to the point where agreement could be reached on a division of investment and labor with regard to the production of mineral fertilizers, synthetic rubber, artificial fibers, and plastic fabrics. Probably the most important decision made then, from the standpoint of the West, was to build the "Friendship Pipeline" for Russian oil from the U.S.S.R. to Poland, East Germany, Czechoslovakia, and Hungary.

This pipeline, now nearing completion, is a considerable weapon in any Soviet economic offensive mounted to meet the pressures generated by E.E.C. or to seduce Western European governments away from European unity. For example, when in mid-1962, the East Germans presented their bid for a $280,000,000 credit in goods from the Federal Republic, part of their bait was repayment in Russian oil flowing into East Germany through the pipeline.

COMECON has also decided to construct an electricity grid system that will link Eastern Europe with the Ukraine by early 1963.

Khrushchev can thus claim that on their side, the Communists have made good progress toward economic integration. There is some substance to this, but not much.

The Council is an advisory body rather than an operational organization like E.E.C. Moreover, it is working in an area where, despite a decade and a half of "Communist unity," national rivalries and antagonisms are still very strong. The Poles dislike the Hungarians, the Hungarians hate the Czechs, and all three look down on the Rumanians and Bulgarians as backward, boorish neighbors. Finally, all the others distrust and even hate the East Germans, partly because of war memories, partly because they feel the Russians have been overgenerous to the East Germans with economic aid in order to narrow the gap between West German opulence and East German poverty.

The Soviet Union has gradually consolidated its position as the main supplier of raw materials to the satellite economies. Meanwhile, the more advanced Communist states, East Germany, Poland, and Czechoslovakia, are now exporting increasing amounts of industrial machinery and equipment to other satellite states. Trade among members of COMECON rose by about 200 per cent between 1950 and 1960. But it started from almost zero, and the rise is less than that registered by the present six members of E.E.C. in the same period.

Specialization in industrial and agricultural production has not proceeded as rapidly as the Russians had hoped.
Again, national rivalries have played a part. Even Communist governments, despite the brotherhood of Marx, are reluctant to tie national well-being to key industries outside
their control. For example, there has been a steady rise in the
production of rolled steel. But trade in this product has not
increased among the members except by a marginal amount.
Some specialization is apparent in secondary industries such
as motor vehicles, chemicals, and machine tools.

Intelligence reports on the state of Eastern Europe indicate that political differences among the Communist governments have also played a part in delaying economic unity. The
Soviet Union, in terms of military and economic strength,
towers over its vassals. But Khrushchev has not convinced
some of his Communist collaborators of the wisdom of his
leadership in international affairs. There is, for example, a
strong Stalinist tint to many of Walter Ulbricht's pronouncements on the future of Germany. Stalinist overtones are also
apparent in Prague and Budapest, where the talks between
the United States and the Soviet Union with regard to Germany fanned the fear, always latent, that some deal might be
made to restore a united Germany to Central Europe. This
would be no more attractive to the Czechs, the Hungarians,
or the Poles than it would be to the British, the Dutch, or the
Italians. There does not appear to be much chance that Germany's reunification is near. But the fact that even talk about
it creates apprehension and doubt about Soviet policy in Eastern Europe reflects the differences that exist with regard to
Khrushchev's attitude toward the West.

The satellites, too, are better informed about conditions

within the Soviet Union than are the Western allies. Russian deficiencies in production, inefficiency in personnel, and internal frictions, only guessed about in the Western nations, are the common currency of gossip within the Communist capitals. And national antagonisms do not begin and end within the satellite system itself. The Russians, particularly the aggressively confident Party and industrial bosses from Moscow, are unpopular throughout Eastern Europe, almost as unpopular as the Red Army was a decade ago.

Despite the space shots and the sputniks, the rocket rattling and the boasting at a thousand Party celebrations, this Soviet Union of Khrushchev's is still prey to grave internal difficulties. How can a country whose agricultural program is a blatant failure hope to compete with the bursting economies of Western Europe?

I do not believe I am painting the present position of the Soviet Union in unduly somber hues. If the union of Western Europe takes shape, the Russian economic, military, and political position will suffer drastically. European strength will be one reason. A second and perhaps equally important reason is that the new Europe will be linked to the United States, and these two powers together will mobilize enough strength not simply to make the West secure but to exert pressures that will curb the extension of Russian power and eventually reduce it.

For various reasons, American involvement in Europe, either in the disunited Europe of the present or in some form of future European union, is resented by some Europeans. This resentment provides part of the emotional basis for the Third Force idea. In the past it had a good deal to do with the brief flowering of European neutralism of a decade ago. Although it may spring from deeply felt convictions about the role of Europe in the world, it is no more in tune with the times than would be a return in the United States to the isolationism of the twenties and early thirties. The irritating difficulty is that so few Europeans understand why America is there and what she represents or have any clear conception of the United States today.

The Soviets know that a greater European community alone will alter the power balances in Europe. They realize that Europe linked with the United States will be an alliance of infinite power. Western safety from Communist military pressure and Western victory in the global contest with the Communist philosophy will follow the establishment of a greater European community and the forging of the closest links between it and the United States. Here is the opportunity for triumph.

· 10 ·

The E.E.C.'s Role in the Struggle for Africa
... Communist Failures in the First Phase ...
African Political Development and Western
Illusions ... Aid and Markets for Africa ...
The Multi-racial Society and Africa's Future

THE DEVELOPMENT of the European Economic Community into a viable political and economic unit is one of the prerequisites for Western success in the struggle for Africa. This struggle, fought over a vast, untutored continent, hungry for material development, will engage the interests and anxieties of the world as much in the sixties as did the struggle for Europe in the late forties and early fifties. Here is an area where Soviet success could vitiate all the gains of the free world in Europe. This is a cold-war battle into which the Russians and the Communist Chinese already have flung impressive amounts of men, matériel, and money.

Africa demands and deserves economic development through Western aid. But the areas to be developed are so vast, the political, economic, and sociological problems so numerous and so varied, that the task cannot be carried out by a single nation. The importance of E.E.C. in this connection is that it concentrates financial resources, industrial and agricultural techniques, and political experience to an unprecedented extent. Here are the tools for building a new Africa. And here is the opportunity for the former colonial powers to prove to Africans that it is the free West, and not the enslaved East, which can lead them to a better life.

Nikita Khrushchev has made it clear that the Russians are aware of this opportunity. As we saw in the previous chapter, he has attacked E.E.C. as a means of reimposing European imperialism and colonialism on the emerging countries of the continent. This could be a potent argument among African leaders, who are invariably sensitive to any suggestion of a return of European control. But it need not be, if the Community is able to deploy its economic resources with a minimum of political emphasis. The emphasis must always be on E.E.C.'s interest in building viable economies in Africa.

Political propaganda and diplomatic pressure are liable to backfire, as the Russians have learned. The Soviet Union, in fact, approached the awakening giant of Africa with curious ineptness. Think back to 1957, when the echoes of the Suez adventure were still rumbling on the horizon. Africa from Algeria to the Cape presented the U.S.S.R. with a great political opportunity. Here were countries freeing themselves of colonialism, often by force of arms. Here were peoples groping for new faiths, new leaders. This was an arena in which the Russian failure to progress in Europe after 1948 might be dwarfed by new Soviet successes. Such was the popular impression, and, in view of contemporary conditions in Africa, there was good reason for it. It was influenced, however, by one illusion: that the Russians and their European allies were a great deal more informed and intelligent than they actually were.

After the Communist spoor in Central and East Africa, it was clear that the Russians, and their allies, had approached the problem with a basic misconception. They believed that the chaotic situation in the Congo and the potential for chaos in other areas, notably the Federation of the Rhodesias and Nyasaland, represented the sort of revolutionary situation they were accustomed and equipped to deal with in Europe or the Middle East.

To be sure, this part of Africa is in ferment. New masters are replacing the old. The black Africans, or at least their leaders, are conscious of freedom without, I fear, much realization of what the word means in terms of responsibility. In these respects, Africa, or that section of it, is awakening. But the giant is only stirring in its sleep.

The Kremlin strategists seem to have exaggerated the ability of the Africans to understand Communism. The first prerequisite for a strong Communist party—an ambitious, and discontented, industrial proletariat—was absent. The African farmer is avid for more land, largely because his present agricultural methods are appallingly inefficient. But he is hostile to any suggestion of collectivization which would modify his or his tribe's control of the land. In black Africa an industrial proletariat exists only in a few widely scattered areas, the copper mines of the Rhodesias and the Congo, the gold and diamond mines of South Africa, and a few other relatively small mining and manufacturing concentrations. Some of the African intellectuals, who provide such political leadership as the new countries can boast, are susceptible to Communism. Politicians seemed generally unmoved by the political aspects of Communism, although they were naturally interested by Russian offers of economic help.

The Russians in these circumstances seemed to take the easy way out. They bought African leaders, chosen as much for their ability to make trouble for the retiring colonial powers and for the new generation of African leaders as for intelligence and ability. These men flaunted their fidelity to Moscow and their venality. As a result, they were easily identifiable to both of the groups they sought to undermine.

A singular omission was the failure by the Communists to exploit the authoritarianism and conformism that are such powerful traits of African character. I am not referring to the intellectuals and political leaders, who are rebellious and disputatious, but to the Africans who have just left or are still living in a tribal society. There authority and conformity are requirements for survival; the chief and, sometimes, the elders decide, and the tribe follows. Joe Stalin would have felt at home among the Bemba.

These characteristics influence even the most worldly African leaders. Men like Tom Mboya, the most intelligent and ablest of the Kenya leaders, believes in a one-party state for his country after independence, the party, naturally, being his own Kenya African National Union. The popular argument is that the new Kenya, facing manifold social and economic problems, will not be able to afford the luxury of an opposition. But a more fundamental argument is that the African himself will not understand a regime which is not in accord with his views of government as an authoritarian institution with which all must conform.

Parenthetically, it should be noted that, though the Russians have made plenty of mistakes, the United States, with more information and experience, has made a few also.

Both the present and the preceding American administrations were quite right to recognize the vital importance of the explosive African scene in the world contest with the Soviet Union. Even if they had not, the Congo would have taught the lesson. Where the United States seems to have gone wrong is in its assessment of the capabilities of the African. There is a tendency among some of the enthusiastic young men in Washington to talk of affairs among Africans in new or emergent African states in the terms customarily applied to Europe. Europe, perhaps—but the Europe of the early middle ages, not the Europe of today. The boundaries of African states, fixed largely by the great European colonial powers late in the last century and early in this, are no more permanent than those of the provinces that the Roman Empire bequeathed to Europe. Considerations of public opinion, the use of an informed and objective press, and the brakes and accelerators of parliamentary democracy are no more applicable to the Africa now emerging than they would have been to the Europe of Charlemagne.

They may in time be accepted. Devoted, selfless men, French, British, Belgian, and American, have tried to show the way. But they could not reach more than a very few Africans, and, inevitably, many of these will go under in the struggles for power. The West must be prepared for the conduct of international affairs with governments whose citizens for the most part are just emerging from the dark ages. To accept the affable, highly educated men who speak with the accents of Cambridge, Massachusetts, or Cambridge, England, who appear at the United Nations or in embassies overseas as representative of their people, or even to care very much about those people, could be a disastrous error.

It would be particularly unfortunate if the United States, in its dealings with the new African governments, equated African with American Negroes. Let me give you an example.

At the Roan Antelope Mine of the Rhodesian Selection Trust Ltd., I watched a group of new workers being trained for work in the mines. They were men from the Bemba tribe who live to the northeast. They had to be introduced to the use of the shovel, the pick, and the hoe; they had to be taught how to climb ladders and how to lift heavy objects. They were willing, eager, handsome men. But they were novices to the rudiments of physical labor.

It can be argued that the British government should have provided the tribesmen with some form of education in these rudimentary skills. So, perhaps, it should, had it been possible to induce the tribesmen to accept any form of education until after they came into contact with white civilization. The fact is, they did not have the scantiest knowledge of modern civilization. The Africans in the Federation and in Kenya have been exposed to Western civilization for, at the very most, ninety years. To think of them in the same terms as American Negroes, whose racial experience with Western civilization dates back to the seventeenth century, is folly.

I am not contending that the African Negro lacks the mental capacity to absorb education and civilization. I am suggesting that he is starting very far back in the race. Political independence and sovereignty, thus, are coming to a very high percentage of the African people before they have more than the vaguest notions—many of these, remember, overcast by deeply held ideas on witchcraft—about the essentials of a modern society. It is not simply that these Africans lack the education to make democracy or perhaps less involved and complicated forms of government work. They lack the education to make a simple agrarian civilization work. That they can do it in the future, that they will evolve their own methods for dealing with their problems, with the economic aid of E.E.C., I have no doubt. But meanwhile there is going to be trouble, and plenty of it.

The educated African in the Federation and East Africa too often is the product of the classical or semi-classical curricula of English or American universities, which fit him, if he has the ability, for a job in the civil service but leave him highly unsuited for the tough task of mastering the great, empty, potentially rich land he will own. What the Africans need is more concentration on agricultural, mining, and mechanical know-how and less of an Oxford or Harvard emphasis. The land-grant college of the United States is one answer.

Once the African realizes that knowledge about such simple things as crop rotation or the maintenance of a tractor means more money, more physical well-being, there is no holding him. At the Roan Antelope Mine I watched a miner returning home off-shift. He was tall, with a commanding head, a member of one of the southern tribes, once the most formidable warriors in that part of the world. After he had greeted his family and changed, he was off with his wife to one of the white schoolhouses set above his compound. There, with twenty or

thirty others, they studied, he to master the intricacies of new
mining techniques—he had already been taught to read and
write and to do a little simple arithmetic—and she to make her
first stumbling, laughing efforts toward mastering the alphabet.

That mine, indeed the whole copper belt, constitutes a
small island of an industrial proletariat between the South
African Republic and the Sahara. Enlightened capitalism, in
the form of the great copper companies, has educated the African and then gradually raised his wages and his job status.
These African miners are living in conditions so infinitely
superior to those of their relatives in the bush that comparisons are worthless. The African miner has entered the twentieth century; his brother in the tribe still lives in the tenth.

The creation of an African industrial proletariat in the
copper belt has its dangers, which will arise elsewhere if the
process is repeated. Intelligent management has formed a relatively small group of men who earn salaries that by African
standards are enormous. Since they are a fertile and polyga-
mous race, these Africans have produced perhaps five times
their number of sons and daughters, the majority of them educated in the schools run by the big mining companies of "The
Belt." Many of them, especially the young men, present a serious problem. Accustomed to a relatively high standard of living, and well-educated, they seek work in the mines. The
number of jobs is limited and would be limited even if all but
a handful of whites were to leave. Aimless and frustrated,
these young people drift into the shady alleys of politics; ready
for anything, a torch thrown through the door of an independent miner, the beating-up of an outspoken veteran who wants
nothing to do with politics as long as his job is safe.

So the elevation of the African in the copper belt has

fathered its own particular problem in the unemployed and educated offspring of the miners.

I make no apology for including in a book primarily concerned with the Western world a discussion of these far-off communities. The main street that runs through Lusaka ends in Louisville and Leningrad; to a very real degree, the salvation of the new African nations may lie in the ability of the new union of Europe to assess and meet its needs.

Aid to the undeveloped countries is a broad, generous slogan that has almost no meaning unless it is defined. The warm hearts of the American and British public respond to appeals for medical aid, for advice on sanitation—something inadequately conceived in popular thinking as a loan, and the general idea that the Anglo-Saxons are beneficent patrons of these new powers. All very nice, but scarcely relevant.

The primary needs of the new African nations are, first, financial and technical help to expand and strengthen their economies and, second, markets for their products, which at the outset will be foodstuffs and industrial raw materials. A recognition of these needs by the Community and by the United States seems as important as the invasions by enthusiastic Peace Corpsmen or dedicated young instructors in agriculture. After economic aid, markets. The most important market will be the European Economic Community when it finally is organized as Big Europe, including Britain and the Scandinavian countries.

Europe will be able to carry on a flourishing trade in finished products within its own frontiers. It can be argued that if Big Europe is established, standardization, wiser direction of investment, and a more efficient use of the means of production will create an intra-European trade as dynamic as that within continental United States. But this should not be allowed to inhibit European purchases of the products of the new Africa.

When you talk this over with enthusiastic proponents of the Common Market, you encounter a certain sensitivity about European products. Some exports from African countries will be cheaper than similar products produced in Europe; and, should the African products enjoy preferential treatment, the European products and the workers who make them will suffer. And, as one German said in Nairobi, "this is not what we have joined E.E.C. to achieve."

At this point enlightened political leadership in Europe should intervene. It is in the interests of all European powers that there should be strong economic ties between the new countries of Africa and the European Community. The relationship must be established methodically. The opening of European markets to the raw products and cheap manufactures of the newly developed countries must be a gradual and regulated process. In this, as in so much else, an arrangement that covers the world, that is, the Western world, and its new partners in Africa is preferable to agreements between a group of European nations and Africa or a group of North American nations and Latin America.

If Europe were to cast the African nations adrift now for narrow economic reasons, it would provide the Russians with an opportunity even more favorable than the one they failed to grasp five years ago.

The relations between the new Europe and Africa need not be one-sided. The West will not be forever exporting aid, in the form of money, goods, and technical assistance, and at the same time buying African products to keep struggling economies there on their feet. The purchasing potential of Africa is enormous.

In Nairobi I lunched with an affable Indian whose grandfather had come across the Black Water to help build the country's first railroad. His son, my friend's father, had opened a tiny shop that sold to Africans the simple products which the first contact with the white man caused them to need. Since then the family had prospered. Not, I was told, because of any particular business acumen. Rather, because year by year and decade by decade the African appetite for Western products had increased. I am told by socialist friends that this process is "sheer mercantilism," a degrading survival of economic colonialism.

That is as may be. But if a common need for soap or ships or sealing wax can bridge the gap between the African and the European, it should be welcomed.

In this excursion into Africa I have said little about the future relationship between the African and the European, or, as he might be called more accurately, the white African. I am constrained to lead the reader further into African affairs at this point because on no other issue has more nonsense been uttered.

From the standpoint of Central and East Africa, the best hope for peace and prosperity lies in a multi-racial society. By this I mean that the three races, African, European, and Asian, will co-operate in the economic and political development of Africa. I do not expect the whites to retain their present political domination in Central Africa; it has already passed away in East Africa. I do believe, however, that both white and black will have sense enough to realize that the passing of white political power should not mean the ousting of the whites from all positions of influence and authority in the economies of the countries concerned.

Why not? Quite simply because the African is not yet equipped to run all the vital primary industries. In time he will be. But the timing, henceforth, will depend on him. If it were clear that President Kwame Nkrumah of Ghana was spending more money on technical education than on some of his sillier projects for national aggrandizement, it would be reassuring. At any rate, it is evident that the present standard of living in Central and East Africa *for the African* as well as for the white man cannot be maintained without whites in large sections of the economy. Without that co-operation it is difficult to see Africa's great riches developed for the improvement and happiness of her people.

In this area, as in some others, the inquiring traveler in Central and East Africa will encounter the idea, among Africans, that any white help in running mines or factories or ports is preferable to that of former colonialists. In this aspect of the African conflict the identity of Russians as Russians helps them. They are not identified with colonialism—a situation that might raise some laughter in Tashkent or Riga. This Russian advantage is balanced by the fact that they are white and consequently equated by the uneducated African with the bad British, French, or Belgians.

Partly because they were not white, the first Communist evangelists sent by China to Africa seem to have been more successful personally than the Russians.

Africa has not given its heart to either West or East. At the moment, despite the rabid outcries about colonialism and the political posturing, some of it well meant and much of it based on emotion, in the United Nations, the lead still lies with the West. But this kind of situation does not remain static. It would be too much to say that the Russians have been repulsed by the West in their first attempt to lead the new African nations into the Communist camp. They failed because they did not understand a situation which differed so greatly from those they had been taught could be exploited by Marxism.

Here is a rather human sidelight on the Soviet campaign in Africa. The Russian points of attack in Ghana, the Congo, and Somaliland are a very long way from the Soviet Union. Although the Communist Party of the U.S.S.R. breeds willing zealots who will serve under any conditions to further the cause, it must also make use of other Russians, relatively untouched by this religious fervor, to pursue its aims. When they arrived in Africa, almost totally unprepared for the climate and equally uninstructed on the diet or clothing necessary to meet it, they gave a sorry performance.

The British would have built clubs and the Americans soda fountains; the Russians, however, sat around, often in long, heavy underwear, drinking, after the vodka ran out, the formidable spirits of the country and singing lugubrious songs about the homeland. The exhortations of the Party's cheerleaders failed to move them. They performed their duties mechanically, treating the Africans with a rudeness and a lack of comprehension that would have earned any young British District Officer instant dismissal. The Somalis, for instance, were at first impressed by the size of the Soviet embassy, but later they concluded sadly that their guests lived like pigs.

My belief is that in the first ten years of freedom neither Communism nor parliamentary democracy will prevail in Africa. The magnitude of the task of economic and social development in the new countries and the inability of the peoples to operate the democratic system will promote the emergence of authoritarian governments. I do not foresee the growth of a group of African Hitlers. But it is possible that the new nations may be ruled for some years by what a former age would have called benevolent despots, leaders anxious to promote economic and social reforms and to build for the future without political interference.

Such authoritarian regimes will always be open to Communist take-overs because no democratic opposition will exist. Hence, there will be no open criticism of the efforts the Communists will make to subvert the governments by political infiltration, by corruption, and by assassination. We can take it for granted that the Russians, chastened by their first failures, will renew their efforts in Africa, and that the West, principally the United States and the European Economic Community, must meet these efforts with an understanding of the political problems which face the leaders and with a continued flow of capital, equipment, and technical assistance.

We cannot expect these to "buy" the Africans. We must not expect the Africans to imitate Western democracy. The best we can hope for is that, as a result of the West's tactful use of its economic resources and political advice, the Africans will understand that Europe and America, and the democratic system, offer the best hopes for the future. The struggle will be a long one. But it is one the democracies can and must win.

· 11 ·

Britain's Great Debate ... The Change in Political Patterns and the Divisions within the Classes ... Party Strengths and Attitudes toward E.E.C.

THE BRITISH, as a people, are slow in reaching decisions. After fifteen months of negotiation in Brussels, there was still a clear division in the country for and against membership in E.E.C. But the British had been committed by the government to seek entry. There is little doubt in my mind that they would have done so, had de Gaulle not broken off the negotiations just when the British and five other governments believed success was near. It may be years before the British are as ready to enter Europe. The Tories will never forgive de Gaulle.

The decision to enter Europe was a sharp departure from Conservative policy. A government elected in 1959 on a platform that put little stress on union with Europe, less than two years later took the vital decision to enter. The popular response was "well, let's see"; the government proposes, but we, the British people, will dispose. Prime Minister Macmillan may have believed he had committed Britain to entry under reasonable conditions. The electorate believed that it was the final arbiter.

At the start of negotiations the British government and people did not understand de Gaulle's hostility to their entry. The General's oracular doubts about British suitability for membership were regarded as the expression of a natural French desire to put the price for entry as high as possible. No one foresaw that these doubts would be transformed into a flat veto in January 1963. This was true as late as the December 1962 meeting between de Gaulle and Macmillan. It is the basis for the British charge that they were deceived by the French into believing that if the negotiations were successful, they would gain admission.

Throughout the negotiations, then, the British proceeded in good faith. The background comments of de Gaulle, Spaak, Adenauer, and others were an accompaniment to a great national debate which began in 1961 and continued through 1962. It has since been supplanted by an even more important one based on a single issue: if Britain cannot enter Europe now, what is she to do? The answer may lie in what was said for and against entering Europe in the preceding two years. In this national discussion we see the old imperial, rural, traditional England in conflict with the new, "European," industrial nation that has developed since the end of World War II.

Politics is an art. Public opinion, which is the driving force of politics, as most intelligent people know, is coarser, rougher, and more interesting than the recording of preferences in a public opinion poll. The student of politics in the United Kingdom could watch the development of a great public debate on a major issue on which the questions of the pollsters and the answers they received had little or no effect.

The amount of information available to the masses was small at the outset. In Britain, and in every country, public opinion is divided into two groups. One might be called informed public opinion—these are the people who read newspapers, talk to M.P.'s, listen to lectures, and have a background of general education on which political judgments can be based. This kind of public opinion exerts a particularly strong influence in Britain. This is partly due to geography. Such opinion tends to center on London, and the United Kingdom is so small that the effect of what is said or written in London today will be a guide to debates in clubs and pubs in Liverpool and Leamington tomorrow.

When I first visited Britain before the war, it seemed to me that public opinion in provincial centers like Manchester or Edinburgh or Cardiff was a much more important factor in British politics than I had been led to expect. A quarter of a century later, I would say that the constant drift to the richer economic and social rewards of London have concentrated informed public opinion in the capital to an unusual degree.

In addition to informed public opinion which operates in London—sometimes, it seems, within a relatively small group of perhaps ten thousand politicians, civil servants, newspaper and television and radio officials, and university professors—there is the great mass public opinion, often incoherent, invariably lethargic, but fundamentally powerful and, ultimately, conscious of its power.

This mass public opinion ultimately will decide whether Britain is to continue to move closer to Europe or whether she is to find economic and political development outside the Continent. "Well, mate," Ernest Bevin used to say, "y' live in a democracy, dontcher; well, that's what it means."

The role played by the responsible newspapers in London, which set the tone for the country, has been and will be an important one. From 1961 onwards, these newspapers provided more and better information than any other media. The popular press, although somewhat slower to grasp the importance of the issue, also contributed.

In this continuing national debate it is clear to an extraordinary degree that the press, under modern conditions, is vital to any thorough discussion of a great, popular issue. Some newspapers advocated moving into Europe, and still do; others have been unwaveringly against, including those controlled by Lord Beaverbrook.

Without the newspapers the people would have been cheated. This was an occasion when the position of the press as a public utility, one as necessary to its well being as electricity or water, was manifest to the most reactionary. In the circumstances, a strike that closed the London newspapers would have been a blow to democracy. We can progress to the axiom that in the troubled world in which the democracies live, any strike that closes newspapers, even if well intentioned, endangers those democratic principles by which both the press and the unions survive.

Opposition to entry into E.E.C. harmed and helped the government. When the debate on entry into Europe was at its height, an old friend said: "Look at it this way, anything that's opposed by Lord Beaverbook, Viscount Montgomery, and Khrushchev *must be the right thing for us to do.*"

Alternatively, many of the arguments raised by Lord Beaverbook and his writers, a highly skilled group of experienced professionals, were cogent and pointed. Repetition, as the advertising men tell us, is an important factor in choice. Purists might lament a lack of objectivity. But those who believe in the role of the popular press can answer that, even in opposition, the Beaverbrook newspapers provided a good deal of information and encouraged the kind of popular discussion of a great issue which is essential to the democratic process.

The other popular newspapers were less biased in their presentation of the issue and less full in their treatment, although all dealt with it in editorials. But the real failure in this challenge to the democratic process came in television and radio.

Perhaps this was inevitable. The Common Market itself and the pro's and con's of Britain's entry are not questions that lend themselves to ten, twenty, or thirty minutes' debate, no matter how well informed. To be understood, the issues must be read about and analyzed. Few people's auditory memories are good enough to enable them to listen to a lecture or a discussion on so complicated a subject and form reasonable opinions. The details, the nuances are missed. And in this question the nuances are terribly important; the details—the effect, for instance, on the British legal system—may involve a whole complex of national interests.

The part played by the information media in the public debate was not matched by that of the government. This was due to a large extent to the government's assumption, taken with reason on its side, that it was in command of the political situation when the application for entry was made in the summer of 1961. As we shall see, this assumption was wrong. At any rate, throughout the last months of that year and in 1962, the government was miserly in the amount of information it gave directly to the people. Prime Minister Macmillan, usually an extremely astute politician, burbled happily through a national television broadcast early in 1962 without once mentioning E.E.C. or Britain's negotiations for admission.

The government may have been right to believe that when negotiations of such importance are under way its wisest course was to keep quiet until something tangible emerged from the talks in Brussels. Yet its reluctance to speak or explain under any sort of pressure clearly retarded the organization of a positive, popular opinion in favor of moving toward Europe. This confused the continental idea of contemporary Britain, giving de Gaulle, and others, the image of a country still stuck to the past and unwilling to take the necessary political plunge.

The Community, originally economic in purpose, is political in its emotional motivation. The economic agreements are the basis for a future political structure. Europe, we know, is divided over the course political unity should take. But the choice before Britain, then, now, and in the future, is not an agreement on economic issues. It is acceptance of a political destiny common to all members. Yet the popular debate at the outset was waged on economic issues.

The Conservatives were slow to realize the interest the issue had generated. Late in 1961 and early in 1962, few were interested. The British were then too immersed in the joys of affluence to be deeply involved. This was natural. The situation changed suddenly. I believe that the change came after President de Gaulle and Dr. Adenauer made known their opposition to Britain's entry on terms which, they thought and said, entailed special favors for the Commonwealth. These statements may have had little relevance to the discussions in Brussels. What they did do was to awaken the British to the fact that entry into Europe was not simply an issue which could be left to Edward Heath, the Lord Privy Seal, and his negotiating team at Brussels. Instead, the issue appeared to be one regarding which nation could be set against nation and government against government.

The better informed might plead that the introduction, on the British side, of national feelings, even passions, was no help, that it muddied the clear waters of negotiation. The plea was in vain. People like to attach policies to persons or causes. And, in the end, the result was good from the standpoint of British democracy. Within six weeks the temperature of the debate had risen.

In the first of the series of by-elections in 1962, there was very little discussion at party political meetings of the Common Market and Britain's proposed entry. By early June, after de Gaulle and Adenauer had had their say, it was one of the major issues. Aidan Crawley, the successful Conservative candidate at West Derbyshire, found it the most important question at his meetings.

Informed by their newspapers of the effect their decision would have on far-away members of the Commonwealth—the Europeans they admired, like the Dutch and the Norwegians, and those they suspected, like the Germans—Britons felt that once more, as in 1939 and 1940, they were at the center of the world. More than that, they believed that the manner in which their support developed might well set a new course for other nations, just as their overwhelming endorsement of the Labor Party in 1945 reinvigorated social democracy in Europe.

"Most of us want something more than this sort of society," a young Englishwoman said. "There are still lots of people in this country who remember 1940 and 1945, when England stood for more than take-over bids and frozen dinners and holidays on the Costa Brava. I think that's why they were attracted to the Common Market. But the same thing, this feeling they must count for something as themselves, is going to argue against co-operation in Europe if they feel they're being pushed around by de Gaulle."

The debate, as it gathered intensity, thus demonstrated that there was a good deal more to British society than the affluence for which it waited so long and of which it has been so comfortably proud.

"It's just like Suez," people said. They meant by this that the issue was one that divided families, set dinner parties squabbling, provoked violent arguments in pubs: "Just step outside, mate, and I'll show yer who loves the bleedin' Jerries." The British were in the process of proving to the world what they themselves always subconsciously remember and the world too often forgets, that there is a great deal of fire and zest, unregulated by socialism, unsatiated by conservatism, beneath that phlegmatic façade. As I look back to the discussions in Europe when the Community was being established, I am impressed by the vigor and vehemence of the British debate.

When a free people move toward a great national decision, the divisions within their society frequently are more illuminating than party alignments. This was especially true in Britain's debate over entry into Europe; the magnitude of the issue undermined political alignments. Since 1945 there has been an increase in Parliamentary party conformism due to the virtual disappearance of independent members and a tightening of discipline by both the Labor and Conservative parties in the House of Commons. The divisions that emerged with regard to entry into E.E.C., therefore, were a welcome change, but not to the government.

The upper classes, those who by birth, education, experience, and money had had the most experience with the world, generally showed a strong bias toward union with Europe. The people in these classes who were opposed were vitriolic in their displeasure over government policy. Their criticisms assayed a high percentage of anti-Americanism and a hatred of what Miss Mitford's "Uncle Matt" called "bloody abroad." But the class with the deepest roots in Britain is also the most venturesome historically. However, its support for entry would not in itself have been important, were it not for reinforcement by a new and significant group.

This new group consisted of the men and women, now in their late forties and early fifties, who had risen to the top in the new industries: electronics, plastics, man-made fibers, aircraft and automobile manufacturing, television. By the nature of its commercial experience and its memories of the war, this group has been more inclined to take a sympathetic attitude toward co-operation with Europe than Britons connected with the older industries: coal mining, cotton, ship building, and some areas of engineering.

Most of the new men and women are now Conservative, although many of them were once a little to the left of center. They are the contemporary examples of a process repeated time and time again in British history: a young, aggressive

social group starts on the dissenting left, gradually wins authority and influence through the exploitation of new techniques
and new inventions in industry, and finally moves into places
of power within The Establishment.

Their greatest strides have been made in the period of
Conservative rule after 1951. But although most members of
this group did well, financially and socially, in that period,
they are all aware of the fundamental precariousness of the
country's position, particularly of the effect of the recurrent
economic crises upon the pound sterling.

The middle class in Britain has expanded faster than any
other group since the war, largely through the influx of families moving out of the industrial working class. The division
within the middle class with regard to entry into Europe appeared even greater than in the other two groups. Fundamentally conservative in their outlook, these people, whether La-
or, Conservative, or Liberal, were suspicious of any alteration
in the status quo which might affect their new prosperity.
When one traveled through Britain, one heard the same question over and over about Britain's entry into the Community:
"But how is it going to affect me?" No one, an elderly Conservative remarked in Middlesbrough, seemed to be thinking how
it would affect the country.

This is an extension of what the British call the "I'm all
right, Jack" mentality. It is distressing, but it is understandable.
Those who might censor this lack of imagination or enterprise
should keep in mind that this class, probably for the first time
in history, has, by and large, financial security, all it wants to
wear, new and better houses, automobiles, television, and lei-
sure. These people are like climbers who, having ascended the
mountain, and gained the plush sanctuary of a new hotel, find

themselves exhorted to don their climbing shoes and start anew on a trail that ends in the mists of obscurity.

The middle class has awakened slowly to the real significance of Britain's new relationship to Europe. Basically it is rather anti-intellectual. It has paid little attention to the arguments on Europe raging among economists and politicians. The primary interest of the class is in the hard facts of how a new relation with the Continent would affect the individual. It took a long time for the political aspect of Britain's position to penetrate.

When it did, after de Gaulle's rebuff to Britain at Brussels and the signature of the Franco-German pact in Paris, the middle class was the most vehement in attacking the French general. More than national pride was affronted. It is unfashionable in left-wing intellectual circles to mention it, nowadays, but the middle class made a tremendous contribution in blood and treasure to the destruction of Germany and the salvation of France in 1939-1945. This class therefore felt that Britain had been scurvily treated by de Gaulle, and it will take a long time for this feeling to disappear.

As a result, the middle class has been and will be the least amenable to suggestions that Britain, despite rebuffs, must at some future date join in the organization of a greater European political and economic group. A basic insularity has been reinforced by suspicion of the Germans and a new and lively distrust of France. For years to come, British governments will have to deal with this legacy of Brussels and Paris.

The attitude of the industrial working class with regard to movement toward Europe has been governed by its political composition. To begin with, it is a mistake, often made by Americans, to regard the class as entirely pro-Labor. In the last general election, at least four million trades-union members voted for the Tories. Another paradox is that this class, which supported Labor's economic and social revolution in the late 1940's, is on the whole parochial and reactionary in its approach to foreign affairs.

There remains a well-advertised minority that carries on the traditions of what might be called "international evangelism," which flowered in the years before World War II when British socialists vehemently, and often indiscriminately, supported anti-fascist governments and parties everywhere in the world. Our world owes a great deal to the people of the working class who, often unemployed and ill-nourished, found the energy to campaign among their countrymen against Hitler's Germany, Mussolini's Italy, and Franco's Spain.

As anyone who listens to Michael Foot in the House of Commons or reads the *New Statesman* will realize, the tradition survives. The difference is that it can no longer rely on the mass support of the industrial working class. It is relevant to note that this group of left-wing leaders—I exclude the secret Communists and fellow-travelers in their ranks—opposed entry into Europe because the union of Europe they saw was Catholic, anti-Communist, and capitalist.

Yet it is doubtful that these misgivings carried much weight with the mass of industrial workers. Their opposition was based on more earthly considerations.

Like the middle class, the industrial working class is enjoying prosperity. For them the difference between today and 1949 or 1939 is greater than for any other class in Britain. Its members are highly sensitive to anything that will change this condition for the worse. In these circumstances, the industrial working class is not simply opposed to change, it is opposed to facing an issue that in the long run will mean change, for good or ill. Many of its members still live, blissfully, in 1935.

The Labor Party equivocated for years about its attitude on entry into Europe. Even now that membership in E.E.C. is temporarily out of the question, the party is still undecided about its basic view of closer relations with the Continent. The only new factor in the situation is increased unemployment in the north of England and in Scotland. This makes the British working man even more hostile to any radical changes. Here is the true reactionary.

When Prime Minister Macmillan addressed his old constituency, Stockton-on-Tees, early in 1962, his reference to the rich rewards that would result from union with Europe had almost no effect upon the industrial workers in that constituency. The middle class showed some interest. Only the party workers were enthusiastic.

Macmillan, of course, could not be specific since the negotiations were then nearing their most important point. But his easy generalities had little or no appeal. People in the pubs wanted to know how entry into Europe would affect their jobs, their pocketbooks, and their hopes. They still do. No government will lead Britain into Europe without thorough explanations of the position, more thorough than the Tory platform of 1962.

At this moment, and for some time to come, any Conservative policy will meet heavy weather. The old belief that a Tory policy is designed by "them" to do "us," the workers, down dies hard. By "them" the proletariat means not only the government but the whole apparatus of authority from the police to the Anglican Church. Despite years of prosperity, despite Harold Macmillan's repeated assertions that the old class distinctions are dying, this ingrown suspicion of "them" and what "they" want to do remains.

As I have emphasized, the government's decision in 1961 to seek entry into Europe did not represent a commitment of the British people to the European Economic Community. The government had committed itself to negotiation with the Community in an effort to determine the terms under which it could enter Europe. At the time, it was supremely confident that if it found the terms satisfactory its judgment would be enough to lead the United Kingdom into the Common Market.

This was probably the high tide of Tory confidence. When I asked a member of the cabinet the basis for this rather imperial gesture, he answered: "We were elected to carry out our policies and this was one of them. The House and the country will go along."

This confidence has been sapped since by the most startling change British politics have undergone since 1945. A series of parliamentary by-elections, local elections, and public opinion polls, coupled with abundant evidence of a new mood in the country, have indicated a significant weakening of the authority and popularity of the Conservative government. This was accompanied by the defection from the government's policy on E.E.C. of a group of about fifty Tory M.P.'s.

The Conservatives' share of the vote in twelve by-elections between November 1961 and May 1962 fell by 17.6 per cent. Even though an especially attractive Tory candidate held the West Derbyshire seat in June, the party's share of the vote in that constituency fell by 25.3 per cent. In these twelve by-elections, Labor's share of the vote dropped in ten. In every case, that of the resurgent Liberals increased.

The Tories have consistently lost ground; Labor has also lost, but to a lesser extent; and the Liberal Party by the summer of 1962 appeared capable of winning between eighteen and twenty-five per cent of the total votes in any by-election.

Taking the by-election results and the polls as their text, the Liberal and Labor parties argued that the government no longer represented the majority of the electorate. The immediate and inevitable effect of this new political fluidity was a weakening of the government's position in its negotiations with the E.E.C. in Brussels.

Should the present political trend continue, which, of course, is by no means certain, there will be more serious changes in the British political scene. Ever since the eclipse of the Liberals in the general election of 1924, when their representation in the House of Commons fell from 159 to 40 members, Britain has had essentially a two-party political system. Conservative and Labor governments, aided by the strict discipline of the modern parliamentary system, have been able to push through sweeping programs without the distraction of a third party strong enough to affect legislation by throwing its support to one faction or the other in an important vote.

This situation may now be altered by the Liberal revival. Even if this trend should continue, it does not seem likely that the Liberals can win enough seats in the House of Commons in the next general election to rival either the Tories or the Socialists in numbers of seats. But the Liberals could achieve great political power by holding the balance between the other two parties.

Should they win thirty or forty parliamentary seats, most of them, it is assumed, at the expense of the Tories, the Liberals would emerge as an influential minority. Their voting strength could be used, as party leader Jo Grimond has promised, to support Labor against the Conservatives on decisive issues. Or they could accept a limited number of Cabinet portfolios and form a coalition government with Labor. This seems remote. In any event, the sort of Liberal-Labor alliance now foreseen would not be the best guarantee of the political stability Britain is supposed to provide the new Europe.

Is this too somber a picture? One can only say that the established patterns of British politics appear to be breaking up in 1962 and that those who foresaw the replacement of the two-party system by the three-party system had the voting figures on their side.

It seems unlikely that in these circumstances Macmillan will go to the country in a general election in 1963. The Conservatives' mandate expires in the autumn of 1964. He can wait, if he wishes, until the spring of that year or even later. By that time, he may believe, the anti-government vote, which has gone to the Liberals rather than to the Socialists in most ballots, will have been retrieved by an improvement in economic conditions, particularly in exports, and by entry into Europe.

Macmillan's position is difficult. He must present voters with a progressive platform that still envisages some sort of link with Europe. And, at the same time, he must recognize and appease his party's bitterness toward de Gaulle. His immediate course may be a new emphasis on the American connection, one not invariably popular among Tories, coupled with an assertion of Britain's intention to enter Europe "next time" not as a supplicant but as a key power in the development of political unity. Such policies are difficult to reconcile in one program. But Macmillan is a consummate politician.

The next British general election, therefore, is going to be of extraordinary importance to the British, to Europe, and to the free world. In the present situation, political prophecy is more difficult than in ordinary times.

If the Liberal revival has been launched on a wave of anti-government votes, as the Tories and Socialists say it has, then the Liberals will have to present a more coherent and forceful program if they are to cut into the Conservative and Labor holdings in the House of Commons in a general election.

The Liberals naturally will benefit from their long-standing espousal of the cause of union with Europe. Events might conspire to make this the key issue of the election. But a party that appeals to all the people rather than to those in a single constituency needs a clear program on a wide range of national policies: defense, education, housing, and pensions. The Liberals have the intellectual resources to provide such a program. Of course, they may think it safer to fight solely on anti-government, anti-Socialism lines.

If they follow this course, the results will not measure up to the Liberals' present expectations. Political rules are no more inviolate in the United Kingdom than anywhere else. But one which has stood the test of time is that at a general election those who in by-elections have defected to another party—and the Liberals have benefited more than any party from such defections—tend to resume their original loyalties, having satisfied their resentment, often on a minor, local point, in the by-election ballot.

The Liberals' best opportunity is to go to the country with a program which will appeal to all those who believe that Britain must be something more than a self-satisfied, materialistic society. The old strain of evangelism still exists in the British political ethos. The party that exploits it should win the next general election.

Until the 1950's it was the Labor Party which made the most out of this appeal. But Labor today suffers from its own accomplishments. To most Britons, although not to the doctrinaire left of the Labor Party, British social democracy completed its revolution between 1945 and 1951. The goals, which generations of Labor speakers had extolled to unthinking passers-by on windy street corners, had been won.

To the extreme left, the party's proper course remains the pursuit of complete nationalization, enshrined in the famous Clause IV of the party constitution as the national ownership of all means of production, distribution, and exchange. But the majority of the party, and certainly the center and right wing, believe that this program has little relevance and almost no appeal in the comfortable, prosperous Britain of today.

Despite one or two successes in 1962, the Labor Party still seemed caught in the receding tide that had held it since 1950. Its electoral position, moreover, is less strong than it appears. Labor candidates undoubtedly will pile up immense majorities in northern, industrial constituencies at the next general election, while the party's candidates elsewhere, if successful, will just squeeze through. In other words, the total Labor vote in the country, although still well over 12,000,000, is not a good guide to the party's ability to elect a majority in the House of Commons.

Labor can hold its own in the ancient industrial strongholds. But it has failed to win voters in some of the new industrial areas or to retain the support of many members of the industrial working class now moving into the middle class.

The Tories have found comfort in the saying that although they have lost a number of by-election battles they have not lost the war. Such comfort may be illusory. The ebb of Conservative fortunes, based on hostility toward government policies, distaste for the Prime Minister, and a desire for a more dynamic, even a more idealistic, approach to the world, may have become so strong that, when the last battle comes, the Tories will find themselves bereft of troops and ammunition.

Public boredom is one price the government had to pay for over a decade of political success. But one dividend of that success has been the flow of able young men into the party and, more recently, into the lower ranks of the ministries. A Tory comeback could be led by these younger men, who in many respects, notably in their understanding of the voters' desperate interest in education and housing, are closer to the electorate than Macmillan or R. A. Butler.

Given a chance to exploit these men and their gifts and to dissect the reasons for their decline, and perhaps with a new leader, the Conservatives could recover. But they must do more than maintain an iron optimism in the face of the rebuffs at parliamentary by-elections. In the case of the Prime Minister, R. A. Butler, Iain Macleod, and other ministers, this optimism was based on the conviction that the government's policies, primarily entry into Europe and wage restraint, would prove successful and would be seen to be successful. Their optimism also was due to the Tory conviction that on any major issue, such as support for the union with Europe, the Labor Party is incapable of attaining a united position and would once again split.

Of course, Labor, now within striking distance of a return to power, cannot afford such a split. But can the movement avoid it? The Parliamentary Labor Party, indeed the whole movement, has been deeply divided on issues much less important than this. Aneurin Bevan used to point proudly to such divisions as proof that the Labor Party represented a real democratic movement whose members were not to be dragooned into servile acceptance of policies proclaimed by party leaders. Perhaps, but such divisions have been a reason, although not the main one, why Labor has been out of office since 1951. And a new schism is in the making now.

The party might survive the continued hostility of the independent Labor M.P.'s like Foot and Sydney Silverman to union with Europe. Will it be able to surmount the continued opposition to this step of many Labor politicians of the center and right? In an ordinary political party, such men might be counted on to close ranks and follow the leader once the party line had been decided. But Labor is not an ordinary political party. Essentially it is a movement, large enough to generate terrific political force but also to admit and even encourage a profusion of views on any single issue.

No single theme united Labor's opposition to the Common Market. The extreme left stressed the anti-Communist, capitalist, and catholic character of the Six. The moderates feared its restrictive effect on the economic planning of a future Labor government. Throughout the movement there are faithful socialists who are highly insular in their approach to the problem. They, more than any other section of the political population, are inclined to the idea of Britain developing into a somewhat larger Sweden, a safe, sound socialist haven.

Other Labor politicians were fundamentally sympathetic to union with Europe—and still are—as long as it is done under Labor auspices.

"The Tories haven't got the authority in the country or the weight in Europe to obtain suitable terms," a Labor front bencher said. "They'll fail and, when we're elected, we'll take the country into E.E.C. in 1964 or 1965."

It looks as though my friend will have a chance to prove the accuracy of his prediction.

One thing is certain. Whatever Labor's leaders decide to do about Europe, the program will be roundly condemned by a large section of the Labor movement. No man will be able to swear that Labor is for or against Europe. Such is the nature of this great, divided, warm-hearted proletarian alliance.

The Liberal's position is better. They have advocated entry into Europe from the start. But had Britain gone into Europe in 1963, and presumably if it enters in 1964, it will be the Tories, not the Liberals, who will reap the benefits at the polls. There is no reason to believe the Tories won't try again.

French and, to a lesser degree, German opposition to British entry in 1962 provoked the fundamental Conservative toughness. Also an elasticity of political outlook. Some Tories argued that if the French kept Britain out, the party could go to the country on a nationalist platform in which emphasis on Europe would be replaced by emphasis on the Commonwealth and "Great" Britain. At the moment there is no sign that the Conservatives will try this. But so great is their political mobility, so astute their leadership, and so strong the vein of nationalism that I, for one, can see them adopting this line and winning with it. An outside chance, but well worth a bet.

Moralists will shake their heads at the thought that such a change of front could be contemplated. But the Tories are not in politics for morality. They are in politics for power. It is quite possible that an approach of this kind would have won a general election.

These combinations and divisions within the British political parties mean more to the rest of the world now than they have since the days when the United Kingdom led the West. The nature and direction of British governments in the next few years will influence events and conditions of far wider import than the simple problem of whether the United Kingdom enters the European Economic Community. The next eighteen months, consequently, will be fateful for the economic and political development of the West and for its long-term stability in the duel with the U.S.S.R. What happens in Europe in the following few years, when its increased economic strength is brought to bear on other continents and its growing political unity begins to affect the great issues between East and West, will be as important for the automobile worker in Detroit or the Kansas farmer as it will be for Australian cattlemen, Dutch shipbuilders, and Russian kolkhozniks.

The problem of Britain's entry, with all the partisanship it encouraged, was only the prelude. Europe and America have other problems to solve as the prospect of an even larger union becomes clearer. It is time now for a last evaluation of the considerations which will affect the Western world.

· 12 ·

Britain's Position in an Evolving Common-
wealth . . . Sovereignty and Europe's Unity
. . . Political Prospects in E.E.C. . . . Europe
the First Step to a Larger Association?

IN ITS DEVELOPMENT, the European Economic Community
employed economic means to reach a political goal; that
goal, it is only too clear, is still unattained, but that it is political, in the form of a united Europe, few will deny. The United
Kingdom's approach to Europe was made along economic
lines, and the considerations that influenced the great debate
in the country were at the outset those of industry and commerce. But the overriding psychological factor was political.
Nationalism, that is, patriotic feeling, affected most Britons'
views of the Community in that phase, just as it will be the

dominant emotion governing any American movement toward E.E.C. in the future. Nationalism may be, as Albert Einstein once wrote, "an infantile disease . . . the measles of mankind," but it continues to disrupt the world.

No sooner do we believe that a long and terrible war has taught civilized people the folly of nationalism than nationalism reappears in France in its most virulent form. Africans and Asians, ready to condemn nationalism in Europe or America, once they are independent embrace its gaudiest and most outdated trappings.

The movement of Britain toward Europe was complicated by the fact that the British, in addition to strong, if often sublimated, feelings about their own islands, bore the additional nationalist burden of the Commonwealth. As the successor to the old Empire, the British Commonwealth was linked to British nationalism in a peculiar way. There is little historical evidence that conscious waves of nationalism in Britain sent soldiers and sailors out to conquer a new Empire after the loss of the first. Commercial or, as they were then called, mercantile interests prevailed. Not until the late nineteenth century was there any conscious urge to add new areas to the Empire.

The tie with British nationalism comes from the strength of popular pride in the Empire and, later, in the Commonwealth, on the part of people who served both and who sincerely believed in their efficacy as instruments for bringing civilization to the back of beyond and peace to the world.

When the original members of E.E.C. rejected proposals that would enable Britain both to enter the Community and to retain most of her economic ties with the Commonwealth, including some adjusted form of preferential trade arrangements, they protested that British entry on such terms would alter *their* economic concept of the Community. But there were deeper, nationalist reasons for their hostility.

To Europe, especially France and Germany, Britain and the Commonwealth added up to British influence verging on dictation within the new and enlarged Community. Macmillan might refer disparagingly to his country as an "off-shore island," and British officials might protest their desire to cooperate within E.E.C; Europe was too old and experienced to be won by such tactics. To many, these protestations seemed only a clever cover for the hope of the achievement of British hegemony within the Community.

In the age of the nuclear missile, such ideas are absurd and irrational. Yet this European resistance to the Commonwealth, because it exacerbated highly charged emotions in Britain with regard to the Commonwealth, possibly was the single most difficult barrier to speedy and successful entry in the first negotiations.

We are familiar with the economic considerations that led the British government to turn toward the Continent. These remain valid despite the efforts made by opponents of the move to picture the rich rewards available to the British economy if only "a new dynamism" could be created in Commonwealth affairs. This phrase was used by Sir Derek Walker-Smith, M.P., and Mr. Peter Walker, M.P., in their pamphlet *A Call to the Commonwealth*. The publication was intended to awaken Britain to the potential of the Commonwealth once the new methods and instruments proposed by the authors had been put to work.

There is little doubt that instruments like the Commonwealth Marketing Board proposed by the two Conservative politicians might have benefited British trade and tightened the ties between mother country and Commonwealth, ties which have loosened with bewildering rapidity in recent years. British political influence and authority in the Commonwealth have declined very rapidly recently. How much is this influence worth? What are its chances of survival, now that Britain is becoming established in Europe?

Unfortunately for those who uphold the Commonwealth cause in Britain against proponents of a united Europe, in the months during which the British were negotiating with E.E.C. a number of Commonwealth countries, by various methods, showed their independence of Britain with alarming frankness. Commonwealth unity may never recover from the shock.

Prime Minister Nehru, who had so bitterly censured Britain for the Suez adventure, sent his troops into Goa despite clearly expressed British advice to the contrary. By the middle of 1962, to the open concern of the United Kingdom and the United States, the Indian government was toying with the idea of buying Soviet MIG aircraft. In the long-drawn controversy in the United Nations with regard to the Congo, the representatives of India almost invariably opposed the United Kingdom and other members of the Commonwealth.

Ghana, moving rapidly toward authoritarianism, despite the protests of the United Kingdom delegation, forced the United Nations to debate the situation in Southern Rhodesia, like Ghana a member of the Commonwealth. Money from Ghana fed subversion in Nigeria, also a member of the Commonwealth.

The attitude of India, Ghana, and other Afro-Asian

members of the Commonwealth toward Britain and her policies should be a sufficient answer to those in the United Kingdom, most of them within the Labor Party, who emphasize
the importance of the Commonwealth as a means by which
British political ideas and experience can be channeled to the
new countries.

Up to a point the importance of the Commonwealth has
been such in the period when British control over these territories was greater than it is now. The first generation of
African or Asian rulers may remember enough of the teach-
ings of Cambridge or Oxford or London to be affected by the
great traditions of parliamentary government. But in some
Commonwealth nations—India is a good example—the old
generation of British-educated leaders is on the way out, and
a newer group less dedicated to the scholarly, political philoso-
phizing of Mr. Nehru is coming to the top. How long will
India reflect British ideas once these men take over? And of
what relevance is the great tradition of British law, of habeas
corpus, for example, to Dr. Kwame Nkrumah in Ghana?

It is nonsense to think that as these countries develop
they will become more, rather than less, influenced by Britain.
Not even economic aid from the United Kingdom on an unprecedented scale will alter the present political development
of the Commonwealth's African and Asian members. This
development leads away from British traditions and ideals
toward new ideas and ideals of their own. It is most unlikely
that any new plan for the Commonwealth, no matter how
generous, astutely conceived, and efficiently administered,
would have more than a superficial effect on this movement.
As a result of their environment and their individual political

and economic problems, the members of the Commonwealth in Africa and Asia are bound to move away from British forms.

Although they have been less spectacular, indications multiply that the "advanced" members of the Commonwealth are increasingly quick to establish and implement policies independent of Britain. This results, partly, from the fact that they *are* "advanced," politically as well as economically. Canada's trade with Cuba in the Caribbean and with Communist China in the Orient is an example of a strongly individualistic policy on the part of one member; a policy, it might be added, which has been as strongly, if less openly, criticized in London as in Washington.

Even Australia, sentimental, emotional about Britain and "home," has established the closest military and political ties with the United States and is seeking in Asia working agreements with some of the Oriental powers. Indeed, Australia's population, ethnically British, has altered rapidly since 1945 with the admission of large numbers of immigrants, known as the New Australians, from Italy and elsewhere in Europe. Logically, this infusion of blood from Europe will affect the view of the next generations of Australians toward Britain. She will not be "home" to as many of them.

The advocates of the Commonwealth cause tended to gloss over these developments in the debate over entry into Europe. Instead, they made great play with the mission of the multi-racial Commonwealth, the debts in blood owed the Canadians, Australians, and New Zealanders, and the unifying role of the Crown.

The debt in blood is there. But those who emphasize it sometimes make history sound as though the last two world

wars had been fought for the British Empire entirely by
Commonwealth troops. The figures of British and Empire
losses, given in an earlier chapter, will correct this impression.
In two great conflicts, Britain and the Commonwealth fought
together for aims they shared and acknowledged as being of
mutual interest to all members of the British family of nations.
The contribution of the Australians in 1915 and the Canadians
in 1942 certainly was important. But these are advanced
political societies whose people knew quite well what would
happen to them if they and Britain lost the war.

The Commonwealth's "advanced" peoples did not spring
to the aid of Britain in the two German wars. They entered
them, as nations do, because they realized that if Britain fell
before the German tyranny, they would fall too. They fought
with great valor—so did the British—but they didn't rescue
Britain. "The debt of blood" is a fine, stirring phrase for the
politician or the editorial writer. But it has precious little relevance to the problem of Britain, the Commonwealth, and
Europe today.

No American can write with much persuasion about the
position of the Crown in Britain; he is dealing with a subject
that is rooted in a millennium of custom, racial feelings, and
inbred attitudes. The British people do not explain their attitude toward the Crown and the Monarch. They feel it rather
than think it.

But a writer from the United States may be on slightly
firmer ground in discussing the supposed "unifying influence
of the Crown in the Commonwealth." This is another of those
phrases that have beclouded discussion of Britain's entry into
Europe. It's greatest weakness is that those Britons who use
it ascribe to Commonwealth subjects, Ghanians or Canadians,

Pakistanis or Rhodesians, sentiments about the Crown and Queen Elizabeth II similar to those they feel themselves. The American may come a little closer to the Commonwealth attitude.

Commonwealth friends may admire the Queen and, quite often, praise the importance of the monarchy as a stabilizing factor in British politics, but they do not believe that these sentiments should be allowed to outweigh the long-term interests of their own countries in relation to Britain or other nations. This feeling has little to do with the personality of the Queen or the merits of monarchy. The Crown is a symbol they would be prepared to respect and cherish even if their ties with the British loosen still further. But the Crown is not a positive factor in uniting them and other members of the Commonwealth.

Just as it is difficult to convince the average suburban housewife in Britain that "our Queen" is Queen of New Zealand as well, so it is hard to induce Canadians to believe that the Queen of Canada was also Queen of "all those naked black men" in Ghana when she visited there in 1961.

Another example of the occasional irrationalities of the Commonwealth attitude toward the Crown is the feeling, strong among some New Zealanders and Australians, that they "understand" the Queen and the monarchy better than do "those socialists beatniks" in Chelsea.

The role of the monarchy in British society too often is underestimated. This is especially true of the pervasiveness of its influence. But the role of the monarchy as a unifying influence within the Commonwealth is too easily and too frequently exaggerated.

The independent members of the Commonwealth clearly

are moving away from political interdependence with Britain. The speed varies, but the movement has begun. It does not seem likely that this trend could be reversed even if a greater measure of economic integration should be established. Nor can I accept the argument that such Commonwealth economic integration would outweigh the economic advantages of Britain's entry into Europe. Indeed, the abandonment by Britain of certain political claims in the Commonwealth will be more than balanced by the political opportunities open to the United Kingdom in the Community.

What might be called "the Commonwealth fixation" was directly connected to the issue of sovereignty—another word, in the popular mind, for nationalism—and everything this means to the British in terms of national identity. Like the contemporary concept of the Commonwealth and its political unity, the popular idea of British national sovereignty has very little relevance to the facts. It is a powerful factor in political affairs none the less.

Since 1945, that is, for eighteen years, successive British governments, Conservative as well as Labor, have surrendered bits of sovereignty in the pursuit of the objectives of British policy. The United Nations, the North Atlantic Treaty Organization, Western European Union, the General Agreement on Trades and Tariffs all have benefited from this willingness on the part of cabinets in London to abandon specific national powers in return for the creation of a stronger international power.

To some extent, the same thing has occurred in the United States. But neither the British nor the American people have ever fully realized how greatly their independence of action is bound by their commitments to international organizations. Parenthetically, it might be noted that great powers, and I mean great because of the resolution of their peoples, in a crisis often flout such commitments. This is a risk which those engaged in building a more closely integrated West must be prepared to take.

The failure of the average Briton to realize the extent to which his government's power to take independent action has shrunk is due to the superimposition upon his native insularity of a tradition of world dominion. To a large degree this remains unshaken in many Britons.

This tradition is still far too strong in one, not unimportant, section of British life—the Tory right—and it nourished the opposition to entry into Europe. Its survival represents a failure in political leadership on the part of the Tories, particularly the Prime Minister.

When Harold Macmillan took office in a Britain shocked and humbled by the withdrawal from Suez, he proclaimed his intention to make certain that it was still "Great Britain." Indeed, this goal was emphasized exactly at the time that the Prime Minister was bowing to American wishes on the Middle East and being most assiduous in following American policy in Europe. Even in 1959, when he made his celebrated and largely fruitless visit to Moscow, he did not announce his plans until they had received the acquiescence of Secretary of State John Foster Dulles.

This continual emphasis on the part of the Conservative government on Britain's supposed independence in international affairs has obscured the realities of the balance of power within the Western alliance for many of its supporters and for many more in each party who like to hear the British Lion roar. Consequently, when the political implications of entry into Europe first became a subject for debate, great stress was laid on the manner in which this would weaken the sovereign power of Parliament, on alleged European inter- ference with the workings of British government, and on the influence of the Continent upon the making of foreign policy.

Although exaggerated, these factors exist. But I do not believe that the limitations which entry into Europe would im- pose on the making of foreign policy are any more likely to shift a government position than those imposed by membership in NATO. For years, the North Atlantic Community has im- plored Britain to increase the British Army of the Rhine to 55,000, a figure to which the Macmillan government is com- mitted. For economic and political reasons the government has refused to fulfill this commitment.

This concentration upon sovereignty, like that upon the weakening of the Commonwealth, reflects the parochialism of British thinking about the country's role in Europe. The gov- ernment is not guiltless. It failed to emphasize the political opportunities in Europe, preferring to stress economic ad- vantages. Perhaps this was tactical. Too much attention to the former might have increased French opposition. But this op- position was not subject to change because of British attitudes.

After the rupture at Brussels, there was nothing in Paris to show that the wholesale surrender by the British of their country's special interests would have made entry possible. Had this surrender been made, I feel sure General de Gaulle would have found other reasons to say the United Kingdom was not yet ready for membership. Whether these reasons would have satisfied his allies is beside the point. They would have satisfied him.

But it is in the political field, I am convinced, that

Britain has the most to gain from union with Europe. Leaving aside the question of the ultimate form of that union, federal or confederal, the political involvement with the Continent offers the United Kingdom exactly the sort of challenge its political energies can accept, the sort of challenge which, since the decline of the old influence in the Commonwealth, the British need if they are to continue to contribute to the evolution of the world.

Since, in the dawn of modern history, the British became a united people, they have shown themselves almost spectacularly responsive to such challenges. Poor, numerically inferior, torn by internal religious dissension, they showed themselves capable, in the sixteenth, seventeenth, and eighteenth centuries, of winning an empire overseas and defending it successfully against the ambitions of Spain and France. There was no more notable or lastingly effective response to the age of exploration than that furnished by the islanders.

Having lost the richest portion of their first empire in the American Revolution, at about the time they were initiating the industrial revolution, the British people went ahead to create an even greater empire out of the energies and industry of its people. This empire may well have been built in a fit of absentmindedness. But twice in a third of a century it withstood the furious onslaughts of great empires.

At this point in any account of British history, writers usually insert a cautionary note. British ardor may be dampened. The stream of creative energy that flowed from renaissance England under the first Elizabeth may now be so reduced as to make no difference in a world dominated by the American and Russian colossi.

As I have noted, there is a strong desire in Britain to stop the world and get off. The easy opulence of a Sweden or a Switzerland with no world responsibilities can be very attractive. But I don't think the desire will survive the growing understanding in Britain of the opportunities offered by a closer relationship with Europe.

The economic opportunity is clear. Britain still is a rich country, rich in an intelligent and energetic industrial work force, an experienced and venturesome financial community, and technicians and techniques which when properly employed in the large industrial complexes are as good or better than anything on the Continent. Movement toward and competition with Europe will further the re-establishment of national economic discipline, for employers as well as for labor, which is necessary if the economy is to progress at its potential rate.

The political opportunity, however, is even more important. Except for that period, historically rather brief, in which Britain at the head of her empire was a dominant world power, the British Isles have always been part of European politics. Despite de Gaulle's rather distorted view of history, the English and the Scots and Welsh have for centuries played a role in Europe no more foreign to the Frenchman than the German or Italian or Spaniard. Britain built a great colonial empire. So, in their time, did the Spanish, the Dutch, the French, and the Portuguese. This did not separate them from Europe.

Now Western Europe, in which Britain has been militarily and politically involved to a greater or lesser degree since the time of the Norman kings, is moving toward unity. Here is Britain's chance, perhaps her last, to play a decisive role as the leader of Europe. And the role is a familiar one for the British.

For centuries the islanders have been prepared to prevent the domination of Europe by any one power. In the days of Elizabeth I or Marlborough, one power meant one nation, Spain or France, and later, to the subjects of George V and his son, George VI, Germany. Today one power means a multi-national community led by France.

This is not the way the British, the Americans, or many Europeans expected the Community to develop. Nor is it the way, in my opinion, which offers the best chance for European unity and peace. Indeed the events in Paris and Brussels in January and February seemed to be leading the West away from the future and back to the ghastly charade of conflicting national aspirations of the nineteenth century.

The rebuff at Brussels should not be allowed to check the British permanently. They must continue to seek entry into the European Economic Community. They must throw all their energies into making Europe a liberal, enlightened, and united force in world affairs.

This is in the interests of the United States. Perhaps the British, when they do join Europe, will not be as responsive to American wishes as the Administration believes. Perhaps they will be more interested in promoting their own policies and influence within Europe than those of the United States. These are risks we must take. The national interests of the two countries have so much in common that Americans can be reasonably sure that on major issues Britain's interests will be ours.

Many grave problems cannot be solved until Britain does enter Europe: the establishment of a European nuclear deterrent, the guidance of European resources to the underdeveloped nations, the development of a policy toward the Communist bloc that combines firmness of purpose with flexibility of method. These are not simply British or American problems. They will confront everyone in the West in the testing years ahead. Their solution is vital to the West in the duel with the East.

Earlier I noted that Britain could give political stability to Europe, although this might be modified by the present changes in the British political scene. Now that the French appear to be rapidly losing touch with political realities at home and abroad, a dose of trans-Channel stability would be all the more welcome.

One of the factors that contributed to de Gaulle's decision to block British entry was his conviction that the Tories would be defeated in the next general election and that the Labor Party would be anti-Europe. He may have been right, although the death of Hugh Gaitskell has affected Labor's electoral chances. But the important thing is that Britain eventually bring to Europe her fidelity to government by parliamentary democracy and her opposition to authoritarianism of the left or right.

The next few years will see some fearful political battles in Britain. New men and new policies will appear. Personal and party reputations will be destroyed. But none of this will involve any shift from democracy. There will be no cries for a general on horseback or for a proletarian dictatorship. This reliance on the democratic process, with all its fumblings and delay, is the lesson the British must teach Europe, by example while outside, by leadership once inside.

The clash of national interests that prompted France to keep Britain out, and the enraged resentment of her five partners in E.E.C., will have a damaging effect on politics within

the Community in the next few years. While de Gaulle rules, it
will take a great deal of faith to believe in the eventual triumph
of European unity.

As this is written, Europe is canvassing alternative solu-
tions to British entry, interim arrangements, a modus vivendi
through Western European union, and the like. Whatever the
eventual outcome, it is painfully clear that France, having kept
the British out of Europe and, in the Earl of Home's words,
"deceived" them, must now prepare for a collision with the
British.

Yet the logic of history points inescapably to the continuation of two courses in Europe: the disappearance of the last
vestiges of colonialism and the development of unity within
one large European community.

There is for Britain no alternative to a closer relationship
with Europe. Nor can she sink back into an apathetic neutrality, alone, proud, and, eventually, poor. This course does
not suit the peculiar genius of the British. And it would leave
Europe to the nineteenth-century notions of General de Gaulle.

Once Britain is in Europe and the political organization
of a larger Europe takes shape, the Western world will be
forced by events to consider a wider association of powers.
Probably the quickest approach will be through economic ties:
the establishment of world markets for key raw products, the
channeling of European and North American technical and
financial resources to the underdeveloped countries of South
America, Asia, and Africa. The West may unite because at
last its leaders understand that they must win the battle with
Communism in those countries or lose the world.

This larger community would be a more certain safeguard
for the tradition of European civilization than the present one.

The ultimate victory in the continuing battle with tyranny is not to be won by force of arms. The great lesson the world is learning is that the ultimate weapon is now the ultimate disaster for all mankind. In these circumstances the West must find the political and economic means of co-operation to provide the strength to match and outlast the Communist bloc. The war, and it is a war, with Communism is being fought on economic, political, diplomatic, and propaganda lines, and victory is on the side of the big battalions.

Britain must return to her task. This means more than making a second and successful effort to join the Community. It means that while that effort is being made, and afterwards, Britain must devote her great energies to the political and economic development of the enlarged Community. Eventual entry cannot be the end for Britain or her associates, but the beginning.

The world that will emerge will be different from the present one. National pressures are strong. So is the resistance to change of well-ordered, prosperous communities like ours. But in the present world situation the risk for the West of standing still is far greater than that of going ahead.

This is a dangerous world for the British and everyone else. The old, orderly world of fixed incomes and steady progress is at the mercy of powerful new scientific and political forces. No nation can expect a free ride through history. What the West believes in and what its people have died for in the last thousand years faces the greatest challenge in history. The challenge can be met only by a united Europe, including Britain, and by the steady progress on that foundation to the establishment of a larger Western community.

· 13 ·

American Policy and the New Europe . . .
Shadow and Substance in Policy Goals . . .
Continental Nationalism versus American
Political and Military Aims . . . New Alli-
ances for Old

THE C-47 DROPPED out of the soft darkness of the summer
night into the pool of light surrounding the airport at
Hutchinson. I shook hands with the automobile dealer with
whom I had chatted on the trip from Kansas City. "Enjoyed
our talk," he said. "Europe sure sounds mighty different from
what it was after the war. Guess we ought to think more about
what it's like today. Have a good time at the fair."

When I talk to my countrymen, I am invariably impressed by the time-lag in their thinking about Europe and its
problems. There is a great deal of confusion, some ignorance,
but far less apathy than might be expected. No European

should underestimate the curiosity and intelligence which a large section of the American people apply to Europe and its problems. At the same time it would be a mistake to exaggerate how informed they are or how relevant their knowledge and feelings are to the great issues in Europe today. Americans who are interested know that Western Europe is prosperous, although they have as yet little idea of its industrial and financial potential. But they remain behind in assessing the political effects of European recovery and unity on themselves and on continental peoples and governments.

There is less confusion in thinking about Britain than about America's other allies abroad. Americans are confident they "know" the country and its people, even if their experience is limited to a few weeks or months of war service in Lincolnshire or three days of sightseeing in London. The absence of a language barrier encourages in Americans a conviction that they understand the British—always a dangerous illusion in international relations. Of course, the British feel the same way about the United States and Americans. Thus distortions prosper.

American thinking about the European Economic Community is affected by the simple faith that it is another form of the United States of Europe. Our own country is a success. Why would it not be a success in Europe? Americans were puzzled by Britain's rather slow approach, angered by de Gaulle's rejection of that approach. Such oversimplification is dangerous. But in the end the Americans found more to blame in Paris than in London. This surprised the French. The vehemence of American criticism of de Gaulle's policy was not anticipated. The French discounted the residual respect and even affection for Britain which colors our attitude toward that country. This attitude is by no means as strong as it once was. But it remains a good deal more powerful than other Europeans think, and surprises them occasionally with its influence and depth.

American confusion about Europe coincides with the emergence of new political attitudes on the Continent which, outside of New York and Washington, seem to be almost totally ignored or misunderstood. Here again the closeness of our relationship with Britain is a factor. It is easier to understand Britons or to read their newspapers, magazines, and books. Hence, our thinking about trends and developments in Europe is influenced unduly by our opinions about Britain.

Many Americans, moreover, have been gratified by the deference, at times verging on servility, showed to United States interests and policies by Prime Minister Macmillan and the majority of his associates in the Cabinet. The reversal of what they were taught, by folklore and ignorant schoolteachers, were the roles of the British Empire and the United States earlier in this century is psychologically satisfying. Even the grandsons and granddaughters of the hyphenated Americans of World War I can now be condescendingly kind to the British, who, after all, try not to make too much trouble for us in the world.

The confusion and uncertainty about Europe affects governmental as well as public opinion. This is especially true with regard to Europe's new nationalism. No other government in the world is as conscious of or as familiar with the bases of military power and political influence as that in Washington. No other government, friendly or hostile, has as much of that power. Naturally, no other government can know or understand even a fraction of the appalling strength of weapons now in American hands or about to be stocked in the nuclear arsenal. Even the British, perhaps the best informed, too often tend to talk of their country as a great power.

The knowledge of the tremendous, truly unbridgeable gap between the strength of the United States and Britain or France or Germany has made it difficult for American statesmen to understand European nationalism. Courteous and civilized men such as Secretary of State Dean Rusk and Secretary of Defense Robert S. McNamara find it hard to credit the pretensions of France to lead Europe as an independent power.

It is not only sheer American strength that beclouds this issue. There is also the historic fact that since the war American thinking has been concentrated, understandably, on the duel with Russia, and all other issues which might weaken Western strategy and unity in Europe have been considered mischievous distractions. There was a great deal of high-flown talk from Washington at the time of Suez about the rights of small nations and the preservation of international law and order. There was also a belief, less well advertised but certainly extremely strong, that the Franco-British adventure in Suez weakened Western unity at a critical period, that of the Hungarian rebellion.

This preoccupation with the Russians, although clearly vital to the preservation of the West, may lead in the next few years to an undervaluation of the role nationalism can play in the formation of a new Europe and of the extreme difficulties which will ensue in the struggle for political unity there. Perhaps it is pertinent here to repeat an earlier warning: no objective evidence exists that French nationalism will die with President de Gaulle or that German nationalism will be kept at bay

by Chancellor Adenauer's successors. Nor should supra-
nationalism in the new Europe be automatically considered a
harmless and beneficial development for us.

One of the most striking changes in European attitudes
toward the United States and its policies has occurred in relation to American views on the Soviet Union. Europeans
from Athens to Edinburgh were grateful in 1949 when the
United States created the NATO alliance and told the Soviet
Union "stop." But gratitude is the least hardy of sentiments.
Europeans are still dimly grateful; many still acknowledge the
danger of Soviet aggression. What they no longer accept is
the argument that their own national policies, their views on
the future of Europe, Africa, and the Middle East, must be
subordinated invariably to America's interests in the struggle
with Russia.

This struggle, they assert, has dominated American
policy-making since the peace of 1945 went sour in 1948.
Policies have been made and projected largely on the basis of
their effect on America's position in relation to the Russian
rival, with scant attention paid to political or economic developments in Europe.

One example: Many European diplomats and politicians believe that the United States pushed too forcefully for
continental acceptance of the European Defense Community,
which would have reinforced the existing military strength
of Europe. Blatant, unrealistic, tactless pressure, they assert,
brought about the rejection of E.D.C. by France and set back
the cause of European unity by at least five years.

American friendship and support for Franco's Spain are
cited by the left in Europe as compromising the United States'
role as friend and defender of democracy. This is especially

true of France, the United Kingdom, Norway, and other European nations where, on the left at least, the memories of that cruel and bloody war fought a quarter of a century ago in Spain remain fresh. And the European right will answer that its faith in the United States as the main bulwark against the Bolshevist hordes has been weakened by United States economic aid to Yugoslavia.

For a decade and a half, the United States has pursued in Europe a policy centered upon the rivalry with the U.S.S.R. The objectives of this policy under John F. Kennedy are very similar to those under Harry S. Truman. The complicating factor, which most Americans ignore, is that Europe has changed. And the principal change, the one that promises the gravest political consequences for the United State, is the Continent's movement toward unity.

The relationship between the E.E.C., during the period of political development, and the United States obviously is of the utmost importance. How can it be reconciled with the basic aims of American policy?

One of these aims is, and has been since 1947, to get the Russian army out of Central Europe. Since there have been considerable withdrawals of Soviet forces from the satellite states, Central Europe now means East Germany. There is a striking similarity between this American policy goal and that Soviet policy which seeks the withdrawal from the European mainland of the American land, sea, and air forces.

If fifteen years of fruitless negotiation have taught the Soviet and American governments anything, it is that neither objective is likely to be reached as the consequence of a single conference dealing with this one point alone. In fact, both the State Department and the Foreign Office now put their faith in the conclusion of lesser agreements, which may in the end lead to a Soviet withdrawal.

It is only sensible to see the Soviet approach in the same light. The Kremlin and the White House probably believe that the conclusion of an interim arrangement on the future of Berlin would lead to a reduction of each other's forces in Europe. It is the fear of this development, rather than any newly developed anxiety for the fate of West Berlin—a city he has never liked and where he has never been particularly popular —that lies behind Dr. Adenauer's opposition to negotiations between the United States and the Soviet Union on any terms but his.

Although the withdrawal of the Soviet forces from Central Europe remains a cardinal point of United States policy, the achievement of this goal is distant. But, for the sake of argument, suppose it occurred. Suppose some transcendent convulsion in Russian society set the tanks and the planes and the long columns of infantry marching eastward. Would the consequences be what we expect? Would one break in the Soviet pattern of control lead to a political ferment behind the Iron Curtain?

At the outset, we can dismiss any expectation of a spontaneous restoration of democratic government. You cannot restore that which has never been. Yet the idea that there exists in the satellite states a furiously energetic movement waiting only to see the Russians' backs before it establishes parliamentary democracy dies hard. The harsh historical fact is that what is known as representative or parliamentary democracy in Britain and the United States has existed only fitfully in Eastern Europe. Those familiar with the pre-war history of Yugoslavia or Poland or Rumania will recall the powerful authoritarian trend that marked their political development. The special pleading of refugees from these countries, usually brave, dedicated, intelligent men, too often leads us to consider their political outlook as representative of the majority of their countrymen.

What should be emphasized about the governments of Eastern Europe in the years before 1939 is that they were accessible to Western influences. The liberal and humanitarian principles of European and American thought did not stop, as they do now, at the Elbe. The governments of the area, although not particularly hospitable to democratic processes, allowed Western ideas to circulate and managed, in most countries, to preserve a façade of democracy. This has gone, and it is extremely doubtful that it can be restored easily or quickly even if the Russians depart.

In the last chapter we noted the economic differences and national rivalries which beset the Russian empire in Eastern Europe. These amount to a plus for our side. But nothing in international affairs is a complete victory. There is always a minus. In this case, the minus is the consequences of seventeen years of Communist rule in the satellites. This constitutes a major problem for the United States and for a united Europe.

To begin, seventeen years is a long time. Hitler ruled for twelve. All things considered, the Communist system imposed upon Eastern Europe is probably more thorough in its application and more restrictive in its practice, although not more terrible in its rigors, than the National Socialist regime. In each case tyranny was imposed upon peoples psychologically prepared for it. The Germans of 1933 had been humiliated by the defeat of 1918 and impoverished and frightened by the inflation of the twenties. Eastern Europe in 1945 was emerging from a nightmare. Pre-war governments of various degrees of fascism had rejected popular government and installed authoritarian regimes. The peoples had either been subjected to a ruthless occupation, as in the case of Poland, or had been dragooned, as were Rumania and Hungary, into a wasting, costly campaign in the east against the Soviet Union. When the pendulum swung back and the Russian armies poured westward, a terrible retribution was exacted. The Red Army looted Eastern Europe as no army has looted since the Mongol invasions. When, satiated, they stopped, Eastern Europe lay stripped, ravished, and forlorn.

Into this vacuum Communism was introduced. Now, seventeen years later, a new generation is assuming the direction of these countries. This generation has no memories of even the superficial kind of democracy which flickered in Eastern Europe before the war. If it remembers any government before the present one, it is the harsh rule of the fascist dictators. More malleable than their elders, the young of this generation are the principal objects of Communist propaganda and training.

East Germany is perhaps the most important example of how Communism has established itself in the satellites. The Russians began their efforts under a disadvantage. Nowhere else in Europe had the Red Army behaved worse than in East Germany. But they also had an advantage. No other people in Europe is as susceptible to regimentation as the Germans. Since, in 1961, the Soviets and the German Democratic Republic built their wall in Berlin, the flow of refugees has ended. The Communist state is now static, and the consequences are depressingly apparent.

Communist officials, most of them in their late twenties and thirties, have focused party activity on the East German generation now in its late teens and early twenties. The officials themselves are the products of the youth program of the forties and fifties, veterans, many of them, of the great Free German Youth demonstration in East Berlin in the summer of 1951. The emphasis naturally is on the new Germany which is to arise as the result of youth's endeavors, the transformation that will come at the end of the present seven-year plan in 1965. Dreams are more digestible for the young than for the middle-aged and old. Despite the shortages of food, building materials, and manufactured goods, the shocking state of the railroads, the lack of skilled labor and industrial technicians, youth in East Germany is working for the fulfillment of a dream.

Aside from the Party cadres, however, there is no enthusiasm for Communism. But there is resignation and a belief that, since no foreseeable solution exists for the problem of a divided Germany, young men and young women must do their best with what Walter Ulbricht and his lieutenants offer.

The Communist bosses, both Russian and German, are clever enough to make available sports facilities and cultural institutions, all carefully supervised, for the rising generation in East Germany. These provide ersatz opportunities for the young. If they cannot express themselves politically, and there are no objective reasons for believing that this is important to any appreciable portion of the population, they may at least express themselves in books, painting, or the 1,500-meters race.

The skeptic will protest that in 1953 the East Germans did rise against the Soviet Union. So they did, and the rising was one of the brightest pages in German history. But the realist will note that the rebellion took place a decade or so ago and that a great deal has happened in East Germany since. Emigration to West Germany drew off many of those bold spirits who participated. The Communist apparatus, frightened by the depth of feeling against it, tightened its restrictions and made greater efforts to attract the young.

Meanwhile, West Germany has rearmed and taken her place in the Atlantic Alliance. This had two effects. The Soviets were forced to increase their economic and political commitments in East Germany to counteract the attraction of a prosperous German Federal Republic. They also had to provide more vigorous support, in public at least, for Ulbricht and his policies than was considered advisable in the past, particularly as Ulbricht at times spoke in the tones of Stalin rather than of Lenin and Khrushchev.

Viewed from the outside, therefore, the East German regime now appears a good deal more stable than it did before the wall went up in Berlin. Are we to assume that a similar political stability now prevails in the other satellites?

Opinion among the informed in the United States and British governments is divided. There apparently is a great deal of grumbling about the inequities of the Communist system throughout Eastern Europe. But those who report this add that there would be a great deal of grumbling about the inequities of any sort of political system. A depressing factor is that, although changes in the way the system works are advocated—more or less openly in countries like Poland, and secretly in Czechoslovakia and Bulgaria—there is very little support for a change in the Communist system itself. No one hopes the system is there to stay. But barring some economic explosion—crop failure and famine might do it—there is every sign that the system can endure the frictions and difficulties to which, like every form of government, it is subject.

The implementation of United States policies toward Russia and her satellites since the war has depended on a firm democratic base in the Western half of the continent. Since 1945 every administration has addressed itself to this *sine qua non* of American policy. At first, naturally, it was viewed as indispensable to the exclusion of the Russians and their allies from Western Europe and to the prevention of Communist seizures of power there. Looking at Europe as she is today, a new generation may find the latter contingency laughable. Yet only sixteen years ago plans were being made in Washington and London to deal with a Communist seizure of power in Paris.

The economic assistance given by the United States to Europe in the decade after 1945 was one of the benefits to Europe of the Russo-American rivalry so many Europeans condemn. We are prone to forget the magnitude of this aid, its timeliness and the enthusiasm and vigor which a generation of American civil servants brought to its distribution. It is easy enough to snipe at the reasons for United States aid. But it was not niggardly and it was provided at the expense of the American taxpayer. The United States, in its present position as leader of the West, cannot, and should not, expect gratitude and affection as a result. But Americans have the right to more understanding of what American aid has meant and what America wants in the world than they have received in recent years.

Of course, there have been mistakes. The blindly optimistic support for the European Defense Community was one of them. John Foster Dulles, in many ways a gifted Secretary of State, appeared unusually indifferent to European sensibilities. The reporter abroad occasionally will still hear echoes of his less felicitous remarks, such as "agonizing reappraisal." This is not the place to discuss the break with Britain and France over Suez, a break which endangered Western unity at a time when the Russian empire was challenged in Hungary; but the faults were not all on the eastern side of the Atlantic.

Yet on the whole, from the Marshall Plan through NATO on to E.E.C., the influence and resources of the United States have been used to build a stable, democratic Europe. What is surprising is that so few understood that, once a united Europe had been created, it would almost instinctively manifest the national characteristics of its member states and, collectively, desire to play a more important role in world affairs than that it occupied in the years of post-war weakness.

It was understandable, in view of the scale of American aid and the protection that American arms gave the Continent, that successive administrations should expect complete co-operation from their allies. A few, a very few, looked accurately into the future. The last time I saw the late General Walter Bedell Smith, in 1959, he remarked: "Boy, they don't know what's going to land on their neck in a couple of years. Those fellas in Paris and Bonn are flexing their muscles now. Wait till we get a real crisis of leadership. We'll spend as much time arguing with them as we do with Khrushchev."

Strong countries produce strong leaders. France and West Germany, the two most powerful continental allies, each has at its head a man of determination and resource with strong ideas on the future organization of Europe. Prime Min-

ister Harold Macmillan in Britain has been unwaveringly loyal
both to President Eisenhower and to President Kennedy.
But Mr. Macmillan will probably be the last British Prime
Minister whose education in statesmanship goes back to World
War II and the powerful maturity of the Anglo-American al-
liance. Henceforth the United States will have to deal with
British leaders less involved, emotionally, in strengthening
and perpetuating the American link and less likely to be
guided by the Churchillian precept that the alliance with
Washington comes first.

The emergence in France of a nationalist, or, as a
Frenchman would say, a patriotic view of that country's interests annoyed a great many Americans. Their annoyance
was exacerbated by the realization that in the military sphere
—for example, with regard to France's coldness toward
NATO—there was precious little they, or anyone else, could
do about it. For France is the most important piece of real
estate in Europe. If there is to be a defense of the continent
with conventional weapons, then France is essential.

But France and French manpower mean something
more. American policy planning for Europe has always shied
from the establishment of any one continental power as a
dominant factor in any of the organizations for military, political, economic, or financial co-operation. Yet if France should
concentrate on building an army, navy, and air force for her
own national interests, then West Germany will become the
dominant power within NATO because she will have more
troops committed to the Alliance. The French military contribution to NATO thus is essential to the maintenance of
the balance of strength within the Alliance. German domina-

tion of NATO, I am convinced, is something Dr. Adenauer himself would reject. We cannot be sure that the next Chancellor in Bonn will find it equally distasteful.

The United States wanted a strong Europe. It has it. But it doesn't like it because this is not the kind of strong Europe Washington envisaged. The resentment in Washington may be due to that excessive optimism with which many Americans look at international affairs. In view of all that had been done for them, the Europeans, in the opinion of Americans, were not expected to act like Europeans, that is like people with hundreds of years of national identity. They did, however, and it seems as though they may continue to do so for some years to come.

Fortunately, the ultimate American objective for Europe coincides with that of an important section of informed public opinion there. This is the attainment of a federal Europe organized supra-nationally, that is, one in which policy decisions can be taken by a majority vote. It is quite possible that America will not like supra-nationalism, once it is established, any more than it likes the recurrent nationalism of the moment. That, however, is beside the point.

We know from our examination of political and public opinion in the present members of the E.E.C. that the supranational, federalist approach, although overshadowed by General de Gaulle's concept of a Europe of Fatherlands, retains strong support. Even if at present the emphasis in the development of a European community is more on the confederal and national approach than on the federal and supra-national, the idea of federalism is so deeply implanted and the historic inevitability of such a moment is so manifest that the latter concept seems bound to be accepted five or ten years hence.

But whether the first form of political association is federal or confederal, Europe and the United States should have certain common objectives. The lowering of trade barriers throughout the world is one. This means the elimination of the system of Commonwealth preferences, long sought by the United States. Again we must wait and see whether the establishment of a Big Europe with a common external tariff will not cause as many or more difficulties for the American economy in the future as the system of Commonwealth preferences has in the past.

Aid to the undeveloped or underdeveloped countries is another mutual interest of Europe and America. But here the United States and some members of the evolving European community are bound to clash on political rather than economic grounds.

Existing differences between Washington and London with regard to the pace toward African independence will widen as the Federation of the Rhodesias and Nyasaland nears that state. Disputes appear inevitable with regard to the source and the character of the economic assistance that should be made available to the first African government there and elsewhere. But these probably can be reconciled by good will and intelligence in the two capitals. The real storm will break when the Africans in the Portuguese colonies, Angola and Mozambique, make their bid for freedom and independence.

This tendency to avoid even a discussion of critical issues until they erupt onto the front pages of the newspapers possibly is inevitable in a government which, like that in Washington, has the whole world as its parish. Uncle Sam often seems like a mechanic in charge of an enormous and intricate machine; he cannot stop the machine to make repairs and consequently must spend his time applying the oil can wherever trouble develops. Just as the police, no matter how numerous and able, can do no more than preserve a semblance of law and order, human cussedness being what it is, so the government of the United States may be able to do no more than maintain a semblance of Western unity.

This, however, does not excuse some illusions that accompanied American pressure on Britain to join the Common Market. When this pressure was being generated in the early days of the Kennedy administration, a visitor remarked to a very senior official of the government that the attitude of the older members of the Commonwealth would present a real problem to any British government in its efforts to negotiate union with Europe. This, the visitor was told, was nonsense. The Commonwealth, if not a figment of the British imagination, was really a minor factor in the affair, affecting only slightly the political and economic interests of the United Kingdom.

Such insensitivity to the feelings of others is surprising but not unusual in a government with a sense of dedication. As *The Economist,* a firm supporter of the United States and a proponent of Britain's entry into E.E.C., remarked in 1962: "American statesmen, tackling the organization of Europe, sometimes appear as innocents abroad. Their zeal for European and Atlantic unity is marked by native boldness, generosity and imagination, and by an endearing sense that what is good for America is good for Europe too. But the disposition to oversimplify, to slip from the idealistic to the doctrinaire, can be irksome to natives whose attachment to their customs goes deep. . . . The impatience and vision of the men of the new frontier could bring dangers now."

This danger was inherent both in the attitude taken toward the movement of Britain and other European powers, especially the three neutrals, Sweden, Switzerland, and Austria, toward the Community and in the ultimate reaction in Washington if the European community that evolves does not measure up to the American vision. By one means or another the administration has worked itself into a position with regard to European integration which provides little room for a flexible policy.

The United States wants a solidly, avowedly anti-Communist Europe. This means that the three neutral powers, which are strongly anti-Communist, cannot be members because they have avoided membership in the North Atlantic Alliance. The fact that Sweden and Switzerland bear a heavy burden of military expenditure and have modern, powerful forces to protect them from attack by the Russians—who else—does not weigh against this doctrinaire thinking in Washington.

The United States admiration for Europa also is rooted in the belief that we will get a girl just like the girl her mother was in 1950, when a wink from Washington was as good as a nod. Whatever the ultimate development in Europe, a big Europe or a little Europe, we are not going to get that sort of co-operation. Individually or collectively, the states that make up contemporary Europe are too strong.

Under the circumstances in Western Europe and given the continued rule of Nikita Khrushchev in the Soviet Union, it is reasonable to look forward to the day when the American military position in Western Europe comes up for review. Political considerations are not the only ones at work. The costs of maintaining an army in Europe are very high and contribute to America's overseas expenses. They will seem higher when the program for Polaris submarines, in itself very costly, is fulfilled. To Americans they will seem astronomical if the Europeans, particularly the French, are more interested in national than in international defense. These factors make a drastic reduction of United States conventional military protection for Europe possible in the next five years.

President de Gaulle is quite right to talk of the colossi of East and West. He is short-sighted to avoid recognition of why they are what they are. The Soviet Union and the United States do bestride the earth like colossi because of their nuclear armaments. Considering the tremendous cost of these to the American taxpayer, it is easy to see a situation in which an administration concludes that in view of the balance-of-payments problem it cannot both provide a nuclear deterrent in terms of rockets, Polaris missiles, and a strategic air force and at the same time maintain a large and expensively equipped army in Western Europe.

In these circumstances one consideration will weigh heavily in American military planning. This is the new system of pre-positioning for conventional forces, by which the equipment for a division can be placed in depots in Europe and the men moved in by air in time of crisis. Of course there is a risk. The division may never get to its equipment. But to planners this risk may appear worth taking compared to the heavy expense of maintaining the division *and* its supplies in Europe.

Europeans may protest that what is needed is the physical presence of American soldiers. The United States can answer that it expects, and should expect under the North Atlantic Treaty, that its European allies will provide the troops to meet the first shock of Soviet attack and that its role is to provide the reinforcements for the continental armies.

This is a logical military argument against too deep an involvement in a nationalist Europe that fails to provide an international defense. But there is also a deep psychological argument in many American minds against support for the kind of Europe de Gaulle and Adenauer favor. Failure on the part of Europeans to answer this argument seems to me as culpable as the American refusal to acknowledge the claims of Europeans to an individual view of the world's problems.

Anyone who travels around the United States must sooner or later realize the hostility of most Americans to the perpetuation of the old national quarrels in Europe. Our country is full of the descendants of people who left the continent because they had had a bellyful of this type of nationalism.

In the two great moments of our history when we were faced with the choice of intervention or neutrality in a European war, this suspicion and distrust of European nations and their rivalries played a major role in the making of public opinion. It was, I believe, a more important factor in American opposition to entry into the first war in 1917 than the Irish-American detestation of England or the German-American loyalty to the Fatherland. And in 1940 this belief that the quarrels of Europe were something which a great many Americans had left behind argued powerfully against involvement in a cause which the majority felt to be just.

Consequently, if, in the presence of the danger from Russia, Europeans fall to quarreling among themselves, if they re-create and nourish the old continental antagonisms, public opinion in the United States inevitably will move toward a new isolationism. It would be a mistake for Europe to take American internationalism for granted. The day is fast approaching when the United States can be defended from the oceans and from the rocket installations in its own territory.

The development of new weapons is only one factor in the equation. Another is the emergence in Europe of a different attitude toward the Soviet Union. To talk about a European Third Force is to imply that this force can act independently, that it is not in all circumstances the unwavering ally of the United States against the Soviet Union.

It seems probable that the stronger Europe becomes, the less willing it will be to follow the American lead in the duel with the Soviets. This does not mean that it will become more tolerant of Communism. But national policies will be based more on the interests of Europe and less on fidelity to the interests of the United States in the struggle with the Soviet Union.

Europe, as we know, is proud of her civilization. This pride does not end with the heritage of Dante, Goethe, Chateaubriand, Rousseau, Milton, and Shakespeare. It extends to the physical expressions of a thousand and more years of European culture, the cathedrals of Cologne and Rheims, the forum in Rome, St. Paul's in London. All these are the essence of Europe. And so, to a lesser extent, is all that Europe has contrived to save and build out of the wreckage of 1945.

The Soviet Union, in a great crisis, may ask Europe whether this heritage is to survive or be incinerated. Survival can be bought at the price of Communist rule, with all its deadening horrors.

The American, for whom the choice is not the same, since he believes that he can escape the worst of a nuclear war, may retort: "Rather dead than red." The European who *knows* he will be dead and that all he and his ancestors have built will die with him may take a different view. In the long history of European civilization, what is a hundred years under the Russians or the Turks or the Mongols compared with the preservation of an irreplaceable culture? Time's belly may hold a dozen Parthenons and artists greater than Leonardo. But they can materialize only if Europe and its people are there to produce them.

The question of what happens if the Russians blackmail Europe with nuclear threats is an important one not to be obscured by high-flown talk about allied solidarity. Its importance will grow as the economic and political strength of Europe grows. The United States would be blind if it did not accept that one of the implications of a European Third Force is a continental alliance strong enough to remain aloof from a war crisis and perhaps from a war which would destroy the Soviet Union and much of the United States.

Those with experience in world affairs would say that no European would be able to remain outside when the conflict between the United States and the Soviet Union was nearing a crisis. But one lesson of history is that governments and their peoples do extraordinary things when they are hypnotized by danger. There is no better illustration than the illusion shared by a number of small European countries in the late thirties that by proclaiming their neutrality they could escape German invasion. A Europe seeking the same sort of escape would, I am sure, be no safer today.

Americans, as a nation of enthusiasts certain that whatever it is we are selling, fountain pens or long-term policies to ensure peace, is the only answer, tend to overlook these potentially explosive situations. The tendency to discount the dangers of Soviet blackmail in Europe, for example, is only one aspect of a certain intolerance toward all views other than those of the United States. We find this intolerance applied to the suggestions that the three European neutrals, Sweden, Austria, and Switzerland, should work out some form of special economic arrangements with the European Economic Community once Britain has joined. The view of the administration in Washington, quite a reasonable one, was that this would adulterate the political character of the Community. In other words, ties with the neutrals would make E.E.C. less of an anti-Communist bloc. Since the United States has spent billions of dollars to establish an anti-Communist bloc in Western Europe, this was a perfectly legitimate objection.

Here is the American diplomatic difficulty. The administration desperately wants European unity. It is, or should be, aware that American pressure for this unity, if exerted in public, can do more harm than good. It is equally clear that the development of a Little Europe would presage a serious setback to American politics, mainly because those who advocate this development in France and Germany are those least responsive to United States leadership.

The conclusion must be that American policies with regard to Europe can be pursued satisfactorily only after Britain has become a member of a larger E.E.C., which in turn will admit Norway and Denmark and perhaps others as full members.

As I have tried to show, such a Community would from the outset be a far more formidable force, politically, economically, and militarily, than Little Europe. But after the entry of the United Kingdom and the two Scandinavian powers, Europe also will be assured of a strong influence of liberal governmental traditions, touched, in Britain's case, by a clear recognition of the importance of maintaining and strengthening ties with the United States and other powers outside Europe. Only such an organization can provide the basis in the future for a wider association of Western powers.

The Administration in Washington recognizes the problems that might arise if Britain enters Europe. The nationalist trends in France and West Germany are not transitory and there is strong, if latent, nationalist sentiment in the United Kingdom, exacerbated at the moment by General de Gaulle's haughty stand. Should the British, as members, become, in their own phrase, "bloody minded," an awkward situation would be created for the United States.

The Anglo-American relationship has been a powerful and continuing factor in the affairs of the West since the signature of the Atlantic Charter in 1941 brought into the open the growing intermingling of British and United States political and military planning in war. But the relationship changed with political developments. Its source, mutual interest, is constant. Its intimacy varies. When and if Britain achieves union with Europe, its continuation may become, for the first time, as important to the United States as it now is to

Britain. This is the moment for a closer inspection of that
relationship as it now stands, seven years after Suez.

That adventure was the great watershed of Anglo-
American relations, not because it found American political
resources arrayed against its closest ally, but because it demonstrated, to all who wished to see, that Britain henceforth
would be incapable of independent military action without the
support, either moral or material, of the United States. This is
clearly recognizable today when the success of British actions,
supported by the United States, in Kuwait, and the joint action
by the two governments in Lebanon in 1958, are compared
with the failure in the Suez adventure, which the United States
opposed.

Winston Churchill as a wartime Prime Minister and
again between 1951 and 1955 was capable of independent
action. So was Clement Attlee. Anthony Eden tried and failed.
Harold Macmillan, his successor, has been the faithful lieutenant of two American presidents. This is galling to many
Britons. But many, many more still do not realize how exten-
sively their own government's freedom of action is restrained
by the all-important need to retain the position of the intimate
ally of the United States. Tory politicos, when they find their
policies balked by American opposition, usually are careful
to point to reasons other than the real one. A revelation of the
true state of affairs, which is completely in accordance with
the power relationships between the two countries, inevitably
produces a storm of anti-Americanism.

This fidelity has its advantages from the British standpoint. In the key area of nuclear defense, for example, America shares more secrets with the United Kingdom than with
any other country. American trust of the British government

has grown in the last five years, especially after that government, without making too much of a fuss about it in Parliament, began to tighten its security measures. The French desire early in 1962 for some share in the American nuclear armory illustrated the difference in United States attitudes toward Britain and toward France, our oldest ally.

"We'll go right down the line with the British," an administration official said, "but I'm damned if we're going to tell the French anything 'hot.' How could we trust the French army with secrets when the whole outfit is riddled with disloyalty and torn with intrigue? The French government itself is uncertain whom it can trust. How can they expect us to trust people they're not sure about themselves?"

Britain, because she is trusted, may well prove to be the best, perhaps the only agency, for the channeling of information about American policies and desires to a new Europe. President de Gaulle sees this clearly, and, equally clearly, he doesn't like it. Yet once Britain, with her wealth, influence, and diplomatic skill is fully established in Europe, it will be almost impossible to prevent this—if Britain accepts the role. The United States will need a friend at court when moves have to be made which are better made quietly than in open conference. What better friend than the British?

For have not a succession of British Prime Ministers, Labor as well as Tory, emphasized the pre-eminence of the American connection in British eyes? Are not the two governments linked by informal working agreements throughout the whole catalogue of diplomacy and intelligence? Only two situations, it would seem to me, might prevent the establishment of Britain in Europe as America's spokesman and advocate.

One is a change in the direction of British interests as the United Kingdom becomes more deeply involved in Europe. Historically the British have always played a major role in the alliances which circumstances have forced them to join. With all their faults, which they are the first to admit, they are a vigorous, inventive, supple, and intelligent people. De Gaulle has challenged them. He may have roused the British. If he has, and they enter Europe, they will then try to run it—very much as the General is doing now.

In this case, London will not be as interested as it is now in maintaining close and intimate relations with Washington.

"Your fellas in Washington may be walking into one of the biggest mistakes in history," an old Irishman said. "You may be taking the English for granted. That's the sort of mistake the Germans are forever making. I thought Kennedy would be smarter. And himself an Irishman, too."

Another event that could sour Anglo-American relations, as Britain nears Europe, is an American raid on the Commonwealth. In a rare moment of conviviality, John Foster Dulles once told a group in Geneva that he had never understood the Commonwealth and that he doubted if any American ever had or would. Americans must understand that any attempt by an American government to shift Commonwealth allegiance from London to Washington would have the most serious effects upon the alliance.

As the British approach Europe anew, the United States may be tempted to increase its economic investment in the Commonwealth. The vitality and productive capacity of American industry could in time allow America to supplant Britain as the foremost exporter to the countries of the Commonwealth. This would weaken, and perhaps snap, the political ties, reputedly as light as gossamer and as strong as steel, with Britain.

The United States government will have to proceed with the utmost delicacy in the next two or three years. If it desires, as it says it does, ultimate British union with Europe, it must be careful not to offend British susceptibilities about the Commonwealth. This would be opposed by the majority of Britons, not simply those who want desperately to enter Europe.

What the United States wants, or should want, is a Britain in Europe that retains its present close relationship with Washington. General de Gaulle doesn't want this. If Washington and London are to achieve the Europe they want, then no dispute over the Commonwealth must be allowed to interfere with their co-operation. The British must understand, as many of them do, that the old relationship with the Commonwealth is passing. The United States must realize that it would be folly to alienate the British for the sake of temporary economic gains in the Commonwealth. And the European Economic Community must accept that political ties between the United Kingdom and the Commonwealth are a valuable source of strength for Europe. This is no time to excite British nationalism by attempting to subvert the Commonwealth. To do so would arouse those forces in Britain who are at once anti-Europe and anti-American. Britain's path into Europe is going to be long enough and hard enough without additional barriers to final union.

Those who accept that Britain's union with Europe is the most important immediate goal and the basis for progress to a true Atlantic union, embracing capitals from Washington to Stockholm, must also accept the possibilities of discord. Again the risk of discord must be run. The concept of a greater West-

ern Community is worth any risk. This is, I believe, the way
out of the present impasse for the West.

In such a community we can see the future salvation of
that civilization born in Athens and Rome which is the common heritage of all the countries of the West. Political salvation, however, is not easily achieved. The United States must
demonstrate a higher degree of political flexibility, a deeper
appreciation of what Britain and the Commonwealth mean to
each other, and a greater understanding of what the Europe of
today wants.

The American record under Kennedy shows a high but
variable degree of sensitivity to other peoples. Praise for Archbishop Makarios or a gracious gesture toward Tom Mboya
must be balanced by a deeper understanding of the relationship
between the Commonwealth governments and peoples. It is
inevitable that, as Britain grows closer to Europe, the Commonwealth will change; this will be shown by a loosening of its
political and economic ties. In this situation, the United States
can best serve the West and its own interests if it works to preserve what is good, and what can be preserved, in the British
Commonwealth. There is no sense in destroying one group
simply to speed the formation of another.

Britain's approach to Europe has created a world situation totally unlike that in which the Anglo-American alliance
has flourished. As Britain moves toward Europe, some aspects
of the old relationship will disappear. The United Kingdom
may speak for Washington in Europe. But it will do so as an
intimate and hopeful associate transmitting the views of a
powerful outsider to governments with whom it hopes to be
more closely associated.

America may have the greatest need for British intervention in Europe at precisely the moment when Britain is being offered an opportunity, as de Gaulle and Adenauer slowly withdraw from the control of their governments, to establish herself as the leader of Europe.

The West is entering a period of extreme difficulty. At all costs a clash must be avoided in Britain between those who believe in the cardinal importance of maintaining the existing political and military ties with the United States and those who wish to exploit, at almost any cost, the new and growing ties with Europe.

Events have placed Britain in a very strong position in regard to American policy for the West and to Europe's future political development. What Americans must balance is the weakening of the trans-Atlantic partnership, inevitable to some extent when Britain finally enters Europe, against the strong, new Europe that will develop once the United Kingdom finds a place there.

The vision of a larger, united Europe, eventually including Britain and others, and extending from the Atlantic to the Elbe and from the North Sea to Malta, is an exciting one. It will produce a new, powerful influence in world affairs and eventually end those national rivalries that have convulsed Europe since the rise of national states.

Yet we must ask whether this splendid vision is to be realized at the expense of two special relationships, America's with Britain and Britain's with the Commonwealth. Both, we know, have been, and still are, powerful forces for peace and stability.

A great deal is in the balance. But I believe that the wit of man can and will find an answer. Working with caution and resolution, with a due deference for Europe's feelings and a sure belief in what the larger, united Europe of the future will produce, a world-wide Western Community can evolve.

The United States, and every other Western country, is moving into a new power situation. Everyone must take risks. For the United States the risk may be more serious than for any other power.

Our most powerful and steadfast ally, Britain, is moving toward a larger, united Europe. We know this Europe will be politically and economically more important than the British Commonwealth. We hope that, once Britain is a member two or three years hence, it will be as appreciative of American policies.

The United States will be in a sorry situation if these hopes are disappointed, if the new Europe thinks of itself as a semi-independent third force rather than as an important component of the Western Community. But the long-term advantages are so great—for America, for Europe, for freedom—that the calculated risk must be run.

INDEX

unity, 156–61, 245, 284–5; and confederation, 160, 161; and federalism, 160, 161; Soviet reactions to, 189–96, 201–8; and struggle for Africa, 209, 210, 217, 218, 222; great debate in Britain on entry into, 223–36; and Communist challenge, 260–1

European Free Trade Area, 102, 103, 109, 133, 186

European Recovery Program, 56

European Third Force, 192, 282, 283

Evening Standard, 88

fascism: French and German, feared by British socialists, 113; British tradition of opposition to, 234

Federal Republic of Germany, *see* West Germany

federalism, European, 276; and E.E.C., 160, 161; opposed by de Gaulle, 172; opposed by Communists, 173; French elements in support of, 173, 174; German attitude toward, 178, 180; Italian attitude toward, 184; supported by Benelux powers, 184

Federation of British Industries, 127

Federation of the Rhodesias and Nyasaland, 35, 211, 214, 215, 277

Finland, 133, 142

Foot, Michael, 109, 234, 242

France, 7, 8, 9, 16, 87, 113, 114, 144, 256, 267, 284; nationalism in, 5, 164, 170, 246, 265, 275, 285; economic dynamism of, 10, 11; Third Republic in, 24; as dominant figure in E.E.C. negotiations, 81, 93, 142; and Algeria, 83, 93, 94, 168, 171; Fourth Republic in, 92, 94; question of political future of, 92–5, 172–4; Communist party in, 93, 167, 173, 192; composition of "left" in, 93, 173, 174; right-wing elements in, 94–5, 173; rise of workers' wages in (1961), 127; apprehensions of, on ability to compete with Britain, 130; labor

shortage in, 131; British exports to, 132; "associated territories" of, 140; exports to Britain, 142; import duties in, to protect farmers, 145; improvement of farming in, 147; prosperity of, 171; military defeats of, 171–2; leadership of Europe claimed by, 171–2, 265; *rapprochement* with West Germany, 174, 175, 176, 177; nuclear program of, 176, 191–2; hostility to Commonwealth, 247; nuclear secrets withheld by United States, 287; *see also* de Gaulle, Charles

Franco, Francisco, 166

Frankfurt, as financial center, 148

"Free Enterprise," built by Dutch, 79–80

French Resistance, 175

"Friendship Pipeline," for Russian oil, 204–5

Gaitskell, Hugh, 111, 112, 259

Gandhi, Mahatma, 22

General Agreement on Tariffs and Trade (GATT), 143, 253

George V, 258

George VI, 32, 50, 258

Germany, 55, 83; nationalism in prewar, 5, 6; Third Reich in, 20, 24, 28, 31; coal and steel production of (1939), 30; in World War II, 50, 52; Weimar Republic in, 91

Germany, East, *see* East Germany

Germany, West, *see* West Germany

Ghana, 16, 35, 122, 133, 141, 220, 221, 248, 249, 252

Gibbon, Edward, 74

Glendower, Owen, 82

Goa, 248

Great Britain, *see* Britain

Greece, 55, 131, 191, 194

Greenwood, Tony, 110

Grimond, Jo, 238

Halifax, Earl of, 53

Hallstein, Walter, 178; quoted, 156
Hardie, Keir, 111, 112
Hearst, William Randolph, 22
Heath, Edward, 81, 119, 229
Henderson, Nevile, 25
Hitler, Adolf, 22, 25, 32, 34, 91, 158, 175, 269
Hong Kong, 140, 142
Hungary, 203, 204, 265, 270, 274

Imperial Chemical Industries, 130
India, 14, 35, 36, 48, 51, 142; British international policies opposed by, 16, 248; British withdrawal from, 33, 48–9, 55; effects on, of Britain's entry into E.E.C., 140; exports to Britain, 140, 141; Goa seized by, 248; British-educated leaders on way out, 249
Indochina, 171
inflation, in Britain, 59, 146; halted by Tories, 127
Ismay, Lord, 165
Italy, 7, 8, 39, 52, 144, 181, 191; economic dynamism of, 10, 11, 181; Communist party in, 95, 167, 192; rise of workers' wages in (1961), 127; apprehensions of, on ability to compete with Britain, 130; labor shortage in, 131; exports to Britain, 142; dangers of nationalism appreciated by, 182; dislike of German tourists in, 182; British admired by, 183

Japan, 21, 39, 48, 52
Jebb, Gladwyn, 25
juvenile delinquency, in Britain, 72–3

Kennedy, John F., 267, 275; administration of, 104, 278
Kenya, 35, 105, 212, 214
Kenya African National Union, 212
Khrushchev, Nikita, 188, 190, 198, 199, 203, 205, 206, 279; quoted, 201–2
Kirkpatrick, Ivone, 25
Kuwait, 286

Labor Party, British, 31, 32, 75, 76, 105, 231; post-war industrial production retarded by, 42; rise to power of (1945), 59, 99, 106; anti-German prejudice of, 88; need for unity within, 109, 242–3; left wing of, 109, 110, 240, 242; eroded by national prosperity, 110–11; need for modernization of, 111–12, 240; pacifists within, 114; arguments of, against E.E.C., 114, 115; "Little Englander" concept within, 115; prospects in next general election, 240, 242–43; *see also* trades unions, British
League of Nations, 5, 33
Lease-Lend, to Britain, 45, 46
Lebanon, 286
Liberal Party, in Britain: re-emergence of, 100, 115–16, 236, 237–8, 239; British entry into E.E.C. supported by, 101, 117, 239, 243; as beneficiary of protest vote, 117–18, 239; prospects in next general election, 237–8, 239, 243; need for forceful program, 239
"Little Europe," 191, 194, 284
London, role as shipping center endangered by strikes, 149–50
London School of Economics, 99
Luxembourg, 8, 184, 191
Lyttelton, Oliver, 53

MacDonald, Ramsay, 31
Macleod, Iain, 100, 106, 107, 241; quoted, 117
Macmillan, Harold, 3, 4, 13, 53, 69, 76, 88, 101, 103, 104, 107, 109, 119, 125, 166, 228, 235, 238, 241, 247, 254, 264, 275, 286
McNamara, Robert S., 265
Makarios, Archbishop, 290
Makins, Roger, 25
Malaya, 20, 48, 133, 141
Malinovsky, Marshal, 198
Malta, 45
Marshall Plan, 56, 274
Maudling, Reginald, 106, 107

A NOTE ON THE TYPE

The text of this book was set on the Linotype in a face called TIMES ROMAN, designed by STANLEY MORISON for The Times (London), and first introduced by that newspaper in 1932.

Among typographers and designers of the twentieth century, Stanley Morison has been a strong influence, as typographical advisor to the English Monotype Corporation, as a director of two distinguished English publishing houses, and as a writer of sensibility, erudition, and keen practical sense.

Composed, printed, and bound by H. WOLFF, New York.